Bettina Peters

Innovation and Firm Performance

An Empirical Investigation for German Firms

Physica-Verlag

A Springer Company

ZEW

Zentrum für Europäische
Wirtschaftsforschung GmbH

Series Editor
Prof. Dr. Dr. h.c. mult. Wolfgang Franz

Author
Dr. Bettina Peters
Centre for European Economic Research (ZEW)
L7, 1
68161 Mannheim
Germany
b.peters@zew.de

Zugl.: Würzburg, Univ., Diss., 2006

ISBN 978-3-7908-2025-6   e-ISBN 978-3-7908-2026-3

DOI 10.1007/978-3-7908-2026-3

Library of Congress Control Number: 2007941521

© 2008 Physica-Verlag Heidelberg New York

Production: LE-TEX Jelonek, Schmidt & Vöckler GbR, Leipzig
Cover-design: WMX Design GmbH, Heidelberg

Printed on acid-free paper

9 8 7 6 5 4 3 2 1

springer.com

To my family.

Preface

The term innovation generally means 'something new' – and this monograph is an innovation in a sense that it provides the reader with some new insights into the consequences of innovation activities at the firm level. In recent years, the importance of innovations for improving competitiveness and stimulating economic growth has increasingly become the focus of public attention. The Federal Government, for instance, proclaimed 2004 as the 'year of innovation' and started several initiatives to foster innovation activities in Germany. This monograph is aimed at the empirical assessment of the impact of the introduction of new products and processes on various firm performance measures using modern microeconometric techniques.

This book represents the written part of my doctoral examinations at the Department of Economics at the University of Würzburg which were concluded with the oral examinations on July 28, 2006. The completion of this thesis was only possible with the assistance and the promotion of numerous individuals and institutions. First of all, I want to express my gratitude to my supervisor Martin Kukuk for supporting my academic research. During all the time he put his trust in me and gave me sufficient freedom to realise my ideas. I would like to thank him and Prof. Dr. Norbert Schulz, who kindly accepted to take on the second report, for their critical comments and constructive suggestions.

In addition, I am indebted to the Centre for European Economic Research (ZEW) and, in particular, to Wolfgang Franz and Georg Licht for providing me with excellent and stimulating working and research conditions. I really appreciate Georg's unswerving support and inspiring comments. I would also like to thank Thomas Kohl, all administrative staff, and, in particular, Heidi Halder and Heidrun Förster for their support making the everyday work life at the ZEW much easier as well as more productive.

This work has been made possible through different research projects carried out at the ZEW. In particular, Chapter 3 of this book originates from the research project *Innovation and Employment in European Firms: Microeconometric Evidence (IEEF)* financed by the European Commission within the Fifth Framework Programme (Project No. SERD-2000-00110). I am especially grateful to my co-authors Jordi Jaumandreu, Jacques Mairesse, and Rupert Harrison for their cooperation, precious ideas, many fruitful discussions and, of course, for organising meetings in Madrid, Paris, and London. The research has also considerably benefitted from joint work with the rest of the IEEF team consisting of Laura Abramovsky, Rachel Griffith, Elena Huergo, Norbert Janz, Elizabeth Kremp, Alberto Lopez, Pierre Mohnen, Tobias Schmidt, Helen Simpson, and Bronwyn Hall (inofficial member). It was a real pleasure for me to work with all of them.

Special thanks go to Ulrich Kaiser – for constructive comments but also for continuously asking me about the progress of my thesis, and for encouraging me to finish it – and to François Laisney. I appreciate his valuable econometric courses at the ZEW as well as the patience he exercised and effort he spent every time I sought econometric advice. Helpful econometric comments and proposals that significantly improved different parts of this study were also put forward by Winfried Pohlmeier and Jeffrey Wooldridge, and are highly appreciated.

I would also like to thank my friends and (present and former) colleagues at the ZEW for the inspiring working environment. In addition to Norbert Janz, I have particularly gained from comments by and discussions with Christian Rammer and Wolfgang Sofka. I am also grateful to Birgit Aschhoff, Patrick Beschorner, Katrin Cremers, Dirk Czarnitzki, Jürgen Egeln, Helmut Fryges, Diana Heger, Oliver Heneric, Katrin Hussinger, and Tobias Schmidt for their help and encouragement.

Data availability and quality largely determine the success of empirical research. This research would not have been possible without the data from the Mannheim Innovation Panel. I am, therefore, grateful to all firms which devote their time to thoroughly fill out the questionnaires. Furthermore, I owe our programmer Thorsten Doherr and all our student assistants ('MIP-Hiwis') a great debt of gratitude for their careful data collection and preparation. I would also like to thank Andrew Flower, Alexis Develle, and Tyler Schaffner for excellent proofreading.

Most importantly, I thank God. I am further deeply grateful to all my friends for their patience, heartening words and prayers over the past six years. Finally, as a sign of my gratitude for their permanent and unconditional support, I wish to dedicate this work to my family and, particularly, to my mother and to the memory of my father.

Mannheim, August 2007   *Bettina Peters*

Contents

1

Introduction

1.1 Motivation

Currently, one of the German economy's main problems is its weak growth performance, which shows up in low growth rates for potential output and for real gross domestic product (GDP) (Sachverständigenrat, 2005). Comparing important economic performance indicators within the EU15 countries, it further becomes apparent that economic development in Germany has lagged behind that of many other European countries since the mid 1990s. For instance, since 1995 Germany has continuously been among the group of the three countries reporting the lowest growth rates in real GDP. Similarly, the average growth rate of labour productivity of about one percent for the period 1995-2004 ranks within the lower third of the EU15 countries. In addition to falling behind other competitors in Europe, Germany – and also Europe as a whole – have been unable to keep pace with the economic development in terms of real GDP growth or labour productivity growth in the US, as can be seen in Fig. 1.1. Fig. 1.2 further shows that the low growth development is accompanied by a steady rise in the rate of unemployment over the last 15 years in Germany, whereas other countries, e.g., the United Kingdom (UK) or Spain, have experienced great success in reducing unemployment. In 2004, the internationally harmonised unemployment rate amounts to 10% in Germany. This is one percentage point above the European average, 4 percentage points higher than in the US and even twice as high as in Japan or the UK (see OECD, 2005a). Furthermore, looking at a longer period of time, it turns out that each business cycle has been accompanied by a rise of the base rate of unemployment in Germany. This phenomenon has not been observed, for instance, in the US (see Sachverständigenrat).

Since productivity and employment are key to micro- and macroeconomic wealth, the poor performance relative to other European countries and in particular to the US has been an important focus for government policy in Germany and has induced widespread reforms aimed at increasing growth and lowering unemployment. The weak productivity and employment perfor-

Fig. 1.1: Real GDP Growth Rate and Labour Productivity Growth Rate in Selected OECD Countries, 1991-2004

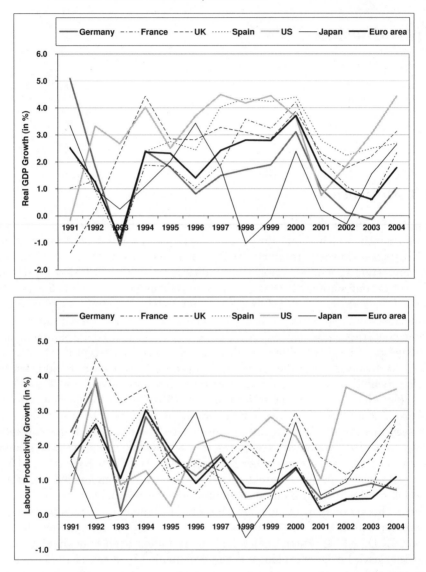

Notes: The Euro area denotes the EU15 countries. Labour Productivity: Real output per employed person in the business sector. Business sector employment is defined as total economy employment less public sector employment. Business output is defined as real GDP less the government real wage bill less net real indirect taxes less real consumption of fixed capital. Thus, business output is valued at factor costs. Source: OECD (2005a); own representation.

Fig. 1.2: Standardised Unemployment Rate in Selected OECD Countries, 1991-2004

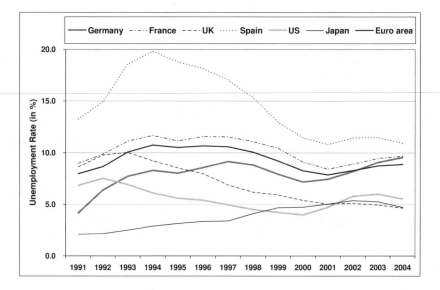

Notes: The standardised unemployment rate is defined as the number of unemployed persons as a percentage of the civilian labour force, where unemployed persons are defined as those who report that they are without work, that they are available for work, and that they have taken active steps to find work in the last 4 weeks (according to ILO guidelines). For Germany, the standardised unemployment rate prior to 1993 refers to West Germany.
Source: OECD (2005a); own representation.

mance is likely to have originated from a set of sources. Institutional conditions on the labour market, high indirect labour costs, a high corporate taxation, but also problems of adjustment due to German reunification are most often mentioned. Another cause, which is likewise adduced in the public debate and which is given a high significance, is that German and, more generally, European enterprises lack innovative ability. The economic relevance of this shortfall is that innovation is widely considered to be a key long-term driving force for competitiveness and growth of enterprises as well as national economies as a whole. For instance, the Sapir report, written on the initiative of the European Commission, argued that Europe's weakness is mainly a symptom of its failure to transform into an innovation-based economy. In the first three post-war decades, Europe mainly grew through adopting and incrementally updating US innovations. But now, Europe is closer to the technology frontier and must grow through innovations rather than imitations (see Sapir et al., 2003; and for a theoretical exploration, Acemoglu, Aghion, and Zilibotti, 2006). Against the background of this discussion, the Federal

Government proclaimed 2004 as the "year of innovation" and started several initiatives to foster innovation activities in Germany.[1]

A lack of innovative ability can find expression in different stages of the innovation process, giving rise to the following questions: (i) Do prevailing circumstances exist which impede or prevent innovation activities within firms? For instance, firms can be forced to refrain from innovating due to amiss venture capital or, more generally, due to financial constraints, a shortage of high-skilled personnel, legal regulations etc.[2] (ii) In view of the fact that investments in research and experimental development (R&D) reach high levels in a world-wide comparison,[3] a natural question is whether German firms are internationally not competitive in translating their R&D investments into new products and production technologies? (iii) Finally, are innovators not able to translate their innovation outcomes into better economic performance? Innovations are not an end in themselves but are aimed at improving the firm's competitiveness and performance. Hence, in the end they have to be assessed on the basis of their economic success or, more generally, on the basis of their impact on relevant firm performance measures (Janz, 2003).[4]

This monograph aims at mainly contributing to the third question in this respect as it empirically studies and reports new results on the following three key topics:

---

[1] The most important initiatives are the *Partner for Innovation Initiative*, in cooperation with industry and science, and the *Innovation and Future Technologies in Small and Medium-Sized Companies – High-Tech Master Plan*. The purpose of the latter programme is, among others, to improve the access to venture capital for small and medium-sized firms.

[2] The role of venture capital in fostering innovation was analysed, for instance, by Kortum and Lerner (2000) for US or Engel and Keilbach (2007) for German firms. The impact of financial constraints were investigated, for instance, by Kukuk and Stadler (2001). Rammer, Peters et al. (2005) examined the importance of different barriers to innovation in Germany.

[3] In 2003, the R&D intensity, i.e., the ratio of R&D expenditure to GDP, amounted to 2.55 in Germany, compared to 1.89 in the UK, 2.19 in France, 3.98 in Sweden, 1.95 in the EU15, 1.94 in Canada, 2.60 in the US, 3.15 in Japan and an OECD average of 2.24 (OECD, 2005c).

[4] Hauschildt (2004) distinguishes three kinds of success which can be associated with the introduction of new products or processes: Technical success, economic success and other effects, like environmental or social effects. The present study focusses solely on the economic success of innovations. Grupp (1997) subdivides economic success indicators of innovations into direct and indirect measures. Direct success or output indicators are the number of innovations, the share of sales due to new products or innovation rents. On the other hand, indirect success indicators measure the impact of innovation on central performance indicators, like productivity, employment, exports or profits, on the basis of an economic model. This kind of analysis is much more common in empirical innovation research.

1. How does innovation affect the employment growth of firms?
2. Does innovation increase firms' productivity performance?
3. Do firms innovate persistently over time?

The outline of this monograph and the research strategy for each topic together with some more background information and the contribution of each topic to the existing literature will be explored in the following section.

1.2 Background, Outline, and Research Strategies

Analysing and quantifying the effects of innovation activities on productivity and employment has a long tradition in empirical research relating to industrial organisation. In the 1990s, research on productivity results in particular was reinforced by new theoretical underpinnings from the endogenous growth theory, emphasising that economic growth is positively correlated with investments in research (Romer, 1986; 1990) and human capital (Lucas, 1988). Surveys by Mairesse and Sassenou (1991), Griliches (1995), and Bartelsman and Doms (2000) provide a useful overview of empirical evidence on productivity effects. An overview of empirical studies linking innovation and employment can be found, for instance, in Spiezia and Vivarelli (2002) or Chennells and van Reenen (2002). But despite a large number of empirical studies, Griliches (1994) argued that innovation research has only been partly "successful" in measuring the effect of innovation on productivity. That is, many studies only found a modest (and sometimes insignificant) coefficient of R&D which is not large enough to account for much of the productivity development in the 1970s and 1980s.[5] These results have caused some concern as to whether the methods and data applied have been accurate since theoretical models would suggest a significantly large contribution of innovation to productivity. In addition to the problem of measuring output in some industries as well as selectivity and endogeneity problems in econometric regressions, one reason for that may be the difficulties of adequately measuring innovation.

For a long time empirical innovation research has focussed on input-oriented innovation indicators when measuring aspects of innovation. In particular, R&D-based indicators, like R&D expenditure or R&D employees or corresponding intensities, served as proxies for innovation. The use of R&D-based indicators has considerably benefited from the development of a unique definition of R&D which was promoted by the US National Science Foundation (NSF) and the OECD and which was codified in the Frascati Manual (see OECD, 2002; first published in 1964). R&D has the advantage of providing well-codified and internationally comparable data. But the literature

---

[5] In many industrialised countries, it has even been observed since the 1970s that, at the aggregate level, R&D expenditure has risen continuously while at the same time productivity growth slowed down. This is known as *productivity paradox* in the literature.

states at least three objections to using R&D. First of all, R&D is not the only way for an enterprise to introduce new products and processes. That is, R&D, although important, is only one aspect of the innovation process, and using R&D indicators tends to lead to the underestimation of innovation activities in small and medium-sized firms as well as service sector firms (see, e.g., Kleinknecht, 1987; Brouwer and Kleinknecht, 1997). Secondly, it is presumably not the input of innovation activities but rather their outcome that exercises influence over the firm performance (Blundell, Griffith, and van Reenen, 1995). Thirdly, R&D or more general innovation expenditure transforms into product as well as process innovations, and, from a theoretical point of view, both affect employment or productivity via different channels.

Patents, most of all patent application counts but, in recent years, also value-based patent indicators, have been used as an option to overcome these deficiencies. But patent-based indicators have been heavily criticised as being a poor yardstick for innovative outcome (see, e.g., Scherer, 1965; Griliches, 1990). Not all inventions are patented and not all patented inventions lead to marketable innovations. Additionally, patents not only represent the outcome of the innovation process but also serve as an instrument to protect the returns of innovation and, hence, are subject to strategic considerations of firms. For many industries, in particular for large parts of the service sector industries, patents only play a minor role in appropriating returns on innovation. Furthermore, a fundamental shift in the role of patents has been ascertained since the beginning of the 1990s. This is expressed in a steep increase in the number of patents which is not associated with an increase in R&D expenditure but accompanied by a decrease in the importance of patents as a method of protection. Hall and Ziedonis (2001) called this the *patent paradox*, and several aspects are blamed for this shift: Firstly, the increasing importance of cumulative technologies implies that a single innovation is increasingly protected by several patents. Secondly, firms use patents more often as a strategic instrument to block competitors. Thirdly, firms use patents as a subject for strategic negotiations, for instance, for merger negotiations, cross-licensing of patents (Eswaran, 1994), or licensing of patents pools (see Shapiro, 2001; Lerner, Tirole, and Strojwas, 2007).

Since the mid 1990s, another strand has become more significant in empirical innovation research, focussing on survey-based innovation indicators. This literature has greatly benefited from the adoption of the Oslo Manual (OECD and Eurostat, 1997; first published in 1992) as well as the release of new and internationally harmonised surveys, which were initiated in the first half of the 1990s and which are known as the Community Innovation Surveys (CIS) in Europe. The Oslo Manual provides a unique definition of innovation and recommendations on some useful direct innovation output indicators. These measures allow me to distinguish the impact of product and process innovations, and – compared to patents – they are less affected by firms' strategic considerations. The studies in the present monograph follow this general line of empirical innovation research.

Since all studies are mainly based on data from the German CIS, which is conducted as an annual panel survey called the Mannheim Innovation Panel (MIP), *chapter 2* starts with a general description of the data set. This includes information on the survey methodology, the innovation concept, and the definition of innovation indicators as well as the variables surveyed. The chapter concludes with some stylised facts on the innovation activities of German firms at the aggregate level over the last 10 years using various innovation input and output indicators.

Chapter 3 examines the impact of innovation on the employment performance of firms. From a theoretical point of view, there are different channels through which product and process innovations can destroy or create employment. After a brief theoretical and empirical literature review, a theoretical multi-product model is developed.[6] The model establishes a theoretical link between the employment growth and both product and process innovation output, and it allows me to disentangle some of the theoretical employment effects under certain assumptions. Furthermore, it is tailor-made for analysing the effects of innovations on employment at the firm level using specific information provided by CIS data. Based on this new model, the empirical analysis pursues three different aims. First of all, I seek to estimate the effects of product and process innovations on employment in German manufacturing and service firms. Despite its rising importance in terms of the number of employees, there is hardly any empirical evidence on displacement and compensation effects of innovation activities in the service sector, and the analysis is intended to fill this gap. In a second step, I extend the model to examine the impact of different kinds of product (new to the market and new to the firm) as well as process innovations (cost reducing or quality enhancing) and to test whether employment effects differ according to the type of innovation. Finally, the question is investigated whether a common pattern in the link between innovation and employment exists among four large European countries (Germany, France, Spain, and the UK), which demonstrated a very different economic development over the last 10 years in terms of employment and productivity growth (see Fig. 1.1).

Chapter 4 studies the impact of innovation on firm-level productivity. Empirical studies traditionally used a production function approach as their theoretical framework, augmented by knowledge capital as an additional input. The knowledge capital was usually measured by an R&D capital stock in the level formulation (see, e.g., Griliches, 1986; Griliches and Mairesse, 1983) or R&D investments (per output) in a growth rate specification (see, e.g., Griliches, 1986; Link, 1981). This traditional approach suffers from at least two main deficiencies. Firstly, the innovation process, that is the link between

---

[6] The theoretical model was developed in a joint paper together with Rupert Harrison (Institute for Fiscal Studies and University College, London), Jordi Jaumandreu (Universidad Carlos III de Madrid), and Jacques Mairesse (Crest-INSEE, Paris) (see Harrison, Jaumandreu, Mairesse, and Peters, 2005).

the resources dedicated to innovation and the innovative outcome, remains a black box. Secondly, only some of the firms are engaged in R&D or in innovation activities in general, and it is well-known that a restriction to the selected (innovative) sample may induce biased estimates (Heckman, 1979). A huge step forward was taken by Crépon, Duguet, and Mairesse (1998) who addressed both of these problems. They developed an empirical model, which is known as CDM model in the literature and which was the first to connect innovation input, innovation output, and productivity. Crépon et al. estimated their model for French manufacturing firms, and a growing number of studies for other countries followed this line of research (see, e.g., Lööf and Heshmati, 2002, for Swedish firms; Klomp and van Leeuwen, 2001, for Dutch firms; Janz, Lööf, and Peters, 2004 for a cross-country comparison between Germany and Sweden). The study presented in chapter 4 will also rely on this model. One drawback of the studies so far is that they only take into account a measure for product innovation output although innovation input is related to both product and process innovation. The empirical analysis aims to extend the model by distinguishing between the output of product and process innovations and to analyse whether different factors are crucial to their success.

The research of *chapter 5* is motivated by the recent empirical evidence that firm performance in terms of productivity is highly skewed and that this heterogeneity is persistent over time (for an overview, see Dosi, Marsili, Orsenigo, and Salvatore, 1995; Bottazzi, Dosi, Lippi, Pammolli, and Riccaboni, 2001; Bartelsman and Doms, 2000).[7] Since innovation is seen as a major determinant of a firm's growth, one hypothesis is that the permanent asymmetry in productivity is due to permanent differences in innovation behaviour. So far, however, little is known about the dynamics in firms' innovation behaviour, and the evidence is mostly based on patents (see Geroski, van Reenen, and Walters, 1997; Malerba and Orsenigo, 1999; Cefis, 2003a). Therefore, chapter 5 particularly focusses on the following two research questions: (i) Do firms innovate persistently over time or is there a steady entry into and exit from innovation activities? Persistence occurs when a firm which has innovated in one period innovates once again in the subsequent period. (ii) If persistence is prevalent, what drives this phenomenon? It might be traced back to a causal effect of past innovation on future innovation (true state dependence). Economic theory suggests several arguments both in favour of and against state dependence at the firm level which will be explored in detail in section 5.2. Alternatively, firms may possess certain characteristics which make them more likely to innovate. To the extent that these characteristics themselves show persistence over time, they will induce persistence in innovation behaviour. To test the hypothesis of true state dependence, the study presented in chapter 5 applies a dynamic random effects binary choice model

---

[7] A related strand of literature investigates the persistence of excess profits. The majority of these studies have found some evidence for profit persistence, e.g., Mueller (1977), Geroski and Jacquemin (1988), or Cefis (2003b).

employing a new estimator recently proposed by Wooldridge (2005) for this kind of model. This panel data approach allows me to control for individual heterogeneity – a potential source of bias which was not taken into account in most of the previous empirical studies due to data restrictions.

Chapter 6 summarises the main findings of interest and draws some conclusions.

2

Data Set and Descriptive Analysis

The subsequent empirical analyses on employment, productivity, and persistence effects of innovation activities are mainly based on the Mannheim Innovation Panel (MIP). This chapter first presents some general background information on the data set including the survey methodology, response rates, and the information collected. It then provides the basic definitions of several innovation indicators which will be applied in the subsequent empirical analyses. The knowledge about the firms can be enriched by merging the MIP with other data sets. Therefore, a short description of the information used from other data sources follows. The chapter concludes by portraying the innovation activities of German firms at the aggregate level over the last 10 years using various input- and output-oriented innovation indicators.

2.1 Mannheim Innovation Panel

2.1.1 Survey Methodology

In Germany, the Centre for European Economic Research (ZEW) in cooperation with infas Institute for Applied Social Sciences runs two different but complementary innovation surveys on behalf of the German *Federal Ministry of Education and Research (BMBF)*.[8] The first covers industrial firms, i.e. firms from the manufacturing, mining, energy, water, and construction sectors. The second survey is the counterpart for services, comprising a great part of the service sector: retail, wholesale, transport, real estate and renting, financial intermediation, computer services and telecommunications, technical services (architectural and engineering activities, technical testing and analysis, R&D), consultancies (legal, accounting and auditing activities, advertising), other business-related services (e.g., cleaning, security, provision of

---

[8] Between 1995-1998, the survey in the service sector was cooperative work of ZEW, infas, and Fraunhofer Institute for Systems and Innovation Research (ISI) in Karlsruhe.

personnel, waste management), and media. Table 2.1 provides the definition of the branches of industry. The surveys are called "Zukunftsperspektiven der deutschen Wirtschaft" and "Dienstleistungen der Zukunft" in the industry and service sector, respectively, and together they make up the Mannheim Innovation Panel (MIP). At the beginning, the questionnaires differed slightly between the two surveys, but since 2001 they have been identical.

Table 2.1: Branches of Industry Covered by the MIP

Industry Sector		Service Sector	
Branches of Industry	NACE[a]	Branches of Industry	NACE[a]
Mining	10-14	Distributive services	
Manufacturing		Wholesale	51
Food	15-16	Retail/repairing	50, 52
Textile	17-19	Transport/storage/post	60-63, 64.1
Wood/paper/printing	20-22	Real estate/renting	70-71
Chemicals	23-24	Business-related services	
Plastic/rubber	25	Banks/insurances	65-67
Glass/ceramics	26	Computer/telecom-	72, 64.2
Metals	27-28	munication	
Machinery	29	Technical services	73, 74.2-74.3
Electrical engineering	30-32	Consultancies	74.1, 74.4
MPO[c] instruments	33	Other BRS[b]	74.5-74.8, 90
Vehicles	34-35	Media[d]	92.1-92.2
Furniture/recycling	36-37		
Energy	40		
Water	41		
Construction	45		

Notes: [a] The industry definition is based on the classification system NACE Rev.1 (Nomenclature générale des activités économiques dans les Communautés Européennes) as published by Eurostat (1992) using 2-digit or 3-digit levels.
[b] Business-related services.
[c] Medical, precision, and optical instruments.
[d] The media industry has been part of the target population since 2003.

For the industry sector, the survey started in 1993, and 2 years later the service sector followed.[9] Both surveys are conducted annually, although there was a break in the service sector in 1996. This study makes use of data from

---

[9] The first two waves in the industry sector already included some selected service industries. Detailed information on the first wave can be found in Harhoff and Licht (1994). A description of the MIP can also be found in Janz, Ebling,

the surveys 1993 to 2004 which means that there are 12 and 9 waves at hand for the industry and for the service sector, respectively.[10] As mentioned before, the survey methodology and definitions of innovation indicators are strongly related to the recommendations on innovation surveys set out in the Oslo Manual (see OECD and Eurostat, 1997; first published in 1992), thereby yielding internationally comparable data on the innovation activities of German firms. In 1993 (CIS 1), 1997 (CIS 2), and 2001 (CIS 3), the surveys represented the German contributions to the Europe-wide harmonised Community Innovation Surveys (CIS), which take place every 4 years under the coordination of Eurostat to investigate firms' innovation activities.

The target population spans all legally independent enterprises[11] with 5 or more employees and their headquarters located in Germany. An enterprise is defined as the smallest combination of legal units operating as an organisational unit producing goods or services. However, very few large firms have their business units merely subordinated rather than organised as legally independent subsidiaries. These large firms constitute an exception as they are split up according to their business units.

In contrast to other European countries, there is no business register available in Germany. The data on firm, employment, and revenue figures for the target population in the industry sector are based on publications of the German Federal Statistical Office.[12] Due to large gaps in the official statistics, the target population for the service sector is constructed using information from the Federal Statistical Office,[13] the German Central Bank, and various federal commissions and associations.[14] The size classification structure in the service sector is mainly based on estimates by the ZEW.

Due to the lack of a business register, the samples cannot be drawn from the target population itself, so the Creditreform database is used as a sampling frame instead. Creditreform (abbreviation of *Verband der Vereine Creditreform e. V.*) is the largest and most important credit-rating agency in Germany

---

Gottschalk, and Niggemann (2001) or Janz, Ebling, Gottschalk, and Peters (2002).

[10] In 2007, the time of publication, two additional waves are available.

[11] Note that in the remainder of this book the terms *enterprise* and *firm* will be used interchangeably.

[12] Publications used are Reihe 4.1.2, 4.2.1, 6.1 and 5.2 of the Fachserie 4; see Statistisches Bundesamt (b; c; d; e).

[13] The information stems from different years of Reihe 4 of the Fachserie 6 (for wholesale and retail trade) and of Reihe 2, 3, 4 and 8 of the Fachserie 8 (for transport); see Statistisches Bundesamt (f; g; h; i; j). Additional information is gained by the turnover tax statistics.

[14] E.g., *Bundesamt für Güterverkehr, Bundesaufsichtsamt für Finanzdienstleistungen, Bundesverband deutscher Banken, Verband privater Bausparkassen, Bundesgeschäftsstelle der Landesbausparkassen, Gesamtverband der Deutschen Versicherungswirtschaft.*

and has the most comprehensive database of German firms at its disposal, which it provides to the ZEW for research purposes. Amongst other information, the database includes the name and address of the firm, contact person, industry classification, region, and the number of employees. Both samples are drawn as stratified random samples and are representative of the corresponding target population. Firm size, industry, and region serve as stratifying variables. Based on the number of employees, 8 size classes are distinguished: 5-9, 10-19, 20-49, 50-99, 100-199, 200-499, 500-999, and 1,000 and more employees. Due to the small number of large service firms, the last two categories are merged in the service sector. With regard to the region, the sample is stratified into West and East Germany. East German firms are defined as those firms that have their head office in one of the following six federal states: Berlin, Brandenburg, Mecklenburg-Western Pomerania, Saxony, Saxony-Anhalt, and Thuringia. Subsidiaries of West German firms in East Germany that are not organised as separate legal entities are not part of the East German enterprise sector as used here. The industry classification scheme used for stratification purposes is generally based on the 2-digit NACE level; however, in the service sector the 3-digit level is applied for some industries (see Table 2.1).

The sampling is disproportional, that is the drawing probabilities vary between cells. Large firms, firms belonging to more heterogeneous cells (according to labour productivity) or to industries with a small number of firms, and East German enterprises have a higher probability of being sampled. The disproportionate sampling of the first three groups is indispensable to produce reliable projections, in particular of quantitative variables. Large firms may, for example, generally be characterised by idiosyncratic innovation behaviour but determine all quantitative variables to a very large extent. The fact that East German enterprises are oversampled is mainly explained by their very different level and dynamic of development compared to West German firms at the beginning of the 1990s. The disproportionate sampling implies that the distribution of firms across cells in the gross sample differs from that in the target population. As an example, the Tables 2.2, 2.3, and 2.4 show the distribution of firms by region, size, and branches of industry in the target population and in the gross sample of the 2001 surveys (CIS 3), which are used for the empirical analyses in the chapters 3 and 4. The pattern is similar for other years.

Tables 2.2-2.4 further show the gross sample rate, which is defined as the ratio of the gross sample to the target population. For the industry sector, this rate amounts to 4.7%. However, the proportions vary considerably between branches, and the low overall rate is mainly due to the dominant role of the construction industry with its minimal value. Excluding construction, the proportion of the target population included in the gross sample comes to 14.5% (see Table 2.3). Similarly, retail is responsible for the low overall proportion of 3.0% in the service sector. Since 2005, both industries have been excluded from the target population.

Table 2.2: Target Population and Gross Sample of CIS 3 by Region, Size, and Industry Branches: Industry Sector

	Population[a]		Gross Sample[a]		
	Number	Share	Number	Share	Sample Rate[b]
		in %		in %	in %
Region					
West	160,954	77.5	7,034	71.4	4.4
East	46,790	22.5	2,821	28.6	6.0
Size					
5-9	92,325	44.4	980	9.9	1.1
10-19	56,401	27.1	1,338	13.6	2.4
20-49	32,444	15.6	1,825	18.5	5.6
50-99	13,219	6.4	1,338	13.6	10.1
100-199	6,789	3.3	1,128	11.4	16.6
200-499	4,475	2.2	1,552	15.7	34.7
500-999	1,233	0.6	795	8.1	64.5
1,000+[c]	858	0.4	899	9.1	104.8
Industry					
Mining	945	0.5	276	2.8	29.2
Food	6,021	2.9	783	7.9	13.0
Textile	3,462	1.7	585	5.9	16.9
Wood	10,589	5.1	873	8.9	8.2
Chemicals	2,214	1.1	640	6.5	28.9
Plastic/rubber	4,416	2.1	640	6.5	14.5
Glass/ceramics	3,118	1.5	477	4.8	15.3
Metals	11,743	5.7	1,354	13.7	11.5
Machinery	8,335	4.0	1,367	13.9	16.4
Electrical engineering	4,068	2.0	789	8.0	19.4
MPO instruments	2,858	1.4	471	4.8	16.5
Vehicles	1,464	0.7	427	4.3	29.2
Furniture/recycling	3,252	1.6	424	4.3	13.0
Energy/water	2,001	1.0	274	2.8	13.7
Construction	143,258	69.0	475	4.8	0.3
Total	207,744	100	9,855	100	4.7

Notes: [a] The target population refers to the year 2000. The gross sample refers to the 2001 survey, which gathers information for the year 2000.
[b] The sample rate denotes the proportion of the target population included in the gross sample which is not identical to the drawing probability, as the sample is drawn from the Creditreform database.
[c] A sample rate of more than 100% can be explored by the split-up of some very large enterprises according to their business units.
Source: Mannheim Innovation Panel; own calculations. Target population: ZEW calculations based on sources referred to in section 2.1.1.

Table 2.3: Target Population, Gross and Net Sample of CIS 3 by Region, Size, and Industry Branches: Industry Sector Excluding Construction

	Population[a]		Gross Sample[a]			Net Sample[a]		
	Num-ber	Share	Num-ber	Share	Sample Rate[b]	Num-ber	Share	Sample Rate[b]
		in %		in %	in %		in %	in %
Region								
West	54,101	83.9	6,784	72.3	12.5	1,262	67.7	2.3
East	10,385	16.1	2,596	27.7	25.0	602	32.3	5.8
Size								
5-9	12,783	19.8	935	10.0	7.3	144	7.7	1.1
10-19	11,893	18.4	1,281	13.7	10.8	245	13.1	2.1
20-49	18,061	28.0	1,739	18.5	9.6	396	21.2	2.2
50-99	9,928	15.4	1,261	13.4	12.7	310	16.6	3.1
100-199	5,740	8.9	1,064	11.3	18.5	244	13.1	4.3
200-499	4,069	6.3	1,490	15.9	36.6	283	15.2	7.0
500-999	1,183	1.8	758	8.1	64.1	128	6.9	10.8
1,000+[c]	829	1.3	852	9.1	102.8	114	6.1	13.8
Industry								
Mining	945	1.5	276	2.9	29.2	50	2.7	5.3
Food	6,021	9.3	783	8.3	13.0	156	8.4	2.6
Textile	3,462	5.4	585	6.2	16.9	110	5.9	3.2
Wood	10,589	16.4	873	9.3	8.2	158	8.5	1.5
Chemicals	2,214	3.4	640	6.8	28.9	125	6.7	5.6
Plastic/rubber	4,416	6.8	640	6.8	14.5	155	8.3	3.5
Glass/ceramics	3,118	4.8	477	5.1	15.3	90	4.8	2.9
Metals	11,743	18.2	1,354	14.4	11.5	281	15.1	2.4
Machinery	8,335	12.9	1,367	14.6	16.4	268	14.4	3.2
Electrical engin.	4,068	6.3	789	8.4	19.4	159	8.5	3.9
MPO instruments	2,858	4.4	471	5.0	16.5	92	4.9	3.2
Vehicles	1,464	2.3	427	4.6	29.2	69	3.7	4.7
Furniture/recycl.	3,252	5.0	424	4.5	13.0	73	3.9	2.2
Energy/water	2,001	3.1	274	2.9	13.7	78	4.2	3.9
Total	64,486	100	9,380	100	14.5	1,864	100	2.9

Notes: [a] The target population refers to the year 2000. The gross and net sample refers to the 2001 survey, which gathers information for the year 2000.
[b] The sample rate denotes the ratio of the gross and net sample to the target population, respectively.
[c] A sample rate of more than 100% can be explored by the split-up of some very large enterprises according to their business units.
Source: See Table 2.2.

Table 2.4: Target Population, Gross and Net Sample of CIS 3 by Region, Size, and Industry Branches: Service Sector

	Population[a]		Gross Sample[a]			Net Sample[a]		
	Number	Share	Number	Share	Sample Rate[b]	Number	Share	Sample Rate[b]
		in %		in %	in %		in %	in %
Region								
West	306,009	83.2	7,812	65.4	2.6	1,335	60.6	0.4
East	61,644	16.8	4,125	34.6	6.7	868	39.4	1.4
Size								
5-9	211,933	57.6	1,929	16.2	0.9	322	14.6	0.2
10-19	86,674	23.6	2,508	21.0	2.9	481	21.8	0.6
20-49	43,253	11.8	2,360	19.8	5.5	502	22.8	1.2
50-99	13,234	3.6	1,194	10.0	9.0	256	11.6	1.9
100-199	6,335	1.7	1,127	9.4	17.8	225	10.2	3.6
200-499	3,777	1.0	1,021	8.6	27.0	178	8.1	4.7
500+	2,447	0.7	1,798	15.1	73.5	239	10.8	9.8
Industry								
Wholesale	35,742	9.7	1,726	14.5	4.8	321	14.6	0.9
Retail	127,795	34.8	1,395	11.7	1.1	233	10.6	0.2
Transport	40,419	11.0	1,892	15.8	4.7	381	17.3	0.9
Real estate	42,395	11.5	937	7.8	2.2	215	9.8	4.0
Banks/insurances	5,365	1.5	1,170	9.8	21.8	142	6.4	1.2
Computer/telec.	12,217	3.3	911	7.6	7.5	317	14.4	0.9
Technical services	35,805	9.7	1,563	13.1	4.4	147	6.7	0.4
Consultancies	41,246	11.2	920	7.7	2.2	301	13.7	1.1
Other BRS[c]	26,669	7.3	1,423	11.9	5.3	146	6.6	0.3
Total	367,653	100	11,937	100	3.0	2,203	100	0.6

Notes: [a],[b] See Table 2.3.
[c] Other business-related services; for a definition see Table 2.1.
Source: See Table 2.2.

Furthermore, the samples are constructed as panels, that is the same set of firms is questioned every year. Of course, firms that no longer exist are removed from the samples (on the pre-condition that this information is available), and a panel refreshment based on a random sample takes place every second year to account for the foundation of new firms and other changes that lead to an inclusion in or exclusion from the sample framework, like changes of the industrial classification or the number of employees.

The innovation surveys are performed by mail.[15] The field phase starts in early spring with the sending out of the questionnaires, followed by two or three reminders in late spring and early summer. Additionally, selected firms are contacted by phone if the response rate is too low in a single stratum. Until 1997, about 10,000 industrial firms and 12,000 service firms were asked to contribute each year. However, due to cost reasons, the collection design was changed in 1998. The new design provides for a long survey in odd years and a short survey in even years. A short survey is marked by a reduced questionnaire (four pages, chiefly limited to the core innovation indicators) which is sent to a sub-sample of the full gross sample. The sub-sample consists of firms which have answered at least once in the previous years or which have been added to the gross sample in the preceding year. In odd years, a long questionnaire (12-16 pages) is sent to the full gross sample. However, to maintain the panel structure with yearly waves, the most relevant variables are asked retrospectively for the preceding year in the long surveys.

Participation in the innovation surveys is voluntary in Germany. Tables 2.3 and 2.4 already provided information on the distribution of firms in the net sample 2001 by size, region, and branches in the industry (without construction) and the service sector. It turns out that the disproportionate sampling also unveils in the net sample (realised sample). In addition, Table 2.5 shows the size of the net samples and response rates by years.

The response rate is defined as the proportion of questionnaires from the corrected gross sample that are actually returned. The corrected gross sample is the gross sample excluding neutral losses. Neutral losses are firms which should not have been part of the gross sample, for instance, those firms which no longer exist or firms which shifted their headquarters abroad. Each year, about 25% of the industry sector firms answered the questionnaire. The distribution pattern in each year is similar to that of the year 2001. Note that the higher response rates in the short surveys (1998, 2000, 2002, 2004) are not directly comparable to those of the long surveys as only the sub-sample of firms which has a higher propensity to participate is contacted. In the service sector, the response rate is even lower at about 21%. Furthermore, the willingness to participate in the survey is slightly decreasing over time. The response rates are the result of the survey's voluntary nature combined with a slight general greater reluctance of German firms to participate in surveys. However, they are in line with response rates of comparable voluntary surveys among firms in Germany. In small enterprises, managing directors usually filled in the questionnaire. In larger firms, it is generally the head of the research and development department who is contacted, or a director whose general responsibilities include technology. However, interviews with large firms show

---

[15] In order to reduce costs and to shorten the field phase, a fax survey was conducted in 2004. However, this experiment was only partially successful and will not be followed up. For more details, see Aschhoff, Rammer, Peters, and Schmidt (2005).

Table 2.5: Gross and Net Samples by Years

| | Gross Sample | | Net Sample | | | | |
| | Total[a] | Corrected[b] | Return[c] | | Plus[d] | Total | |
Year	No.	No.	No.	in %[e]	No.	No.	in %[e]
			Industry Sector				
1993	13,316	12,792	2,860	22.4	11	2,871	22.4
1994	12,664	12,236	3,065	25.0	6	3,071	25.1
1995	10,001	9,718	3,080	31.7	3	3,083	31.7
1996	9,935	9,590	2,281	23.8	12	2,293	23.9
1997	9,852	7,867	2,452	31.2	22	2,474	31.4
1998	5,476	5,234	1,965	37.5	16	1,981	37.8
1999	10,566	9,875	2,487	25.2	16	2,503	25.3
2000	5,497	5,276	1,988	37.7	25	2,013	38.2
2001	10,039	9,253	2,066	22.3	62	2,128	23.0
2002	5,524	5,023	1,935	38.5	77	2,012	40.1
2003	12,037	10,771	2,456	22.8	84	2,540	23.6
2004	9,809	7,930	2,088	26.3	189	2,277	28.7
			Service Sector				
1995	11,596	11,157	2,553	22.9	16	2,569	23.0
1997	11,704	10,818	2,337	21.6	14	2,351	21.7
1998	4,035	3,804	1,739	45.7	15	1,754	46.1
1999	11,821	10,773	2,299	21.3	19	2,318	21.5
2000	6,154	5,890	2,005	34.0	26	2,031	34.5
2001	12,539	11,464	2,443	21.3	52	2,495	21.8
2002	5,973	5,365	1,942	36.2	77	2,019	37.6
2003	13,753	11,747	2,082	17.7	72	2,154	18.3
2004	9,680	7,543	1,790	23.7	153	1,943	25.8

Notes: [a] Number of questionnaires which were sent out.
[b] Gross sample less neutral losses; for a definition see section 2.1.1.
[c] Number of returned and utilisable questionnaires.
[d] Number of firms of which information was gathered by the ZEW on the base of face-to-face interviews, business reports, or the internet.
[e] In % of the corrected gross sample.
Source: Mannheim Innovation Panel; own calculations.

that very often more than one department is involved in filling out the questionnaire.

It is not clear at first glance whether the response behaviour depends on the innovation behaviour itself and whether innovative firms are more likely to answer because they are more responsive to the questions or whether the opposite holds because the time for filling out the questionnaire is much shorter for non-innovative firms or because innovative firms want to keep their information secret. In order to control for a response bias in the net sample, non-response analyses are carried out in Germany. Each year, a random sample of the non-participating firms is drawn and questioned on their core innovation indicators by telephone. The number of realised interviews varies between 2,000 and 4,000 each year. The non-response analyses suggest that the share of innovators is slightly underestimated in the net sample.[16] The results of the non-response analyses are used to correct the weighting factors of the firms (for details on the methodology, see Rammer, Peters et al., 2005).

The MIP differs from several other panel data sets with respect to the individual response pattern. That is, it is not a typical unbalanced panel for which information on individuals is available for a certain time period without gaps. Instead, one observes a lot of firms which, for example, respond in a certain year but then refuse to participate for one or more years, only to join in the survey again at a later date. This means that the time span for firms under observation is marked with gaps. It further implies that panel attrition is often not permanent and not necessarily the result of the fact that the firm has died. If the latter were the case, this could induce a selection problem as firm closures might be correlated with firms' innovation behaviour, that is the objective of the investigation itself. More information about the individual response behaviour and, therefore, the panel structure is given in chapter 5.

2.1.2 Innovation Concept

The object of the surveys is to record information on the innovation behaviour of firms in a comprehensive way. Therefore, various innovation indicators are collected. This section describes their basic definitions and boundaries which correspond to those set out by the OECD in the Oslo Manual and which are used throughout this study. However, I start with a brief literature review of innovation concepts highlighting some of the relevant aspects and problems of how to define innovations.

Literature Review

Innovation is a complex phenomenon and, thus, not surprisingly, various definitions of innovation have emerged in the economic literature (for an overview, see, e.g., Stoneman, 1995; Hauschildt, 2004; as well as the references cited therein). Empirical studies on innovation behaviour in particular have long

---

[16] The result that the probability of innovating is significantly higher for non-response firms in each year has been confirmed to hold in a multivariate analysis. To show this, a simple probit estimation has been performed. The binary indicator variable to innovate or not was regressed on industry dummies, firm size, a dummy variable for East Germany, and a dummy variable indicating an observation that stems from the non-response sample. Results are not shown here but are available upon request.

suffered from the lack of a consensus on appropriate definitions and measuring concepts. Common to all definitions is the notion that something new is successfully introduced. In his seminal papers, Schumpeter (1934; 1947) was one of the first to define innovation as "simply the doing of new things or the doing of things that are already being done in a new way" (Schumpeter, 1934: 65). He made this statement more precise by identifying an innovation as one of the following five events: the introduction of a new product or a qualitative change in an existing product, the implementation of a new production or transportation method new to an industry, the opening of a new market, the development of new sources for raw materials and other inputs, and changes in the industrial organisation (such as a monopolisation of an industry). However, the fields of changes to which an innovation might refer to is not standardised in the literature. Almost all definitions encompass the implementation of new products and processes, though some authors use broader concepts and additionally include, for instance, improvements in material and intermediate inputs, changes in business organisations, changes in marketing methods, or even social, contract, legal, or system changes.[17] This issue is closely related to the question of whether an innovation must be technological.

Another important aspect addressed in the literature is whether an innovation is conceptualised as an outcome or a process and, if it is a process, where it starts and ends.[18] As a process, innovation is often depicted as continuous and cyclical in contrast to a discrete event, as it is seen from the outcome perspective. Also based on Schumpeter's work is the usual distinction between invention, innovation, and diffusion (also called "Schumpeterian trilogy"). While *invention* describes the phase in which new ideas are generated, the term *innovation* covers the realisation of new ideas into marketable products and processes. The diffusion stage follows in which the new product or process spreads through certain channels across the social system.[19] This trilogy is also called the sequential or linear model in the literature.[20] With respect to this, it must be noted that a selection process occurs at each stage, i.e. inventions do not automatically lead to innovations which do not automatically diffuse. Furthermore, from a chronological point of view, these

---

[17] See Stoneman (1983) or Brockhoff (1998) for a more detailed discussion of innovations in a narrow and broad sense.

[18] The innovation management literature usually considers innovation as a process, and much research is focussed on the normative question on how enterprises ought to manage this process to be able to successfully introduce new products, processes, organisational forms, or management methods.

[19] See, for instance, Rogers (1995) for a closer look at theories explaining the diffusion of innovations.

[20] Some authors further subdivide this process, such as Maidique (1980), who distinguishes between recognition, invention, development, implementation, and diffusion.

three stages do not necessarily take place one after another, and the clear distinction between the phases is potentially misleading since it ignores the feedback loops from diffusion to both innovation and invention (see Patel and Pavitt, 1995).[21] In contrast, Roberts (1987) defined innovation as the sum of the invention and its exploitation implying that the invention is an integral part of the innovation.

A further issue in identifying an innovation is to specify the sphere within which the innovation must be "new". Stoneman (1995) distinguished between global and local innovations. Global innovations encompass the first occurrence of an event – for example the first use of a production technology or the first launch of a new commodity – in an industry (or, even wider, in a national or world market). This is in line with the definition of innovations by Schumpeter (1934), Schmookler (1966), or Knight (1967). In contrast, local innovations are new for the unit of observation (generally the plant or enterprise), irrespective of whether the same product or process has already been introduced in other units. This second concept is chiefly focussed on by the business management literature (see, e.g., Witte, 1973).

It is also common in the literature to distinguish innovations by their novelty content into radical and incremental innovations. However, a more or less unique definition of this concept is lacking. Freeman and Soete (1997) depicted radical innovations as discontinuous events which embody fundamental technological changes whereas incremental innovations describe improvements in existing products or processes. While this definition is strongly technology-oriented, other authors focus on the competitive consequences of innovations. This can be explained by the fact that there is strong empirical evidence that there are numerous innovations that involve just moderate changes in technology but have dramatic competitive consequences (see Clark, 1987). Tirole (2000) called a process innovation radical if the firm is able to reduce its production costs and, as a consequence, the price of the product to such an extent that it achieves a monopoly under free market entry; otherwise the process innovation is incremental. An analogous definition is employed for product innovations.

Innovation Survey

The Mannheim Innovation Panel is based on the recommendations of the Oslo Manual (see OECD and Eurostat, 1997). The surveys operationalise an *innovation* as a technologically new or significantly improved product, which an enterprise has introduced to the market or a new or significantly improved

---

[21] For a more detailed discussion about the boundaries and interrelationships between invention and innovations, the drawbacks of linear models and alternative models including feedback effects between the different stages, see Schumpeter (1947), Kline (1985), or Grupp (1997) and the references cited therein.

process implemented within the enterprise.[22] Thus, an innovation is characterised by the following four aspects: Firstly, it is technological, i.e. the innovation has to be based on the results of new technological developments, new combinations of existing technologies, or the utilisation of other knowledge acquired by the firm. Secondly, it is implemented, i.e. it is introduced to the market (product innovation) or used within the production process (process innovation). This further implies that only Schumpeter's first two categories are covered (and ideally measured) by this concept. Thirdly, it is subjective, meaning that the innovation should be new to the enterprise but not necessarily to the market or the industry. Thus, from a business management point of view, the innovation concept used here includes the imitation of products or processes which have already been introduced by competitors, and at the same time it captures the diffusion of innovations from an economic point of view. And fourthly, it does not matter who develops the innovation: the enterprise itself and/or another enterprise.

A *product innovation* is a product (good or service) which is either new or significantly improved with respect to its fundamental characteristics, technical specifications, incorporated software or other immaterial components, intended uses, or user-friendliness. Changes of a solely aesthetic nature and the act of simply selling innovations wholly produced and developed by other enterprises are not included.

A *process innovation* includes new and significantly improved production technologies or methods of supplying services and of delivering products. This includes significant changes in techniques, equipment, and/or software. The outcome should be significant with respect to the level of output, quality of products, or costs of production and distribution. Purely organisational or managerial changes do not fall into this category.[23] New processes or procedures which are sold to other enterprises are product innovations.

Process innovations can be intended to decrease unit costs of production or delivery, to increase quality, or to produce or deliver new or significantly improved products (see OECD and Eurostat, 2005). This implies that not each implemented process innovation is accompanied by a new product. On the other hand, firms may introduce a new or significantly improved product without major changes in its production process. For instance, significant improvements to existing products can be achieved through changes in mate-

---

[22] The third edition of the Oslo Manual extended the definition of innovation: In addition to technological innovations, new marketing and organisational methods are now included (see OECD and Eurostat, 2005). However, the new definition was first applied in the 2005 survey (CIS 4) while this study uses data from the 1993 to 2004 surveys only.

[23] An exception presents the first innovation survey in the service sector in 1995 in which organisational changes are included in the definition of innovations. Due to the reduced comparability, the 1995 survey will, therefore, not be employed for the empirical analysis.

rials, ingredients, or components (maybe solely produced outside the innovating firms) which require no or only incremental adjustments to the production process. Likewise firms can offer a new service or new characteristics of a service without significantly changing the method of providing the service. For instance, one might think of a new customer-oriented software programme where the process of developing the new software is nearly unaltered compared to the one applied for previous software programmes.

In manufacturing, the distinction between product and process innovation does usually not cause any problems. In the service sector, however, identification problems may arise because it is often difficult to distinguish between products and processes as the production, delivery, and consumption of many services can occur at the same time. In addition, services are more often customised to specific demands, and in many cases a clearly structured production process is missing. The Oslo Manual proposes some guidelines how to identify product and process innovations in the service sector (see OECD and Eurostat, 2005):

- If the innovation involves new or significantly improved characteristics of the service offered to customers, it is a product innovation.
- If the innovation involves new or significantly improved methods, equipment, and/or skills used to perform the service, it is a process innovation.
- If the innovation involves significant improvements in both the characteristics of the service offered and in the methods, equipment, and/or skills used to perform the service, it is both a product and a process innovation.

Examples for both product and process innovations can be found in Appendix A2.

2.1.3 Definition of Innovation Indicators

Output Indicators

Based on the innovation concept, an *innovator* is a firm that successfully introduced at least one innovation within the previous 3 years. *Product innovators* and *process innovators* are defined accordingly.

In view of the definition of product innovations, the data set further distinguishes between *enterprises with market novelties* (new-to-the-market products) and *firm novelties* (product imitations). Market novelties are new or significantly improved products that have been launched onto the market by a firm prior to any competitor. The relevant market is defined from the firm's own perspective. In contrast, a firm which offers new or significantly improved products to its customers that are new to the firm but not new to the market is labelled as an enterprise with firm novelties. The distinction between enterprises with market novelties and firm novelties corresponds to the definition of global and local innovators used in the innovation literature. Yet, there has been no counterpart to incremental and radical innovations in the surveys up to now. Since 2003, it has further been possible to identify *product-range novelties* which are product innovations that have no predecessors in the innovating firm. Such innovations, which can be new to the market and/or solely to the firm, thus, enlarge the product range of the enterprise and allow to address customer demand not covered by the firm's supply so far. The three indicators also refer to a period of 3 years.

Firms can introduce new processes for several purposes which largely reflect their different innovation strategies. They may aim to improve the quality of products or to assure that products or production processes meet new legal requirements. Enterprises may also install new technologies simply to be able to produce a new commodity. Last but not least, process innovations may be intended to promote rationalisation in terms of reducing average production costs. Based on the Oslo Manual but in contrast to innovation surveys in other European countries, the German survey, therefore, additionally asked firms whether they have introduced *cost-saving process innovations* (rationalisation innovation). These are defined as new processes that have led to a reduction in the average unit costs of production or service delivery and are part of an innovation strategy to raise the firm's price competitiveness. *Quality-improving process innovations* are new or significantly improved production, delivery, or distribution methods that improve the quality of a good or service and as such are often linked to product innovations. Both indicators again refer to a 3-year period. Whereas the surveys include information on rationalisation innovations since 1993, quality-improving process innovations were initiated in 2003.

In addition to the aforementioned qualitative output-oriented indicators concerning whether an enterprise has introduced a specific innovation, the surveys also gather quantitative information on the direct success involved. A direct performance measure of product innovations is given by the *share of sales due to product innovations*, which refers to the proportion of turnover in a particular year that stems from new or significantly improved products introduced within the previous 3 years.[24] The *share of sales with market novelties*, *with firm novelties*, and *with product-range novelties* are defined accordingly. Measuring the success of new processes is by far more difficult and not possible for all different types of process innovations. With respect to rationalisation innovations, it can be measured by the *share of cost reduction in unit costs*, which is defined as the cost saving in unit costs in percent in a particular year achieved through new processes implemented within the previous 3 years.

Note that all output-oriented innovation indicators refer to a 3-year period. This reference period is to some extent arbitrary but it reflects the process-oriented view of innovations. It takes into account that, firstly, the whole innovation project might carry on for several years, secondly, differ-

---

[24] From 1993-2000, the survey separately asked for the turnover share with new products and with significantly improved ones. Since 2001, both variables are summarised.

ent innovation activities (e.g., R&D, patenting, product launch) possibly take place in different years, and thirdly, the economic effects often appear with a certain delay. It further implies that the measurement of innovation activities is smoother over time and less dependent on random effects in a given year.

Unlike innovators, a *firm with innovation activities* is identified as a firm having at least one innovation project in a 3-year period, regardless of whether the project was successfully completed, abandoned, or not yet completed.

Input Indicators

Developing innovations requires various inputs and can encompass the following activities:

- Intramural R&D;
- Extramural R&D;
- Acquisition of machinery and equipment related to implementing new or significantly improved products and/or processes;
- Purchase of external knowledge (patents, licences, software etc.);
- Internal or external training directly aimed at the development and/or introduction of innovations;
- Internal or external marketing activities directly aimed at the market introduction of new commodities (market research, market tests, launch advertising etc.);
- Product design and other preparations to realise the actual implementation of product and process innovations.

R&D activities are usually regarded as the most important input, at least in manufacturing. R&D is creative work undertaken on a systematic basis in order to increase the stock of knowledge and the subsequent use of this stock of knowledge to devise new applications, such as new and improved products and processes (including software research).[25] Thus, it provides a hint as to the extent of new knowledge production in the course of innovations.

The *innovation expenditure* is the sum of all current expenses for innovation itself (personnel, material etc.) as well as investments associated with these innovation activities. Unlike the output measures, this input indicator relates to a 1-year period in the innovation surveys. The ratio of innovation expenditure to total turnover is usually referred to as the *innovation intensity*.

2.1.4 Surveyed Information

The surveyed information can broadly be classified into structural and innovation-related variables. Structural variables exist for all firms (on the condition that the firm has not refused to answer the question). Each year all firms

---

[25] This definition of R&D in the Oslo Manual corresponds to that given in the Frascati Manual, on which the national R&D surveys are based (see OECD, 2002).

are questioned on sales, number of employees, the main (in terms of sales) business activity of the firm in order to identify the industry assignment on a 3-digit NACE level, location, and ownership structure (part of a national or international group). The long surveys additionally collect data on exports, the skill structure of employees, labour costs, material costs, training expenditure, tangible assets,[26] gross investment in tangible assets, and investment in information and communication technologies.[27] These variables are also collected retrospectively for the preceding year. Other general firm information is only at hand for some cross-sections – e.g., the share of sales for the most important product, mergers and acquisitions, selling or closing down of a part of the business, most important market etc.

With respect to innovation-related variables, it is necessary to be aware of the fact that the questionnaires include a filter. That is, information on whether a firm has introduced a new product or new process or has been involved in an innovation project which was abandoned or not yet completed exists in each year for all firms. But only for those firms which have innovation activities, additional innovation-related variables are observed. Besides the input and output indicators set out in the preceding section, these include several behavioural and technology policy-related innovation variables like cooperation, public funding, hampering factors, protection methods, information sources etc. Some of these additional innovation-related variables only exist for certain cross-sections. Definitions of these variables are given in the subsequent chapters when they are used.

2.2 Additional Data Sources

The knowledge about the firms can be enriched by merging the MIP with other data sets. At the ZEW, this was done with data from Creditreform.[28] This data set has already been briefly introduced in section 2.1.1, and more details can be found in Almus, Prantl, and Engel (2000). In addition to the variables already mentioned in section 2.1.1 (addresses, industry classification, number of employees, turnover), it provides some further structural variables like the date of firm foundation which can be used to calculate the firm age, the legal form of the firm or the district. More importantly, this data set contains information on credit ratings of firms which will be used and explained in more detail in the chapters 4 and 5 as a measure of the availability of financial resources.

---

[26] In the service sector, tangible assets are only asked since the 2003 survey.

[27] In manufacturing, this information is only available since the 2001 survey.

[28] The MIP has also been merged with data from the German and European Patent Office and with a data set on publicly funded research projects.

2.3 Descriptive Analysis: Innovation Activities in Germany

Before analysing the impact of innovation on employment or productivity at the micro level, this section aims at providing a very few key stylised facts of the innovation activities at the aggregate level over the last 10 years in Germany. Tables 2.6, 2.7, and 2.8 in Appendix A1 summarise the development of the core input and output indicators in manufacturing (including mining), business-related, and distributive services.[29]

Fig. 2.1: Share of Innovators in Germany, 1993-2003

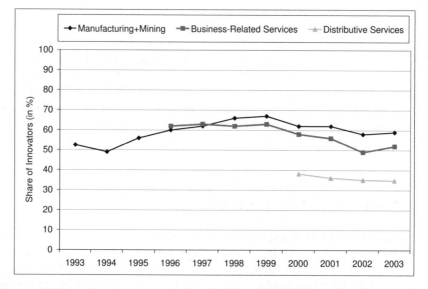

Notes: All figures are expanded to the target population of German firms with 5 or more employees. At the aggregate level, comparability of figures before 2000 is limited for distributive services.
Source: Rammer, Aschhoff et al. (2005); own representation.

Fig. 2.1 shows the share of innovators as a percentage of all firms in Germany in the period 1993-2003. First of all, it reveals a high and quite stable share of firms with new products or processes in manufacturing as well as in the service sector. In manufacturing the share of innovators has ranged between a minimum of 49% and a maximum of 67%. This proportion has been similarly high in the business-related service sector, ranging between 49% and

---

[29] For more details see Rammer, Aschhoff, Doherr, Peters, and Schmidt (2005) or Rammer, Peters et al. (2005).

62% but has been considerably lower for distributive service firms at about 36%. Between 1999 and 2002, one observed a moderate decline in the proportion of firms introducing new products or processes in all three sectors, mainly due to the withdrawal of innovation activities of small and medium enterprises, particularly in less export-oriented industries (see Rammer, Aschhoff et al., 2005). This trend, however, seems to have stopped in 2003, and Germany still occupies a leading position with respect to innovation compared to other European countries. In 2000, the most recent year for which comparable data exists, Germany exhibited the highest share of innovators both in manufacturing and in services whereas for instance France, Spain, and the UK all ranked low down the list (see Fig. 2.2). From a dynamic perspective, there is one interesting question which emerges from these figures but which cannot be answered by such macroeconomic numbers: Does a core group of firms exist which continuously innovates, or is there a steady entry into and exit from innovation activities at the firm level, with the aggregate level remaining more or less stable over time? This question will be addressed in more detail in chapter 5.

Fig. 2.2: Share of Innovators in EU15, 2000

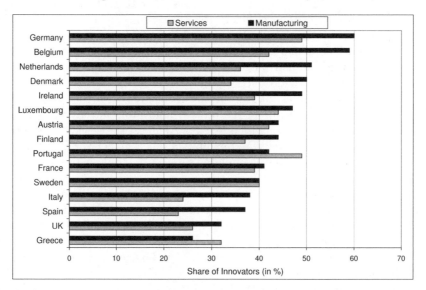

Notes: All figures are expanded to the target population of firms with 10 or more employees. Services include wholesale trade (51), transport/storage (60-63), post and telecommunication (64), financial intermediation (65-67), computers and related activities (72), research & development (73), and technical services (74.2+74.3). Source: Eurostat (2004); own representation.

Secondly, product innovations are more common than process innovations in all three sectors (see Tables 2.6, 2.7, and 2.8).[30] In manufacturing the share of firms which have introduced a new product remains around the 50% mark whereas the share of process innovators fluctuates between 30% and 38% between 2000 and 2003.

Thirdly, the share of product innovators which have launched market novelties is high both in manufacturing and in business-related services compared to other European countries (see Eurostat, 2004) but has substantially decreased since the end of the 1990s. In manufacturing, nearly six out of ten product innovators launched at least one market novelty in 2000, but this ratio had fallen to one half by 2003. The decrease has even been more severe in business-related services, where the ratio shrank from one half to one third. This may indicate that, in view of the unfavourable economic conditions, innovating firms are currently attempting to take fewer market risks by introducing fewer new products in general and more product imitations amongst them.

Fourthly, looking at the innovation success indicators, one can ascertain that firm novelties (product imitations) contribute more to turnover than market novelties in all three sectors. Between 2000 and 2003, manufacturing enterprises earned on average 28% of their turnover with product innovations introduced during the preceding 3 years, nearly 8% thereof with market novelties and 20% with firm novelties. In the business-related service sector, the share of sales due to new products amounted to an average value of 20%, 6% thereof attributable to market novelties. The less frequent occurrence of product innovations in the distributive service sector is accompanied by a lower share of sales due to new products (8%).

Fifthly, not all process innovations are associated with cost savings. Between 2000 and 2003, 60-70% of the process innovators introduced new production technologies to rationalise processes. Amongst the service sector firms, this proportion is clearly lower and exhibits a much higher variance, ranging between 40% and 54% in business-related services and only between 25% and 48% in distributive services.

Looking at the quantitative importance of rationalisation innovations, one can find that the percentage cost saving in unit costs ranges between a minimum of 4% and a maximum of 7.5% in manufacturing over the last 10 years, with an average value of 5.5%. In the service sector, saving potentials turned out to be lower with an average value of 4.5% in business-related services and 2.2% in the distributive service sector.

Turning to the input side of the innovation process, innovation expenditure accounts for 4.5 to 5% of sales in manufacturing. In business-related services the innovation intensity has steadily increased, reaching 3.3% in 2003. Not surprisingly, the innovation intensity is considerable lower in the distributive

---

[30] Note that a reversal in the ranking order of product and process innovations has been observed in the distributive service sector since 2002.

service sector (0.7%). Furthermore, one can observe that R&D activities show an increasing trend over the last 10 years, not only in terms of the amount of money spent in the course of R&D activities (a number which is mainly determined by a few very large firms) but also in terms of the number of firms engaged in R&D. Between 1993 and 2003, business enterprises and co-operative research institutes stepped up their R&D budgets from 29.6 to 46.7 billion € (see Stifterverband für die Deutsche Wissenschaft, 2004).[31] This corresponds to an increase in the ratio of R&D expenditure to GDP from 1.75 to 2.16.[32] In the same period, the share of firms engaged in continuous intramural R&D activities rose from 16% to 25% in manufacturing. This implies that, for instance, in 2003, 42% of the innovators were permanently engaged in R&D. A further 34% of the innovators occasionally conducted their own R&D activities in 2003. In the business-related service sector, the share of firms which conduct R&D rose from 13% in 1996 to 18% in 2003. Here, computer/telecommunication and technical services are the most committed to research.

---

[31] Cooperative research institutes mean Institute für Gemeinschaftsforschung (IfG).

[32] Note that the figures include intramural and extramural R&D expenditure of the business enterprises sector. The ratio of intramural R&D outlays to GDP was about 1.75 in 2001. Intramural R&D expenditure together with the R&D expenditure of government research institutes and universities constitute total R&D expenditure, which amounted to 2.55% of GDP in 2003 (see also footnote 3). Within the context of the Lisboa process, the countries of the European Union are endeavouring to increase this percentage to 3% by the year 2010.

Appendix A1: Tables

Table 2.6: Innovation Activities in Manufacturing and Mining, 1993-2003

	1993	1994	1995	1996	1997	1998	1999	2000	2001	2002	2003
Output Indicators											
Innovators	52	49	56	60	62	66	67	62	62	58	59
Product innovators	–	–	–	–	–	–	–	50	50	51	47
Firms with market novelties	n.a.	22	25	23	24	31	33	29	28	28	23
Firms with product-range novelties	n.a.	n.a.	n.a.	n.a.	n.a.	n.a.	n.a.	n.a.	n.a.	27	26
Process innovators	–	–	–	–	–	–	–	38	34	30	35
Cost-reducing process innovators	32	25	28	34	34	35	36	25	20	21	24
Quality-improving process innovation	n.a.	n.a.	n.a.	n.a.	n.a.	n.a.	n.a.	n.a.	n.a.	22	27
Share of sales with new products	–	–	–	–	–	–	–	31.4	28.5	27.7	24.9
Share of sales with market novelties	n.a.	5.1	4.8	3.8	6.1	7.9	8.6	8.3	7.7	7.6	7.6
Share of sales with product-range nov.	n.a.	n.a.	n.a.	n.a.	n.a.	n.a.	n.a.	n.a.	n.a.	5.9	4.7
Proportion of cost saving	7.1	4.1	4.4	6.2	7.5	6.2	7.2	6.7	5.4	4.8	4.6
Input Indicators											
Firms with continuous R&D activities	16	18	17	25	n.a.	20	22	24	24	23	25
Innovation expenditure	48.1	44.5	48.6	52.2	52.9	55.7	58.1	59.8	64.1	67.9	71.2
Innovation intensity	4.8	4.2	4.4	4.9	4.5	4.7	4.7	4.4	4.6	4.8	5.0

Notes: All figures are in percent and are expanded to the target population of German firms with 5 or more employees. "nov." stands for novelties. " –": The European harmonisation in the course of the 2001 Community Innovation Survey (CIS 3) has led to changes in the way some questions were posed, which has in turn made comparisons with values from previous years more complicated or even impossible at the aggregate level. Among the indicators affected were the number of product and process innovators and revenues from product innovations. Therefore, only the values since 2000 are shown. " n.a.": not available.
Source: Rammer, Aschhoff et al. (2005).

Table 2.7: Innovation Activities in Business-Related Services, 1996-2003

	1996	1997	1998	1999	2000	2001	2002	2003
Output Indicators								
Innovators	62	63	62	63	58	56	49	52
Product innovators	–	–	–	–	45	41	43	39
Firms with market novelties	n.a.	n.a.	22	21	23	17	19	13
Firms with product-range novelties	n.a.	n.a.	n.a.	n.a.	n.a.	n.a.	24	23
Process innovators	–	–	–	–	36	29	30	34
Cost-reducing process innovators	n.a.	24	20	17	17	16	12	16
Quality-improving process innovators	n.a.	n.a.	n.a.	n.a.	n.a.	n.a.	23	26
Share of sales with new products	–	–	–	–	19.3	23.4	19.6	16.0
Share of sales with market novelties	n.a.	n.a.	6.1	6.0	6.0	7.1	6.5	4.9
Share of sales with product-range novelties	n.a.	n.a.	n.a.	n.a.	n.a.	n.a.	5.8	6.1
Proportion of cost reduction	n.a.	3.8	4.3	4.5	4.3	5.1	5.1	3.9
Input Indicators								
Firms with continuous R&D activities	13	n.a.	11	12	16	15	16	18
Innovation expenditure	11.2	11.5	14.5	15.6	15.5	14.9	17.2	15.4
Innovation intensity	2.8	2.7	2.9	3.1	3.1	3.0	3.2	3.3

Notes: See Table 2.6. For the definition of business-related services, see Table 2.1.
Source: See Table 2.6.

Table 2.8: Innovation Activities in Distributive Services, 2000-2003

	2000	2001	2002	2003
Output Indicators				
Innovators	38	36	35	35
Product innovators	29	27	20	15
Firms with market novelties	9	12	8	7
Firms with product-range novelties	n.a.	n.a.	10	4
Process innovators	25	20	24	28
Cost-reducing process innovators	9	8	6	13
Quality-improving process innovators	n.a.	n.a.	13	17
Share of sales with new products	7.3	8.2	8.0	7.2
Share of sales with market novelties	2.7	2.7	1.6	2.0
Share of sales with product-range novelties	n.a.	n.a.	4.1	1.6
Proportion of cost reduction	1.9	1.7	2.5	3.1
Input Indicators				
Firms with continuous R&D activities	2	2	2	1
Innovation expenditure	9.7	9.5	9.1	9.5
Innovation intensity	0.7	0.7	0.7	0.7

Notes: See Table 2.6. The European harmonisation in the course of the 2001 Community Innovation Survey (CIS 3) has also influenced all distributive service indicators at the aggregate level. Therefore, only the values since 2000 are shown. For the definition of distributive services, see Table 2.1.
Source: See Table 2.6.

Appendix A2: Examples of Product and Process Innovations

The following list of selected examples of product and process innovations is taken from the German 2001 questionnaire (CIS 3).

- Manufacturing:
  - Product innovations:
    - ~~Bio-technologically produced bricks for the life-science field~~
    - Ceramic composite disc brakes
    - Use of electronic data transmission in cars (GPS navigation systems)
    - Gas-insulated power lines
    - Microwave ceramics and surface wave filters for mobile communications
    - Low-emission vehicles
    - Electronic stability programme (ESP)
    - Sensor-protected emission reading devices
  - Process innovations:
    - Production use of powder paint for the varnishing of auto bodies and frames
    - New techniques for acid production on the basis of cheaper raw materials
    - Implementation of computer protected methods of product development
    - E-Commerce (e.g., NetBank with personal offers, e-Shopping, introduction of B2B)
    - Production optimisation through the use of finite element simulation programmes
- Retail and wholesale:
  - Product innovations:
    - 24-hour availability of customer services
    - Electronic accounting system
    - Cashless payment methods with chip cards
    - E-Commerce
    - Ecologically sound products
    - Environmental consulting/environmental disposal consulting
    - Electronic ordering systems
    - Digital identification of goods
    - Remote maintenance
  - Process innovations:
    - Implementation of networked data processing systems (SAP and others)
    - Implementation of ecological audits
    - New computer-aided design system (CAD)

- · Electronic ordering systems
- · Digital identification of goods
- Financial services:
  - Product innovations:
    - · Telephone/direct banking
    - · Online banking
    - · Qualified customer consulting in securities and investments
    - · Execution of concurrent policies at point of sale (bank branch)
    - · Introduction of fund-connected life insurance
    - · Counter insurance of risks using the stock market
    - · Cat-bonds, asset-backed securities
    - · Expansion of self-service techniques
  - Process innovations:
    - · Euro-capability of transactions
    - · Paperless offices
    - · Computer-protected consulting and information systems
    - · Electronic archives, optical-electronic receipt archiving
    - · New scoring, rating methods
- Other services:
  - Product innovations:
    - · Customer orientation and service (service teams, later opening times, direct contacts etc.)
    - · 24-hour assistance and emergency services
    - · After-sales service
    - · Consulting in eco-audit regulation
    - · Complementary financial services
    - · Development of customer-specific software
    - · Contracting-services in environmental and energy fields
    - · Use of chip cards as payment method
    - · Statistical summaries for consumers
  - Process innovations:
    - · Internet presence
    - · Electronic data bank systems
    - · Introduction of CAD
    - · Implementation of an electronic business management system (restructuring, PC solution)
    - · Supply chain management

3

Employment Effects of Innovation Activities*

3.1 Introduction

The question of how technological progress affects the employment situation is an old one and has long been the focus of theoretical and empirical industrial organisation research as well as lively public discussions.[33] The controversial debates on this issue mainly result from the fact that, from a theoretical point of view, different channels exist through which innovations can destroy existing jobs (displacement effects) but that there are also several mechanisms through which innovations may create new jobs (compensation effects). In addition, product and process innovations influence employment via different channels. The overall impact depends on a number of firm-, sector- as well as country-specific factors.

The empirical answer to this long-standing question, however, is more topical than ever. This is based on the incessantly high rate of unemployment not only in Germany but in several other Western European countries as well. High unemployment induces severe problems such as those facing the German social security system or public budgets. In addition to mere economic recovery, politics hope that innovations could provide an important contribution to strengthen the competitiveness of firms and, consequently, to the preservation or creation of new jobs. Policies to stimulate innovation activities are, therefore, high on the list of priorities. For instance, the German government proclaimed 2004 as the "year of innovation".

Recently, Jaumandreu (2003) proposed a new simple multi-product model well-suited for analysing the employment impacts of innovations using the specific information provided by Community Innovation Surveys (CIS) data.

---

* This chapter is largely based on Peters (2004). The model in section 3.4.1 and the international comparison in section 3.6 largely draws on a joint paper with Rupert Harrison, Jordi Jaumandreu, and Jacques Mairesse, see Harrison et al. (2005).

[33] For a historical overview, see Petit (1995) or Freeman and Soete (1997).

Further details of the model have been worked out in a joint paper by Harrison et al. (2005). One interesting aspect of the approach is that it establishes a theoretical link between employment growth and innovation output in terms of the sales growth generated by new products as well as efficiency gains attributable to process innovations. As far as employment is concerned, it seems especially useful to lean on indicators that emphasise the economic success because they also incorporate the demand situation which is an important factor to the firms' employment decisions (see Blechinger, Kleinknecht, Licht, and Pfeiffer, 1998). The second advantage is that it allows to disentangle some of the theoretical employment effects under certain assumptions. A third notable feature shown here is that the CIS data are harmonised for the European countries included and, thus, allow firm-level cross-country comparisons.

The first aim of this chapter is to empirically analyse the employment effects caused by innovations in Germany using this theoretical multi-product model. The investigation reports new results on the relationship between innovation and employment growth for German manufacturing firms and is the first to provide empirical evidence for German service firms using data from the third Community Innovation Surveys (CIS 3). The sample includes data on more than 2,200 German manufacturing and service sector firms observed in the period 1998-2000. Despite the dynamic development of the service sector in highly industrialised countries within the last two decades and the fact that new employment was especially created within this sector, firm-level evidence on displacement and compensation effects of innovation activities scarcely exists for the service sector (see section 3.3).

As a second stage, further insights into the innovation-employment nexus are gained by considering different types of product as well as process innovations, as employment effects are expected to differ according to the type of innovation. In case of product innovations, they are likely to depend on the product novelty degree. Falk (1999) has found evidence that new jobs are mainly created in firms that have positioned themselves on the cutting edge by launching products that are new to the market (market novelties) while no significant employment effects can be found in enterprises pursuing an imitation (follower) strategy, that is in firms which offer new products that are new to the firm but not new to the market (firm novelties). However, the latter firms are important for the diffusion of new technologies and the structural change within an economy. Moreover, most theoretical as well as empirical studies assume that process innovations work on the supply side by reducing unit costs. But, the implementation of new production methods is not necessarily intended to afford increased productivity and reduced costs (rationalisation innovations); it can also be a result of product innovations or legal regulations or serve to – incrementally or significantly – improve product quality. Displacement effects are assumed to be stronger for firms which introduce new processes for rationalisation reasons while process innovations aimed to improve the product quality should have an effect similar to product innovations. Despite the large body of empirical work discussing the innovation-employment link, there is still a dearth of studies that focus on different innovation indicators at the firm level. Using the above-mentioned multi-product framework, I am, therefore, extending the model and the analysis by distinguishing between (i) two different product innovations according to their novelty degree (sales growth generated by market novelties and sales growth stemming from product innovations only new to the firm) and (ii) two different process innovation indicators (rationalisation and other process innovations, respectively).

As a third stage, an international perspective is adopted, and firm-level employment effects caused by innovations are compared between the four large European countries France, Spain, the UK, and Germany using the internationally harmonised CIS data, the same econometric model as well as the same estimation method. Despite the ongoing globalisation and European integration, firms in these countries still operate, at least partly, in different economic and institutional environments, which is especially true for the service sector. Differences, e.g., in national market structures might have an impact pertaining to the extent to which firms pass on cost reductions due to process innovations to their customers and, thus, on the amount of compensating effects.

To sum up, five questions are addressed in this chapter:

1. Do product and process innovations spur or diminish employment at the level of the innovating firm in Germany?
2. Can a pattern common to industry and service firms be perceived regarding this topic?
3. Do employment effects differ between different kinds of process innovations?
4. Do firm-level employment effects differ between products new to the firm and those new to the market?
5. Is there a common international pattern discernible in the link between innovation and employment?

The outline of this chapter is as follows: Section 3.2 sketches some theoretical considerations about the channels through which innovations affect employment, and section 3.3 summarises the main empirical firm-level results so far. The basic theoretical and econometric model developed as well as its extension is explored in section 3.4. Section 3.5 presents the econometric evidence on the employment effects of different innovation activities in German firms using the multi-product model. The chapter is round off by an international comparison of the employment effects between the four European countries France, Spain, the UK, and Germany in section 3.6. Finally, section 3.7 draws some conclusions on the relation between innovation and employment growth.

3.2 Theoretical Considerations

From a theoretical viewpoint, the impact of innovation activities on employment is not clearly determined. There are different channels through which technological change can destroy or create new labour: The overall impact depends on several factors and might differ in short- and long-run perspectives. First of all, it depends on the existing production technology and the nature of the technological progress itself, i.e. the type (product or process innovation), direction (labour- or capital-saving, neutral, skill-biased etc.), dimension (radical or incremental innovation), and manifestation (disembodied or factor-embodied) of the technological change. Moreover, consumer preferences, the competition on commodity and labour markets, and the qualification structure of the labour force are of importance to the employment impact. The link between innovation and employment can be analysed on different levels: firm, sector, and aggregate level. The following empirical analysis is restricted to employment effects at the level of the innovating firm, representing one of the main instances where the according mechanisms are more or less explicitly supposed to work. On a sector or aggregate level, technological progress is associated with further impacts on firms' labour demand, which are beyond the scope of the present study.

Both product and process innovations influence employment via different channels (see Stoneman, 1983; Katsoulacos, 1984; Blechinger et al., 1998). An overview of potential effects at the level of the innovating firm is given in Table 3.1.

If process innovations lead to an increase in productivity (rationalisation innovations), firms are able to produce the same amount of output with less input and, ceteris paribus, lower costs. The immediate extent of the employment effect in the innovating firm depends on the current production technology and, thus, the substitutability between input factors as well as on the direction of the technological change. As a rule, this effect negatively affects employment in the short run and is, thus, called the displacement effect of process innovations. At the same time, the innovative firm can pass on the cost reduction to output prices which results – from a dynamic perspective – in a higher demand for and output of the product. This compensating price effect depends on the amount of price reduction, the price elasticity of demand, the degree of competition as well as the behaviour and relative strength of different agents within the firm. The more intense the competition on the commodity market is, the higher is the extent to which cost reductions are passed to output prices. On the other hand, managers may be tempted to use market power to increase profits while unions may seek to transform any gains from innovations into higher wages which lessen the size of compensation effects (see Nickell, 1999). The compensating mechanism enhances labour demand, and thus, the overall employment change at the level of the innovating firm is not clear. Unlike rationalisation innovations, process innovations directed to improve the quality of an existing product or process innovations which

Table 3.1: Theoretical Employment Effects of Product and Process Innovation at a Glance

Type	Effect	Transmission Mechanisms	Direction[a]	Determinants[b]
Process innovation (rationalisation)	Productivity effect	Less labour for a given output	−	Substitutability between input factors, direction of technical change
	Price effect	Cost reductions can be passed on to output prices, enhance output	+	Amount of price reduction, price elasticity of demand, competition, agents' behaviour
Product innovation	Demand effect	Demand increase by new product	+	Competition, reaction of competitors, synergies in production
	Indirect effect	Demand effects on old products	+/−	Demand relationship between old and new products
		Productivity differences between old and new products	+/−	Production technologies

Notes: [a] + indicates a positive employment effect and − a negative one. +/− means that the employment effect can be positive or negative.
[b] List of determinants is not necessarily complete.
Source: Own representation.

accompany the introduction of new products should work more explicitly on the demand side. Their employment effects should essentially correspond to those pertaining to product innovations.

Additional employment effects may occur in upstream or downstream firms. If the firm acquires new machines to improve its production process, this directly stimulates labour demand in the corresponding supplier firm. Furthermore, if the innovative firm is able to increase its output, all its suppliers benefit and may boost their labour demand as well. On the other hand, competitors which cannot keep pace with the technological progress will lose market share or even disappear, implying a deterioration of jobs in those firms. Furthermore, the competition on commodity and labour markets have to be taken into account when analysing employment effects on a sector or aggregate level.

Employment impacts of product innovations are essentially a result of demand effects. When a new product has successfully been launched to the market, it creates new demand for the firm. The demand effect is likely to be the result of a market expansion as well as a business-stealing effect (crowding-out effect, that is the innovating firm's extension of its market share at the expense of its competitors). As a consequence, product innovations increase the labour demand of the innovating firm. The amount and sustainability of such compensation effects resulting from demand increases depend on the competition and the way and delay with which competitors react (see Garcia, Jaumandreu, and Rodriguez, 2002). If the innovating firm produces more than one good, the amount depends on synergies in production as well. The higher the synergy effects are, the lower, ceteris paribus, the effect on labour demand is, as common production implies economies in input factors. Additionally, indirect employment effects occur which depend on the substitutability between the old and new products. If the new product (partially or totally) replaces the old one, labour demand for the old product will decrease, and the overall effect is again not clear for the innovating firm. However, in the case of complementary demand relationships, the innovation in question causes the demand for previously existing products to rise as well, and employment will increase. Product innovations may also have productivity effects, even if they are not associated with simultaneous process innovations. The new or improved product may imply a change in production methods and input mix, which could either reduce or increase labour requirements. The extent and direction of the effect must be empirically determined (see Harrison et al., 2005).

Employment effects of product innovations are also likely to depend on the product novelty degree. From a theoretical point of view, the product life cycle theory of Vernon (1966), which states that each product or sector follows a life cycle, provides one explanation. By definition, market novelties initiate the cycle of the product or even the sector. According to this theory, younger sectors are less mature as consumers are not yet well-equipped, and thus, they experience higher demand increases (see Greenan and Guellec, 2000). As a consequence, market novelties should, ceteris paribus, result in higher output and employment growth.

On the other hand, firms develop innovations to alter market structures and to reduce the competitive pressure. This intended change is an important incentive for innovation activities. If firms are successful, that is if the own price elasticity for their new commodity is lower compared to that for the old product, then product innovations should, ceteris paribus, result in higher prices and decreasing output and employment (see, e.g., Smolny, 1998). This effect should be more pronounced in case of market novelties as they define an at least temporary monopoly. Moreover, market novelties are usually associated with a higher uncertainty and a higher risk of failure which might also lead to a lower employment growth.

In summary, it is suggested that the total effect of process as well as product innovations is not explicitly inferable and, therefore, must ultimately be ascertained on the basis of empirical analysis.

3.3 Survey: Previous Empirical Findings

The large body of empirical work discussing the innovation-employment link has concentrated on two major questions: The first one is related to the impact of technological change on total employment, mainly on aggregate or industry level, but there is also a growing number of firm-level studies. The second strand of empirical literature focusses on the question whether innovation activities induce a change in the skill structure of employees, referred to as the technological skill bias, as it is hypothesised that technological changes increase the demand for high-skilled labour and reduce that for low-skilled persons.[34] In what follows, only studies dealing with the first question will be taken into account. For an overview of empirical studies on technological skill bias, see Chennells and van Reenen (1999), Kaiser (2000; 2001) or Falk and Seim (2000; 2001), and the references cited therein.

For a long time, empirical innovation research has focussed on input-oriented innovation indicators when measuring aspects of innovation, that is mainly productivity but also employment effects (see, e.g., Griliches, 1995). This means that, traditionally, conditional labour demand functions are estimated using factor prices, output, and a measure of innovation input (like R&D capital stock, R&D expenditure, or ICT investment) as explanatory variables. R&D is often found to be positively correlated with employment growth (see, e.g., Blechinger et al., 1998; Regev, 1998) although not always (see Brouwer, Kleinknecht, and Reijnen, 1993; Klette and Forre, 1998). However, the innovation input transforms into product as well as process innovations, and both affect labour demand via different channels. In the 1990s, the focus changed to more output-oriented innovation indicators.[35] One obvious reason for this trend is connected to the greater availability of large firm databases and especially the development of the Oslo Manual (OECD and Eurostat, 1997) and the release of new, internationally harmonised survey data, known as the Community Innovation Surveys (CIS), which began in the first half of the 1990s.

Reviewing previous econometric firm-level studies which explicitly focussed on the distinction between employment impacts of product and process

---

[34] Closely related to the aspect of the shift in the labour demand from low- to high-skilled personnel is the increasing inequality of the relative wages across skill groups (see, e.g., Fitzenberger, 1999).

[35] Traditionally, patents have been used as an indicator to measure innovation output. However, patent-based indicators have been heavily criticised as being a poor measure of innovative outcome (see Griliches, 1990).

innovations, one can ascertain that the majority of them have found a stimulating effect of product innovations on labour demand in manufacturing. For West Germany, this was shown in the studies of Entorf and Pohlmeier (1990), König, Licht, and Buscher (1995), Blechinger et al. (1998), Rottmann and Ruschinski (1998), or Smolny (1998; 2002).[36] The same qualitative result was confirmed by van Reenen (1997) for the UK, by Garcia et al. (2002) for Spain, or by Greenan and Guellec (2000) for France.

As Falk (1999) pointed out, this effect depends on the novelty degree. Using German CIS 2 manufacturing data covering the period 1994-1996, he showed that firms launching market novelties expected an increase in labour demand. Contrarily, no significant employment effects were found in enterprises which had solely launched imitative products that are new to their own firm but not to the market. However, Falk analysed the expected instead of the realised employment change. Brouwer et al. (1993) found that firms with a high share of product-related R&D experienced an above average growth of employment. They interpreted their innovation indicator as a proxy of R&D related to industrial activities in an early stage of the life cycle. All in all, there is currently little empirical evidence of how employment effects depend on the degree of product novelty.

Moreover, there is no clear evidence of a robust effect of process innovations on jobs in manufacturing. In the studies of van Reenen (1997) and Entorf and Pohlmeier (1990) the impact of process innovations turned out to be small and not significant at all while König, Licht, and Buscher (1995), Smolny and Schneeweis (1999), Smolny (2002), or Greenan and Guellec (2000) reported that process innovators experienced significantly higher employment growth rates. The latter study even found evidence that process innovations, compared to product innovations, were of greater importance to create new employment at the firm level.[37] Contrarily, Blechinger and Pfeiffer (1999) found evidence that the introduction of new production technologies led to a reduction in employment in manufacturing firms in West Germany in the mid 1990s – the effect being more pronounced in larger firms. With the exception of van Reenen (1997), who used the number of major innovations, the above-mentioned studies estimated reduced-form equations including dummy variables for product and process innovations.

So far, there is hardly any econometric evidence on the overall employment effects of technological change for service firms, Jaumandreu (2003) being an exception. Using the model described in the next section, he found some indication that the net outcome of process innovation was employment displacement in the Spanish service sector although the effect was not significant. Like in manufacturing, product innovations were associated with employment growth.

---

[36] The result of Zimmermann (1991) is an exception.

[37] However, the reverse relationship was detected on the sectoral level.

3.4 Theoretical and Econometric Model

The model developed by Jaumandreu (2003) and Harrison et al. (2005) allows to disentangle some of the theoretical employment effects mentioned above and is highly applicable in analysing firm-level employment impacts of innovation activities using the specific information provided by CIS data. The share of sales due to product innovations serves as the key output indicator in this data. One interesting aspect of the approach is that it establishes a theoretical relationship between employment growth and results of innovation activities at the firm level. That is, it postulates a link between the employment growth rate and the innovation output in terms of sales growth stemming from innovative products. The latter can be directly calculated by means of CIS data.

3.4.1 Basic Model

Theoretical Model

The theoretical framework is a simple multi-product approach, that is the model is based on the idea that firms can produce different products. It further assumes that one can observe a firm j at two points in time t ($= 1, 2$), which defines the beginning and the end of a reference period. At the beginning of this period, the firm produces one or more products which are aggregated to one product; the corresponding output is $Y_{it} = Y_{11}$, with i denoting the product (for ease of presentation, firm indices j are suppressed here and in the following terms). In what follows, this aggregate product is called the "old product". In the period under consideration, the firm can decide to launch one or more new (or significantly improved) products, with the aggregate output of the new products at the end of the reference period being Y_{22}.[38] By definition, Y_{21} equals zero whereas Y_{22} may be equal to or greater than zero. It is assumed in the remainder of the text that the innovation decision is prior to the employment decision, that is we do not model the firm's choice to innovate or not and assume that it is predetermined.[39] The new product can (partially or totally) replace the old one if they are substitutes or enhance the demand

---

[38] This set-up does not mean that the model is only restricted to firms that change their status from non-innovator to innovator. The label "old product" is justified as viewed from the end of the reference period (here, the reference period is 1998-2000), because the Oslo Manual defines innovators as enterprises that have successfully completed at least one innovative project within a 3-year period. That is, new products introduced, for example, by firm j in 1997 define said firm as an innovator at the beginning of the reference period in 1998 but are not viewed as innovations in 2000 any longer.

[39] The possible simultaneous determination of innovation and employment might induce an endogeneity problem in the estimation.

of the old product if complementarity exists. Thus, in the same period, the output of the unchanged product increases or declines by $\Delta Y_1 = Y_{12} - Y_{11}$.

To produce the different outputs, it is assumed that firms must replicate the conventional inputs labour L and capital C and that the production function F is linear homogeneous in these conventional inputs. To keep the model as simple as possible, we assume that labour is a homogenous input factor, that is we do not distinguish between different skills. Moreover, knowledge capital is accounted for as a non-rival input to the production processes which drives specific efficiencies for each process and its evolution over time. Assuming that (i) knowledge proportionally raises the marginal productivity of all conventional inputs by an efficiency parameter θ_{it} for $i = 1, 2$ and $t = 1, 2$, (ii) the efficiency in the productive process for the old product can increase by $\Delta\theta_1 = \theta_{12} - \theta_{11}$, for instance, due to process innovations, organisational changes or learning effects, and (iii) economies of scope are absent, this leads to the following eq. (3.1) and (3.2) for the old product's output at the beginning and the end of the reference period, respectively:

$$Y_{11} = \theta_{11} \cdot F(L_{11}, C_{11}) \tag{3.1}$$

and

$$\begin{aligned} Y_{12} &= \theta_{12} \cdot F(L_{12}, C_{12}) \\ &= Y_{11} + \Delta Y_1 \\ &= (\theta_{11} + \Delta\theta_1) \cdot F(L_{11} + \Delta L_1, C_{11} + \Delta C_1). \end{aligned} \tag{3.2}$$

The corresponding end-of-period output of the new product is given by eq. (3.3):

$$Y_{22} = \theta_{22} \cdot F(L_{22}, C_{22}). \tag{3.3}$$

According to the duality theorem and the assumptions of linear homogeneity and separability, these production functions correspond to the cost function:

$$\begin{aligned} C_{it}^* &= \begin{cases} c(w_{11}, r_{11}) \cdot \frac{Y_{11}}{\theta_{11}} & \text{at } t = 1 \\ c(w_{12}, r_{12}) \cdot \frac{Y_{12}}{\theta_{12}} + c(w_{22}, r_{22}) \cdot \frac{Y_{22}}{\theta_{22}} & \text{at } t = 2 \end{cases} \\[2ex] &= \begin{cases} c(w_{11}, r_{11}) \cdot \frac{Y_{11}}{\theta_{11}} & \text{at } t = 1 \\ c(w_{12}, r_{12}) \cdot \frac{Y_{11} + \Delta Y_1}{\theta_{11} + \Delta\theta_1} + c(w_{22}, r_{22}) \cdot \frac{Y_{22}}{\theta_{22}} & \text{at } t = 2 \end{cases} \end{aligned} \tag{3.4}$$

with the input prices wage $w(.)$, the interest rate $r(.)$, and marginal costs $c(.)$. We further assume that the input prices are the same for both products and are constant over the time period.

Denoting $c_L = c_L(w,r) = \partial c(w,r)/\partial w$ and applying Shephard's Lemma, we can derive the conditional labour demand functions for the different products for each point in time. The labour demand for the old product and, thus, the firm's overall employment at the beginning of the reference period is:

$$L_{11} = c_L \cdot (Y_{11}/\theta_{11}). \tag{3.5}$$

At the end of the period, firm j demands L_{12} for the old and L_{22} for the new product with L_{12} and L_{22} given by:

$$
\begin{aligned}
L_{12} &= L_{11} + \Delta L_1 \\
&= c_L \cdot (Y_{12}/\theta_{12}) \\
&= c_L \cdot [(Y_{11} + \Delta Y_1)/(\theta_{11} + \Delta\theta_1)]
\end{aligned} \tag{3.6}
$$

and

$$L_{22} = c_L \cdot (Y_{22}/\theta_{22}). \tag{3.7}$$

Thus, the growth in total employment $\frac{\Delta L}{L}$ is given by eq. (3.8):

$$\frac{\Delta L}{L} = \frac{L_{12} - L_{11} + L_{22}}{L_{11}} = \frac{c_L\left(\frac{Y_{11}+\Delta Y_1}{\theta_{11}+\Delta\theta_1}\right) - c_L\left(\frac{Y_{11}}{\theta_{11}}\right) + c_L\left(\frac{Y_{22}}{\theta_{22}}\right)}{c_L\left(\frac{Y_{11}}{\theta_{11}}\right)}, \tag{3.8}$$

which can be rearranged to:

$$\frac{\Delta L}{L} = \left(\frac{Y_{11} + \Delta Y_1}{\theta_{11} + \Delta\theta_1}\right) \cdot \frac{\theta_{11}}{Y_{11}} - 1 + \frac{\theta_{11}}{\theta_{22}} \cdot \frac{Y_{22}}{Y_{11}}. \tag{3.9}$$

Using a first order (linear) approximation for the first fraction, employment growth can be written as:

$$\frac{\Delta L}{L} \simeq \frac{-\Delta\theta_1}{\theta_{11}} + \frac{\Delta Y_1}{Y_{11}} + \frac{\theta_{11}}{\theta_{22}} \cdot \frac{Y_{22}}{Y_{11}}. \tag{3.10}$$

Note that the growth rate of total real output is equal to $\frac{(Y_{12}-Y_{11})+(Y_{22}-Y_{21})}{Y_{11}}$ where $Y_{21} = 0$. Hence $\frac{(Y_{12}-Y_{11})}{Y_{11}} = \frac{\Delta Y_1}{Y_{11}}$ is the growth in total real output due to old products, and $\frac{Y_{22}}{Y_{11}}$ captures the growth in total real output due to new products.[40] According to eq. (3.10), employment growth stems from three different well-known sources: (i) from the efficiency increase in the production of the old product, which negatively affects labour demand; (ii) from the rate of change in the production of the old product (which is provoked by the new product to a certain degree, the induced change being negative for substitutes and positive for complements); and (iii) from starting production of the new product (positive sign). The employment effect of the latter depends on the efficiency ratio between both production technologies.

Econometric Model

Transforming the above theoretical result into an econometric model and taking into account that efficiency gains are likely to be different between process innovators and non-process innovators, we arrive at eq. (3.11):

$$l = \alpha_0 + \alpha_1 \, d + y_1 + \beta y_2 + u \qquad (3.11)$$

with

l : employment growth rate;

α_0 : (negative) average efficiency growth for non-process innovators;

α_1 : average efficiency growth for process innovators;

d : dummy variable indicating process innovations;

y_1 : real output growth due to old products $\frac{\Delta Y_1}{Y_{11}}$;

y_2 : real output growth due to new products $\frac{Y_{22}}{Y_{11}}$;

β : efficiency ratio between old and new production technology: $\frac{\theta_{11}}{\theta_{22}}$;

u : error term with $E(u \,|\, d, y_1, y_2) = 0$.

Eq. (3.11) implies that even non-process innovators can achieve efficiency gains, possibly due to organisational changes, the sale of less productive firm components, acquisitions of higher productive firms, improvements in human capital endowment as well as learning or spill-over effects or minor improvements in the production methods.[41]

Two effects of interest in the literature can be identified on the base of the theoretical relationship in eq. (3.11). Firstly, β measures the gross effect

---

[40] The rate of change in the output of the old product and the growth in total real output due to old products is identical because total output only consists of old products in $t = 1$. For new products, however, it is not possible to calculate a growth rate in the production of new products, i.e. $\frac{(Y_{22} - Y_{21})}{Y_{21}}$ is not defined.

[41] Remember that minor changes in the production process as well as pure organisational changes are not counted as process innovation in the innovation surveys; see section 2.1.2.

of product innovation on employment. Gross effect means that indirect demand effects on old products are not taken into account. Secondly, α_1 allows us to identify the productivity or displacement effect of process innovation. Unfortunately, y_1 captures three different effects which cannot be separated without additional (demand) data: (i) the possible autonomous increase in firm demand for the old products due to cyclical or industry effects; (ii) the compensation effect induced by price changes following a process innovation; and (iii) the indirect demand effects resulting from the introduction of new products.

One problem in estimating eq. (3.11) is that we do not observe real output growth but nominal sales growth. The problem that prices are unobserved is common in productivity analysis, but it is particularly relevant in this case since we are attempting to separately identify the productivity effects of old and new products, which may be sold at different prices. However, we can split the firm's (observed) sales growth rate g into sales growth due to old (g_1) and new products (g_2). Using the subsequent definitions of g_1 and g_2, we can derive eq. (3.15) in nominal variables, which serves as the basic estimation equation. Concerning the nominal rate of sales growth due to old products, the following relationship

$$g_1 = \frac{p_{12}\,Y_{12} - p_{11}\,Y_{11}}{p_{11}\,Y_{11}} = y_1 + \pi_1 \tag{3.12}$$

holds approximately, where p_{1t} is the price of the old product at time $t = 1, 2$, and $\pi_1 = \frac{p_{12}-p_{11}}{p_{11}}$ represents the corresponding price growth for old products over the period.[42] On the other hand g_2 is defined as the ratio of sales of new products to sales of old products measured at the beginning of the period:

$$g_2 = \frac{p_{22}\,Y_{22}}{p_{11}\,Y_{11}} = y_2 + \frac{p_{22} - p_{11}}{p_{11}}\,y_2 = y_2 + \pi_2 y_2, \tag{3.13}$$

with π_2 denoting the ratio of the price difference between the new and old product to the price of the old product.[43] This leads to the following equation:

$$l = \alpha_0 + \alpha_1\,d + g_1 + \beta\,g_2 + v, \tag{3.14}$$

where $v = -\pi_1 - \beta\pi_2 y_2 + u$ is the new composite error term.[44]

---

[42] The exact relationship is $g_1 = y_1 + \pi_1 + \pi_1 y_1$, where we assume that the last term as the product of two growth rates is close to zero.

[43] Like the output growth rate, the price growth rate for new products $\frac{p_{22}-p_{21}}{p_{21}}$ is not defined.

[44] If the inflation rate π_1 has a non-zero mean, one could include $-E(\pi_1)$ in the intercept and $-(\pi_1 - E(\pi_1))$ in the error term.

For estimation purposes we use $l - g_1$ as left-hand variable since new products cannibalise the old ones to some extent and are, therefore, to a certain degree responsible for the old products' change in sales. That is, the basic estimation equation is:[45]

$$l - g_1 = \alpha_0 + \alpha_1\, d + \beta\, g_2 + v. \tag{3.15}$$

As mentioned by Jaumandreu (2003), the relationship (3.15) implies endogeneity as well as identification problems for the estimation. The endogeneity problem occurs because, by definition, g_2 is correlated with the error term v. We assume that $E\left(\pi_2|y_2\right) = 0$. Then $E\left(\pi_2 y_2\right) = 0$ and y_2 is uncorrelated with $\pi_2 y_2$. The assumption that π_2 is mean independent of y_2 means that the relative price difference between new and old products is not a function of the relative output growth of new products. This assumption seems to be justifiable since the price of the new product may be affected by many other unrelated factors (quality improvements, substitutability among the goods, demand shifters, market power etc.), and it puts us in a position to look for suitable instruments which are correlated with y_2 but uncorrelated with the error term. The identification problem results from the fact that we cannot observe firm-level price changes, which leads to π_1 being included in the error term. As a consequence, it is not possible to identify the gross employment effect of efficiency (productivity) gains but merely the net employment effect which has been accounted for indirect price effects. If efficiency rises by the factor a, marginal costs decline by the same factor. Depending on competition and market power, firm j passes on the cost reduction to its clients by the factor δ so that the price is reduced by δa. As long as we cannot control for firm-level price changes of the unchanged product, we are only able to estimate the net effect $-a - \pi_1 = -(1 - \delta)a$. To overcome this hindrance, Jaumandreu proposed to use the disaggregate price indices $\widetilde{\pi}_1$ and $l - (g_1 - \widetilde{\pi}_1)$ as dependent variable. This method leads to an identification of the average gross productivity effect if firms behave according to the sector average. However, the identification problem is still valid for firms that deviate from the average price behaviour.[46] In the empirical analysis, I will rely on eq. (3.15) using $l - (g_1 - \widetilde{\pi}_1)$ as dependent variable.

3.4.2 Extended Model

It is expected that employment effects may not only depend on the type (product or process) but also on the dimension of technological change. Therefore,

---

[45] This implies that the coefficient of the sales growth due to unchanged products is assumed to be 1. A more flexible alternative would be to estimate the coefficient of this variable, too, but this was not done here.

[46] Hall, Lotti, and Mairesse (2006) modified the model by specifying two relationships between the observed price from the statistical office and firm-level prices for old and new products.

the analysis is simply broadened in a second step by distinguishing between different kinds of product as well as process innovations.

I use the the above-mentioned multi-product framework and assume that, depending on its innovation strategy, firm j decides upon the product novelty degree by launching new products that are new to the market (market novelties) and/or by introducing products which are new to the own firm but not to its relevant market (firm novelties) with the aggregate output of the respective products at the end of the reference period being Y_{i2m} and Y_{i2f}. The innovation decision is still assumed to be predetermined.

Most theoretical as well as empirical studies assume that process innovations reduce unit cost. However, as already explored in section 3.1, the introduction of new production technologies may have several different purposes. Process innovations may aim to improve the quality of products or to assure that products or production processes meet new legal requirements; firms also introduce new technologies simply to be able to produce a new product. Last but not least, process innovations may be intended to rationalise in terms of reducing average production costs. I allow for the fact that efficiency and, thus, employment effects may differ according to the type of process innovation.

Both considerations lead to the following estimation equation in the second step:

$$l - (g_1 - \widetilde{\pi}_1) = \alpha_0 + \alpha_c\, d_c + \alpha_{nc}\, d_{nc} + \beta_m\, g_{2m} + \beta_f\, g_{2f} + v \qquad (3.16)$$

with g_{2m} and g_{2f} denoting the sales growth generated by market novelties and firm novelties, respectively, d_c meaning a rationalisation innovation and d_{nc} other process innovations. The hypothesised relationship is $\alpha_c < \alpha_{nc}$ because we expect that the displacement effects are higher for firms with rationalisation innovations. As was set forth in section 3.2, the employment consequences of introducing new products are likely to depend on the product novelty degree. But from a theoretical point of view, the expected relationship between β_m and β_f is ambiguous.

3.5 Empirical Analysis for Germany

Based on this multi-product approach, this section carries out estimates of the employment effects of different types of innovation activities in Germany. Subsection 3.5.1 describes the data set used for the empirical analysis and holds some descriptive statistics. The estimation procedure used is clarified in subsection 3.5.2, and the econometric results are shown and discussed in subsection 3.5.3. A decomposition of the employment growth based on the econometric estimates is presented in subsection 3.5.2; a sensitivity analysis with respect to the cyclical influence completes this empirical investigation.

3.5.1 Data and Descriptive Analysis

The data set used is based on the 2001 official innovation surveys in the German industry and service sectors, which made up the German part of the CIS 3 (see chapter 2 for a more detailed data description). Firms were observed for the reference period 1998-2000. In Germany, the innovation surveys cover firms with at least 5 employees, but to facilitate an international comparison of the German results with those of Spain, France, and the UK, I include only firms with 10 or more employees.[47] Furthermore, I restrict the sample to manufacturing (NACE 15-37) and to those service sectors which are covered by CIS 3, i.e. wholesale trade (51), transport/storage (60-63), post and telecommunication (64), financial intermediation (65-67), computers and related activities (72), research & development (73), and technical services (74.2+74.3).

For estimation purposes, I further exclude (i) firms established during 1998-2000 (i.e., if employment or sales are 0 or missing for 1998) and (ii) firms which experience an increase or decrease in turnover of more than 10% due to mergers or due to the sale or closure of a part of the enterprise. Besides that, a few outliers (in which employment growth or labour productivity growth turned out to be higher than 300%) were eliminated, and firms with incomplete data for any of the relevant variables were dropped. The total number of observations remaining for the empirical analysis is 1,319 for manufacturing and 849 for services. An overview of the sectors and the distribution of innovating and non-innovating firms is given in Table 3.27 in Appendix B. Table 3.28 contains information on the distribution by size classes in the estimation sample.

To compute price growth rates, I use producer price indices on a 3-digit NACE level for manufacturing. For a few 3-digit NACE classes no indices are published; here, the producer price indices on the corresponding 2-digit NACE level are used as proxy.[48] For service firms, I am only able to apply 7 different price indices.[49] All indices are elaborated and published by the German Statistical Office (Destatis).

In general, employment consists of the number of employees and the number of hours they work. Here employment is measured as the number of em-

---

[47] However, estimations for the whole sample, including firms with at least 5 employees, show that the results do not substantially differ from those reported for the restricted sample. These estimation results are available on request.

[48] In Germany, producer price indices are available for 87 3-digit NACE classes in manufacturing. However, no producer price indices are published for the classes 17.3, 18.3, 20.5, 21.1, 22.3, 23.3, 28.5, 28.6, 29.6, 33.3, 35.3, 35.4, 35.5, 37.1, 37.2.

[49] Producer price indices are available for wholesale trade, shipping, and air as well as railway transport, which were applied for NACE 51, 61, 62 and 60.1. For NACE 60 (except 60.1) and 63 I use the transport component of the consumer price index, for 64 the corresponding telecommunication component. For all other service sectors, price growth rates are computed from the services component of the consumer price index.

ployees in full-time equivalents, where I assume that part-time employees are represented by halves of full-time worker. EMPLOY measures the employment growth rate for the period 1998-2000. The empirical definition of other variables derived from the econometric model as well as of some additional control variables subsequently used are described in great detail in Tables 3.2 and 3.3.

Regarding the descriptive statistics, Table 3.4 introduces the means and standard deviations (s.d.) for the major variables used in the study. Additionally, Table 3.5 depicts the growth rates of employment, sales, and prices of the sampled firms by their innovation status in the period 1998-2000. Since mean values can, of course, be strongly influenced by lone outliers, the median is also presented for comparison.

Some interesting similarities and differences between the two total samples, that is samples including both innovative and non-innovative firms, for manufacturing and services are displayed. Starting with the differences, the average employment growth rate between 1998 and 2000 is nearly two times higher in the service sector (10.2%) compared to the manufacturing sample (5.9%). However, I find that in both sectors the average employment growth is higher in innovative firms. Yet, this does not clearly indicate a causal relationship in that innovations lead to more employment. These statistics could, for example, be attributable to industry effects. The correlation between employment development and innovation activities at the firm level will, thus, be investigated using multivariate methods in the following section. The average employment growth rates exceed the official figures released by the German Federal Statistical Office (labour force growth rate in Germany between 1998-2000: 4.7%, i.e. an average growth rate of 2.3% p.a.; see http://www.destatis.de). But of course, these figures are not directly comparable due to (i) different definitions and calculation methods, (ii) the sample restriction, and (iii) a selectivity problem. The latter is due to the fact that only surviving firms as of 2000 are covered by the survey. However, the figures are consistent with the stylised fact that services in Germany have gained in importance since the mid 1980s and that employment shifts from manufacturing to the service sector.[50] Similar differences between manufacturing and service firms can be found in sales and price growth rates. On average, nominal sales mounted by 15% in manufacturing between 1998 and 2000 while prices increased by 1.3%. The corresponding figures for services are 18% and 4%. However, this implies that real sales grew roughly by 7% p.a. in both sectors.

Concerning the innovation behaviour, the sample reflects quite well such characteristics as on the national scale (see section 2.3) and does not give any obvious cause for selectivity concerns in this respect. About 60% of the manu-

---

[50] See figures on the labour force development in Fachserie 1, Reihe 4.2.1 published by Statistisches Bundesamt (a) or Peters (2003). Moreover, one can observe an employment shift within the manufacturing as well as service sector to more knowledge-intensive branches; see Pfeiffer and Falk (1999).

Table 3.2: Definition of Qualitative Variables

Variable	Model	Type	Definition
PROD		0/1	Product innovation: Introduction of at least one new or significantly improved product during 1998-2000.
FIRM		0/1	Firm novelty: Introduction of at least one new or significantly improved product during 1998-2000 which was new for the firm but not for the market.
MARK		0/1	Market novelty: Introduction of at least one new or significantly improved product during 1998-2000 which was new to the firm's market.
PROC	d	0/1	Process innovation: Introduction of new or significantly improved production technologies or methods of supplying and delivering products or procedures during 1998-2000.
COST	d_c	0/1	Introduction of at least one process innovation intended for rationalisation purposes in terms of reducing production costs in 1998-2000.
OTHER_PROC	d_{nc}	0/1	Dummy variable being 1 if PROC=1 and COST=0. It primarily captures quality-improving process innovations.
PROD_ONLY		0/1	Dummy variable being 1 if PROD=1 and PROC=0.
PROD&PROC		0/1	Dummy variable being 1 if PROD=1 and PROC=1.
PROC_ONLY	d	0/1	Dummy variable being 1 if PROD=0 and PROC=1.
COST_ONLY	d_c	0/1	Dummy variable being 1 if PROD=0 and PROC=1 and COST=1.
OTHER_PROC_ONLY	d_{nc}	0/1	Dummy variable being 1 if PROD=0 and PROC=1 and COST=0.
COST&PROD		0/1	Dummy variable being 1 if PROD=1 and PROC=1 and COST=1.
NON_INNO		0/1	Dummy variable being 1 for non-innovators between 1998-2000.
SIZE	x	0/1	System of 3 size class dummies: Firms with 10-49, 50-499 and >=500 employees.
IND	x	0/1	System of 11 and 7 dummies grouping manufacturing and services, respectively (see Table 2.1, electrical engineering and MPO instruments have been summarised).

Notes: PROC and PROC_ONLY are alternative definitions of d in the regression as are COST and COST_ONLY of d_c and OTHER_PROC and OTHER_PROC_ONLY of d_{nc}. x stands for additional control variables.

Table 3.3: Definition of Quantitative Variables

Variable	Model	Type	Definition
EMPLOY	l	c	Growth rate of the firm's overall employment for period 1998-2000 (in full time equivalents).
SHARE_NEWPD		c	Share of sales in 2000 due to new products introduced between 1998-2000.
SHARE_MARK		c	Share of sales in 2000 due to market novelties introduced between 1998-2000.
SHARE_FIRM		c	Share of sales in 2000 due to firm novelties introduced between 1998-2000.
SALES		c	Growth rate of the firm's turnover for the period 1998-2000.
SALES_NEWPD	g_2	c	Growth rate of the firm's turnover due to product innovations for the period 1998-2000. Computed as: [SHARE_NEWPD * (turnover in 2000/turnover in 1998)].
SALES_MARK	g_{2m}	c	Growth rate of the firm's turnover due to market novelties for the period 1998-2000. Computed as: [SHARE_MARK * (turnover in 2000/turnover in 1998)].
SALES_FIRM	g_{2f}	c	Growth rate of the firm's turnover due to firm novelties for the period 1998-2000. Computed as: [SHARE_FIRM * (turnover in 2000/turnover in 1998)].
SALES_OLDPD	g_1	c	Growth rate of the firm's turnover due to unchanged products for the period 1998-2000. Computed as: [SALES - SALES_NEWPD].
PRICE	$\widetilde{\pi}_1$	c	Price growth for the period 1998-2000 on a 3- or 2-digit level (see also the explanations in section 3.5.1).
LAB_COSTS	x	c	Rate of change of the firm's average labour costs (total remuneration plus social contributions) per employee during 1998-2000.
INVEST	x	c	Sum of investments in tangible assets in 1998, 1999, and 2000 per employee in 1998.

Notes: c denotes a continuous variable. x stands for additional control variables.

Table 3.4: Descriptive Statistics for Total and Innovative Sample

	Unit	Manufacturing				Services			
		Total sample		Innovative sample[a]		Total sample		Innovative sample[a]	
Variables		mean	s.d.	mean	s.d.	mean	s.d.	mean	s.d.
Quantitative									
Employment[b]	No.	275	1,168	389	1,506	531	8,044	990	11,515
EMPLOY	%	5.9	24.7	8.4	27.3	10.2	34.9	14.9	35.7
SALES	%	15.2	34.4	18.2	36.2	18.5	51.0	22.8	48.9
SHARE_NEWPD	%	–		23.5	23.4	–		25.0	27.7
SHARE_MARK	%	–		8.5	14.9	–		9.3	16.2
SHARE_FIRM	%	–		14.9	19.1	–		15.7	22.8
INVEST	1000 €	26.3	47.8	29.8	50.3	39.6	17.6	40.7	18.5
Qualitative									
Innovator	[0/1]	0.585	0.493	1.000	0.000	0.486	0.500	1.000	0.000
PROD	[0/1]	0.484	0.499	0.826	0.379	0.393	0.488	0.808	0.394
PROD_ONLY	[0/1]	0.210	0.407	0.359	0.480	0.177	0.381	0.363	0.482
PROD&PROC	[0/1]	0.274	0.446	0.468	0.499	0.217	0.412	0.446	0.498
MARK	[0/1]	0.318	0.465	0.543	0.498	0.248	0.432	0.511	0.500
PROC	[0/1]	0.375	0.484	0.641	0.478	0.309	0.463	0.636	0.482
PROC_ONLY	[0/1]	0.101	0.302	0.174	0.379	0.093	0.291	0.191	0.394
COST	[0/1]	0.270	0.444	0.461	0.499	0.164	0.371	0.339	0.474
Obs.		1319		772		849		413	

Notes: [a] Innovative firms are defined as firms with product and/or process innovations.
[b] Employment denotes the absolute number employees in full-time equivalents.

facturing enterprises introduced at least one product or process innovation in the reference period, compared to only 50% of the service firms. New products were launched by 48% of all firms in manufacturing. In the service sector just 40% of the enterprises supplied new services to their clients. However, in both samples two out of three product innovators launched at least one market novelty. Process innovations are less common with 38% and 31% in manufacturing and services, respectively. The German CIS data set provides an additional distinction between firms applying rationalisation innovations and those utilising other process innovations. Just 26% of all manufacturing firms, that is nearly three out of four process innovators, introduced new production

Table 3.5: Employment, Sales and Price Growth Rates for Innovators and Non-Innovators, 1998-2000

Type	Employment growth			Sales growth																		Price growth		
				Total			Old product			New product														
										Total			Firm novelty			Market novelty								
	m	s.d.	md	m	s.d.	md	m	s.d.	md	m	s.d.	md	m	s.d.	md	m	s.d.	md				m	s.d.	md
Manufact.																								
NON_INNO	2.4	20.0	0.0	10.8	31.2	6.0	10.8	31.2	6.0	–	–	–	–	–	–	–	–	–				1.1	4.8	1.2
PC_ONLY	6.0	22.7	2.3	21.7	44.1	11.4	21.7	44.1	11.4	–	–	–	–	–	–	–	–	–				2.4	7.0	1.6
PROD	9.0	28.0	3.5	17.5	34.3	10.8	-17.0	32.9	-14.8	34.5	35.3	24.0	21.4	24.6	14.2	13.1	26.6	5.3				1.3	4.5	1.8
thereof																								
PD_ONLY	8.1	28.2	2.6	15.2	31.8	8.7	-18.4	31.5	-16.1	33.6	35.1	22.6	21.6	25.8	12.6	12.0	23.6	4.3				1.4	5.5	1.8
PD&PC	9.4	28.2	4.1	19.3	36.0	12.5	-15.9	34.0	-13.9	35.2	35.5	25.3	21.2	23.6	14.8	14.0	28.7	5.6				1.2	3.4	1.8
Total	5.9	24.7	1.6	15.2	34.4	8.7	-1.5	36.9	-1.2	16.7	30.0	0.0	10.3	20.2	0.0	6.4	19.6	0.0				1.3	4.9	1.7
Services																								
NON_INNO	5.9	33.7	0.0	14.4	52.8	4.6	14.4	52.8	4.6	–	–	–	–	–	–	–	–	–				5.0	5.8	4.2
PC_ONLY	6.1	28.8	0.0	11.2	32.6	5.4	11.2	32.6	5.4	–	–	–	–	–	–	–	–	–				4.7	5.8	1.8
PROD	16.9	36.9	7.1	25.6	51.6	13.3	-15.9	44.3	-11.9	41.5	48.4	24.0	25.1	34.8	11.9	16.4	33.9	6.0				3.0	2.9	1.8
thereof																								
PD_ONLY	17.9	34.3	8.8	25.8	55.8	12.5	-11.3	49.2	-11.9	37.2	42.4	23.0	22.1	31.9	10.1	15.1	29.1	6.6				3.2	3.1	1.8
PD&PC	16.1	38.9	5.9	25.4	48.1	13.4	-19.6	39.6	-11.6	45.0	52.8	25.7	27.5	36.9	15.9	17.5	37.4	5.7				2.8	2.8	1.8
Total	10.2	34.9	0.0	18.5	51.0	8.0	2.2	50.1	0.0	16.3	36.5	0.0	9.9	25.0	0.0	6.5	22.7	0.0				4.2	5.0	1.8

Notes: Entrants and firms strongly affected by merger, sale or closure are excluded as are firms with less than 10 employees in 2000 or those lacking complete information. m, s.d. and md denotes mean, standard deviation and median of the variables. For lack of space, PROD_ONLY is abbreviated as PD_ONLY, PROC_ONLY as PC_ONLY, and PROD&PROC as PD&PC.

technologies to rationalise processes. However, amongst service sector firms, only one half of all process innovators experienced cost reductions due to new processes. In both sectors nearly one half (45%) of all innovative firms introduced new products as well as new production technologies while amongst the other half, one third solely concentrated on process innovation and the remaining two thirds on pure product innovation activities.

Looking at the innovation performance, it turns out that in both sectors innovative firms earned approximately 25% of their turnover in 2000 with product innovations introduced during 1998-2000, including about 9% with market novelties. This corresponds to a sales growth rate due to product innovations of nearly 35% in manufacturing: 33.6% for firms only launching new products and 35.2% for firms introducing both new products and processes. In the service sector these growth rates are even a little higher, at 37% and 45%, respectively. Thus, product innovations are important for sales growth in both sectors, and firm novelties contributed more to sales growth than market novelties. At the same time, sales for old products substantially decreased for product innovators, revealing that new products replaced old ones to a large extent. All in all, this induced the sales growth rate of product innovators to be roughly 11 and 14 percentage points higher than that of non-innovative firms and pure process innovators in the service sector, respectively. Note that the sales growth recorded by non-innovators and firms innovating only with respect to processes must be attributed to old products. Furthermore, it should be mentioned that the German economy experienced a considerable upswing in economic activity during this period, the peak being in the year 2000.

3.5.2 Estimation Method

As mentioned above, the relationship (3.15) implies an identification and an endogeneity problem. To address the identification problem, industry price growth rates were subtracted from the nominal sales growth of unchanged products, that is $l - (g_1 - \widetilde{\pi}_1)$ was used as the dependent variable.

Due to the likely endogeneity problem, applying OLS to eq. (3.15) would yield biased and inconsistent parameter estimates. Based on the first regressions in Tables 3.7 and 3.8, the estimates for the coefficient of sales growth due to new products appeared to be downward biased.[51] The Durbin-Wu-Hausman (DWH) test confirmed the endogeneity problem and rejected the

---

[51] Notice, in general, the downward bias may show up because of the endogeneity or as a result of weak instruments. The problem of weak instruments will be further discussed at the end of this section.

null hypothesis that the OLS estimator is consistent.[52] Hence, the model is estimated applying the instrumental variable (IV) method.

Instruments for the endogenous right-hand-side variable sales growth due to new products (g_2, i.e. SALES_NEWPD) should be correlated with the real rate of sales growth stemming from innovations (y_2) but should be uncorrelated with the error term. Factors which have been found to be important in explaining the success of product innovations in the theoretical as well as empirical literature are, among others, R&D and innovation input (see, e.g., Crépon et al., 1998; Lööf and Heshmati, 2002; Love and Roper, 2001; Janz, Lööf, and Peters, 2004), technological opportunities (see Cohen and Levinthal, 1989), technological capabilities (see, e.g., Dosi, 1997; König and Felder, 1994), absorptive capacity (see, e.g., Becker and Peters, 2000), market demand (see Crépon et al., 1998), network relationships, especially with customers (see, e.g., von Hippel, 1988; Beise-Zee and Rammer, 2006), corporate governance structure (see Czarnitzki and Kraft, 2004a), or knowledge capital of employees (see Love and Roper, 2001). Thus, the success of product innovations in terms of sales growth is likely to be correlated to the following factors, where the variables in parentheses are tried as instruments in the empirical analysis to measure these factors (see Table 3.6 for a more detailed variable definition and Table 3.29 in Appendix B for descriptive statistics):

- innovation input (RD_INTENS or INNO_INTENS);
- effects of product innovations (RANGE, QUALITY, or MARKET);
- degree of product novelty (SHARE_MARK; only attempted in the basic model);
- appropriability conditions (PATENT);
- technological capabilities (CONT_RD);
- technological opportunities (SCIENCE);
- integration of customers into the innovation process (CLIENT);
- competitiveness (EXP_INTENS).

However, it is not clear how these factors are linked to price changes, so instrument validity has to be checked for which was done by performing the Sargan-Hansen overidentification test.[53] Additionally, the validity of subsets of instruments has been tested using a difference-in-Sargan statistic, which is also

---

[52] The DWH test is based on an artificial regression by including the predicted value of the endogenous right-hand-side variable (as a function of all exogenous variables) in a regression of the original model and applying an F test for significance of the additional regressor (see Davidson and MacKinnon, 1993). Using, for instance, the instruments proposed in regression (2) in Tables 3.7 and 3.8, the DWH statistic was 44.74 (p-value: 0.000) in manufacturing and 8.60 (0.003) in services; using the preferred instruments of regression (6), the corresponding figures were 4.46 (0.035) and 7.14 (0.008).

[53] It is well-known that the Sargan test statistic is not consistent if heteroskedasticity is present. This problem was addressed through the use of the heteroskedasticity-consistent Hansen statistic.

Table 3.6: Definition of Alternative Instruments

Variable	Type	Definition
CONT_RD	0/1	Firm was continuously engaged in intramural R&D activities during 1998-2000.
CLIENT	0/1	Clients have been a high- to medium-sized information source of innovation.
SCIENCE	0/1	Science (universities, public research institutes) has been a high- to medium-sized information source of innovation.
PATENT	0/1	Firm applied for a patent during 1998-2000.
RANGE	0/1	Innovations has had a high- to medium-sized impact on an increased range of goods.
MARKET	0/1	Innovations has had a high- to medium-sized impact on increased market or market share.
QUALITY	0/1	Innovations has had a high- to medium-sized impact on improved quality in goods or services.
RD_INTENS	c	R&D expenditure/sales in 2000.
INNO_INTENS	c	Total innovation expenditure/sales in 2000.
SHARE_MARK	c	Share of turnover in 2000 due to market novelties introduced during 1998-2000.
EXP_INTENS	c	Export/sales in 1998.

Note: c denotes a continuous variable.

called C statistic. This means, the C statistic allows a test of the exogeneity of one or more instruments. It is defined as the difference of the Hansen statistics of the unrestricted equation (with the smaller set of instruments) and the restricted equation (with the larger set of instruments). Under the null hypothesis that the subset of orthogonality conditions is valid, the C statistic is distributed as chi-squared in the number of instruments tested. The acceptance of the null hypothesis that the subset of instruments are valid, requires that the full set of orthogonality conditions is valid (see Wooldridge, 2002).

For Spanish firms, Jaumandreu (2003) proposed the variables RD_INTENS, RANGE, and MARK_SHARE as instruments. To compare results, I used the same instruments in regressions (2)-(3) of Tables 3.7 and 3.8. However, in several regressions the test of overidentifying restrictions rejected the null hypothesis of valid instruments for the German data set. Using the difference-in-Sargan statistic, I found that it is the RD_INTENS which is often rejected as a valid instrument. In regression (4) the INNO_INTENS was used instead but Hansen's J statistic again rejected the null hypothesis of the validity of the moment restrictions. After testing the different above-mentioned instruments, CONT_RD, PATENT, CLIENT, SCIENCE, and, in addition, RANGE in manufacturing were used as instruments in specifications (5) and (6) of Tables 3.7 and 3.8 and in all estimations of Tables 3.9 and 3.10. Using this set of instruments, the null hypothesis regarding the validity of the orthogonality restrictions was accepted for all estimations.

The search for appropriate instruments is essential for estimation. As mentioned above, appropriateness here refers to the instruments' *validity* in terms of zero correlation ($\rho = 0$) between the instruments and the error term of the structural model as well as *strength* as in showing strong partial correlation with the endogenous right-hand-side variable. In recent years, several authors have been emphasising that particular problems and pitfalls in inference arise if the instruments are weak and conventional (first-order) asymptotic inference techniques are used, for instance, the Sargan test or the traditional Hausman specification test (see Staiger and Stock, 1997; Shea, 1997; Hausman, 2001; Hahn and Hausman, 2002). A situation of weak instruments can emerge when the instruments have a low explanatory power for the endogenous right-hand-side variable or when the number of instruments becomes large (see Hahn and Hausman).

The first problem associated with weak instruments is that they can cause large finite sample biases: Regardless of whether the instruments are valid, the IV estimator is likewise biased (in the same direction as OLS) in finite samples because the parameters of the reduced form are unknown and have to be estimated. Bound, Jaeger, and Baker (1995) already showed that *assuming instrument validity* the bias of the IV relative to the OLS estimator is approximately inversely related to the F-statistic F of the first-stage regression.[54] That is, when the instruments have a high degree of explanatory power for the jointly endogenous variable and, thus, F is sufficiently large (a value of at least 10 was put forward in the literature as a rule of thumb), IV performs better than OLS and should be given preference. Even when instruments are weak, yet still valid, IV nevertheless has a smaller bias compared to OLS as long as the number of instruments is sufficiently small in proportion to sample size (see Hahn and Hausman, 2003). First-step regression results for the preferred set of instruments are presented in Table 3.30 in Appendix B. The instruments are positively and significantly correlated with the endogenous variable(s), and throughout, F is evidently greater than 10. However, as may be applicable with the instruments identified here, larger problems can emerge when instruments are not truly exogenous. Both IV as well as OLS are then biased in finite samples and inconsistent. Hahn and Hausman (2002)

---

[54] More precisely, if there are no exogenous variables in the structural model, the F-statistic of the first-stage regression is applied. If the structural equation contains exogenous variables, the latter have to first be partialled out by premultiplying with an appropriate projection matrix. In this case, the partialled-out reduced-form regression delivers the correct F-statistic.

demonstrate that the finite sample bias of the IV is monotonically increasing (i) in the correlation between the error terms of the structural and reduced form (ρ), (ii) in the number of instruments, and decreasing (iii) in the sample size and (iv) in the R^2 of the reduced form. Hahn and Hausman (2003) found that IV does still better than OLS under a wide range of conditions but if instruments are weak, even a small correlation between the instruments and the stochastic disturbance of the structural model can produce a large finite sample bias in the IV estimator, potentially even larger than in OLS. A similar result was shown for the inconsistency of the IV estimator in such a case by Bound, Jaeger, and Baker.

The second problem of weak instruments is that conventional asymptotic theory breaks down because it treats the coefficients of the first-stage regression as non-zero and fixed (see Staiger and Stock, 1997). That is, the classical asymptotic distributions are not only very poor approximations for the exact finite distributions, but even if the sample size is large they are poor approximations.

Thus, IV-based inference can be highly misleading in a particular application when weak instruments are a problem. Recently, Hahn and Hausman (2002) suggested a new specification test for the appropriateness of IV which *jointly* addresses exogeneity and weakness. The general approach is that of the well-known Hausman-type specification test comparing two different estimators for the same parameter(s). Here, the forward (standard) IV and reverse IV (by exchanging the endogenous variables) estimators are used. Under the null hypothesis that conventional first-order asymptotics provide a reliable guide, the two estimators should be very similar. However, when second order asymptotic distribution theory is used, the two estimators will differ due to second order bias terms. Thus, if the null hypothesis is rejected, one cannot trust the conventional inference techniques. Rejection can occur due to false orthogonality assumptions of the instruments and/or due to weak instruments. The proposed test statistic HH is shown to have a normal distribution under the null hypothesis.[55] Using the set of preferred instruments, the estimated test statistics are 1.211 (p-value: 0.226) in manufacturing and 1.432 (p-value: 0.152) in the service sector (see Tables 3.7 and 3.8). Thus, this test clearly indicates that the problem of endogenous or weak instruments does not exist here and that reliance on the IV estimates is not misleading.[56] The

---

[55] See Hahn and Hausman (2002: 166-169) for the calculation of the test statistic.

[56] Hahn and Hausman (2002) suggest a sequential test procedure. If the null hypothesis of this test has been rejected, a similar specification test based on second-order unbiased Nagar-estimators should be carried out. If the second test has not led to a rejection of the null hypothesis, the limited-information maximum likelihood (LIML) estimator as the optimal combination of Nagar-estimators should be applied. If the second test has likewise failed, none of these estimators should be used at all.

interpretation of the results in section 3.5.3 will be based on this preferred set of instruments.

On a final note it needs to be addressed that the conventional IV estimator, though consistent, is inefficient if heteroskedasticity is present. When facing heteroskedasticity of unknown form, efficient estimates can be obtained by applying General Method of Moments (GMM) techniques. I test the null hypothesis of homoskedasticity performing the test proposed by Pagan and Hall (1983) (see also Baum, Schaffer, and Stillman, 2003). Using two different sets of indicator variables that are hypothesised to be related to the heteroskedasticity (levels, squares and cross-products of all exogenous variables or levels only), both statistics PH_{all} and PH_{lev} did not reject the null hypothesis of homoskedasticity. Thus, IV was considered as an appropriate method, and corresponding results are reported in the next section. Nonetheless, a comparison of GMM and IV results was carried out and can be found in Table 3.31 in Appendix B. As expected, the GMM results are more or less the same compared to IV.

3.5.3 Econometric Results

The empirical results revealing the relationship between employment growth and product and process innovations are reported in Tables 3.7 (basic model) and 3.9 (extended model) for manufacturing and in 3.8 and 3.10 for services, respectively. All in all, I arrive at plausible and, in the first part, very similar estimates for the employment effects of product innovations compared to the results for Spain, France, and the UK; however, there are discernible differences concerning the impact of process innovations (see Jaumandreu, 2003; Harrison et al., 2005).

The main result, which is quite robust to different specifications, is that successful product innovations have a significantly positive employment impact, that is the higher the sales growth rate due to product innovations, the higher the employment growth rate. This impact tends to be larger in manufacturing than in services. Recall that β measures the relative efficiency across production processes, that is if new products are produced more efficiently than the old ones, this ratio is less than unity, and employment does not grow one-for-one with the sales growth accounted for by new products. Jaumandreu (2003) found a unit elasticity of employment with respect to innovative output in terms of sales growth due to new products for Spanish firms. The t-tests show that the null hypothesis of a unit elasticity cannot be rejected for German firms in all estimations, even in the service sector. At the same time, one must consider that product innovations can displace existing products to a considerable extent; this leads to downsizing as well. An estimation of the net employment effect of product innovations will be undertaken in the following section 3.5.4.

Furthermore, the estimation results of the extended model given in Tables 3.9 and 3.10 suggest that new jobs are created not only in firms with mar-

Table 3.7: Employment Effects of Product and Process Innovations for Manufacturing Firms, 1998-2000 (Basic Model)

Basic Model: $l - (g_1 - \tilde{\pi}_1) = \alpha_0 + \alpha_1 \, d + \beta \, g_2 + v$

Regression	(1)	(2)	(3)	(4)	(5)	(6)
Method	OLS	IV	IV	IV	IV	IV
Constant	-5.492***	-7.605***	-7.301***	-7.282***	-6.414***	-6.433***
	(1.101)	(1.261)	(1.339)	(1.330)	(1.343)	(1.336)
PROC	-1.251	-3.943**	—	—	—	—
	(1.673)	(1.763)				
PROC_ONLY	—	—	-5.881**	-5.898**	-6.712**	-6.684**
			(2.967)	(2.963)	(2.905)	(2.910)
PROC&PROD	—	—	-2.697	-2.658	-0.851	—
			(2.349)	(2.322)	(2.592)	
SALES_NEWPD	0.883***	1.071***	1.077***	1.075***	0.993***	0.980***
	(0.064)	(0.085)	(0.101)	(0.100)	(0.085)	(0.063)
Adj. R^2	0.483	0.462	0.463	0.464	0.478	0.480
Root MSE	27.3	27.8	27.6	27.6	27.2	27.2
W_{IND} (p-value)	—	—	0.160	0.160	0.245	0.238
W_β (p-value)	0.069	0.407	0.447	0.452	0.936	0.747
PH_{all} (p-value)	—	—	—	—	0.950	0.745
PH_{lev} (p-value)	—	—	—	—	0.140	0.120
HH (p-value)	—	—	—	—	0.221	0.226
Hansen J	—	3.52	4.17	6.10	1.11	1.08
(df)		(2)	(2)	(2)	(4)	(4)
p-value		0.172	0.125	0.047	0.893	0.897

Notes: ∗ ∗ ∗, ∗∗, and ∗ indicate significance on a 1%, 5%, and 10% level, respectively (standard errors robust to heteroskedasticity in parentheses). Number of firms: 1,319. Regressions (3)-(6) include 10 industry dummies, and Suits' method is used to calculate the overall constant (see text). Instruments: RD_INTENS, RANGE, and SHARE_MARK in (2)-(3), INNO_INTENS instead of RD_INTENS in (4). CONT_RD, RANGE, PATENT, CLIENT, and SCIENCE in (5)-(6). Root MSE denotes the root mean squared error and adj. R^2 is the adjusted R^2. The Wald test statistic W_{IND} tests for the null hypothesis that the industry dummies are jointly equal to zero and is asymptotically $\chi^2(10)$ distributed under H_0. W_β is the Wald test statistic of the test $H_0 : \beta = 1$ and is asymptotically $\chi^2(1)$ distributed under H_0. PH_{all} and PH_{lev} test the null hypothesis of homoskedasticity. In (5) $PH_{all} \sim \chi^2(107)$ and $PH_{lev} \sim \chi^2(17)$ and in (6) $PH_{all} \sim \chi^2(91)$ and $PH_{lev} \sim \chi^2(16)$ under H_0. HH is the Hahn-Hausman specification test. Here, only

Notes are continued on next page.

Table 3.7 – *continued from previous page*

Notes (cont.): the corresponding p-values are reported. J reports the test statistic of a test of overidentifying restrictions. Under H_0, J follows a $\chi^2(m)$ distribution with m as the number of overidentifying restrictions. Testing the orthogonality of RD_INTENS in (3), I yield a C statistic of 4.158 (p-value: 0.041). For regression (6) the corresponding C statistics are: $C_{CONT\_RD} = 0.031$ (p-value: 0.861), $C_{RANGE} = 0.705$ (0.401), $C_{PATENT} = 0.000$ (0.998), $C_{CLIENT} = 0.552$ (0.458), $C_{SCIENCE} = 0.104$ (0.747).

---

ket novelties but also in those which successfully pursue imitation strategies. Both variables are significant, and using an F-test, the null hypothesis that both coefficients are equal cannot be rejected. This result suggests that the employment effects do not significantly vary with the product novelty degree. This conclusion is valid for manufacturing as well as service firms. Hence, at least for the German manufacturing sector, this result is partly in contrast to previous conclusions drawn by Falk (1999).[57]

Note that industry dummies are included in most of the regressions. The estimation equation is specified in growth rates, i.e. in first differences. This implies that time-invariant firm-specific (observable and unobservable) effects in the employment levels are already eliminated. However, the inclusion of industry dummies enlarge the flexibility of the specification by allowing for an unspecified form of heterogeneity in the growth rates between industries.

Based on the theoretical model, the constant α_0 can be interpreted as the average real productivity growth (with negative sign) in the production of old products in the reference period that is not traceable to own process innovation activities of that period but to organisational changes, sales of less productive parts of the firm, acquisitions of higher productive firms, improvements in human capital, learning or spill-over effects.[58] Inclusion of industry dummies, of course, implies that the constant term cannot be interpreted as average real productivity growth since it is related to the respective reference industry. To get an estimate of the average value, I, thus, use Suits' method. Suits (1984) suggested that once the equation has been estimated, one can choose a value k and add it to each of the coefficients of the industry dummies (including the zero coefficient of the dropped-out industry) and subtract

---

[57] Using CIS 2 data covering the period 1994-1996, Falk (1999) showed that only market novelties have stimulated the expected labour demand. The expected employment change was an ordinal variable in the data set which required a different estimation method (ordered probit model). Furthermore, he used dummy variables for both kinds of product innovations. Replacing the continuous variables in eq. (3.16) with their dummy counterparts, however, did not alter the qualitative results.

[58] Since I control for (industry) price changes of the old product, the value of the constant is an estimate of average real productivity growth, after any compensating price effects.

Table 3.8: Employment Effects of Product and Process Innovations for Service Firms, 1998-2000 (Basic Model)

Basic Model: $l - (g_1 - \tilde{\pi}_1) = \alpha_0 + \alpha_1\, d + \beta\, g_2 + v$

Regression	(1)	(2)	(3)	(4)	(5)	(6)
Method	OLS	IV	IV	IV	IV	IV
Constant	-1.402	-2.403	-6.010**	-5.903**	-7.814***	-7.870***
	(1.521)	(1.611)	(2.591)	(2.590)	(2.691)	(2.695)
PROC	4.777	2.472	—	—	—	—
	(2.387)	(2.392)				
PROC_ONLY	—	—	1.353	1.273	2.724	2.792
			(2.959)	(2.958)	(2.982)	(2.989)
PROC&PROD	—	—	3.041	3.283	-1.057	—
			(3.256)	(3.257)	(4.081)	
SALES_NEWPD	0.746***	0.851***	0.833***	0.825***	0.965***	0.955***
	(0.054)	(0.074)	(0.090)	(0.090)	(0.098)	(0.075)
Adj. R^2	0.402	0.395	0.416	0.417	0.391	0.394
Root MSE	34.0	34.1	33.4	33.4	34.1	34.0
W_{IND} (p-value)	—	—	0.013	0.013	0.016	0.013
W_β (p-value)	0.000	0.046	0.064	0.053	0.721	0.547
PH_{all} (p-value)	—	—	—	—	1.000	1.000
PH_{lev} (p-value)	—	—	—	—	0.714	0.714
HH (p-value)	—	—	—	—	0.150	0.152
Hansen J	—	7.95	9.84	10.21	0.11	0.12
(df)		(2)	(2)	(2)	(3)	(3)
p-value		0.019	0.007	0.006	0.990	0.990

Notes: $* * *$, $**$, and $*$ indicate significance on a 1%, 5%, and 10% level, respectively (standard errors robust to heteroskedasticity in parentheses). Number of firms: 849. Regressions (3)-(6) include 6 industry dummies, and Suits' method is used to calculate the overall constant (see text). Instruments: RD_INTENS, RANGE, and SHARE_MARK in (2)-(3), INNO_INTENS instead of RD_INTENS in (4). CONT_RD, PATENT, CLIENT, and SCIENCE in (5)-(6). For the definition of W_{IND}, W_β, PH_{all}, PH_{lev}, HH and J, see Table 3.7. For all tests the corresponding p-values are reported. W_{IND} is asymptotically $\chi^2\,(6)$ and W_β is asymptotically $\chi^2\,(1)$ distributed under H_0. In (5) $PH_{all} \sim \chi^2\,(59)$ and $PH_{lev} \sim \chi^2\,(12)$ and in (6) $PH_{all} \sim \chi^2\,(48)$ and $PH_{lev} \sim \chi^2\,(11)$ under H_0. Furthermore, testing the orthogonality of each instrument in (6), I yield the following C statistics: $C_{CONT\_RD} = 0.099$ (p-value: 0.753), $C_{PATENT} = 0.001$ (0.977), $C_{CLIENT} = 0.036$ (0.849), $C_{SCIENCE} = 0.033$ (0.857).

it from the constant term. The value k is chosen so that the resulting new industry dummy coefficients average zero.[59] Estimating the equation with all industry dummies and this restriction would yield identical statistical properties as the original estimation. The estimates of the constant $\widehat{\alpha_0}$ show the expected negative signs and reasonable magnitudes for a 2-year period, implying an average real productivity growth of about 3.2% p.a. in manufacturing and 3.9% in the service sector. However, the estimates of the constant in the service sector are less robust.

In the theoretical model, the process innovation dummy should pick up additional efficiency gains and, thus, employment changes due to changes in the production process of the old product. However, the information in the data set does not allow to distinguish between process innovations applied to old or new products. To partially address this problem, I divide process innovators up into two groups: firms with process innovations only (corresponds by definition to old products) and firms with both product and process innovations, where changes in the production technology could be related to both old or new products.

The empirical analysis shows differences between the manufacturing and service sectors regarding the impact of process innovations: Process innovations were responsible for an employment reduction in the period 1998-2000 in the manufacturing but not in the service sector. From a theoretical point of view, this can be interpreted in a way that displacement effects outweigh compensation effects in manufacturing, resulting in a negative employment effect. Conversely, the results suggest that service firms tend to react more aggressively and to pass on to prices the productivity gains derived from innovations to a larger extent which may be a result of less market power of service firms on average. However, the results for services should be interpreted more carefully as innovation processes in the service sector exhibit substantial differences compared to the manufacturing sector. In the service sector, the distinction between old and new services or processes is hindered by the fact that services are more often customised to specific demands and that in many cases a clearly structured production process is lacking (see section 2.1). Innovations in services are, therefore, more difficult to identify than in the manufacturing sector (see, e.g., Hempell, 2003).

Moreover, the estimates show that only manufacturing firms which solely carried out process innovations experienced negative employment effects while this was not the case for firms that introduced both new products and new processes. This result leads to the conclusion that different innovation strategies appear to be associated with different price behaviour. However, column (10) of Table 3.9 further reveals that this is not true for all firms that exclusively introduced process innovations but rather only for those firms which merely concentrated on rationalisation innovations. These varying effects of

---

[59] Since the new coefficients are linear combinations of the original coefficients, their variance can easily be calculated from the original variance-covariance matrix.

Table 3.9: Employment Effects of Different Types of Product and Process Innovations for Manufacturing Firms, 1998-2000 (Extended Model)

Extended Model: $l - (g_1 - \tilde{\pi}_1) = \alpha_0 + \alpha_c\,d_c + \alpha_{nc}\,d_{nc} + \beta_m\,g_{2m} + \beta_f\,g_{2f} + v$

Regression	(7)	(8)	(9)	(10)	(11)	(12)
Constant	-6.823***	-6.822***	-6.488***	-6.484***	-6.467***	-7.157***
	(1.266)	(1.266)	(1.343)	(1.342)	(1.345)	(1.527)
PROC	-2.891	—	—	—	—	—
	(1.903)					
COST	—	-3.075	—	—	—	—
		(1.951)				
OTHER_PROC	—	-2.459	—	—	—	—
		(3.222)				
PROC_ONLY	—	—	-6.614**	—	—	—
			(2.897)			
COST_ONLY	—	—	—	-8.081**	-8.102**	-7.621**
				(3.452)	(3.449)	(3.368)
OTHER_PROC_ONLY	—	—	—	-3.179	-3.203	-3.193
				(4.956)	(4.959)	(4.975)
COST&PROD	—	—	—	—	-0.362	—
					(2.269)	
SALES_FIRM	1.055***	1.052***	1.045***	1.044***	1.042***	1.006***
	(0.177)	(0.178)	(0.168)	(0.168)	(0.170)	(0.175)
SALES_MARK	0.986***	0.992***	0.877***	0.878***	0.891***	0.990***
	(0.277)	(0.278)	(0.265)	(0.265)	(0.278)	(0.268)
SIZE: 10-49	—	—	—	—	—	0.995
						(1.190)
SIZE: 50-499	—	—	—	—	—	1.263
						(1.050)
SIZE: 500+	—	—	—	—	—	-2.258*
						(1.360)
INVEST	—	—	—	—	—	-0.013
						(0.037)
Adj. R^2	0.472	0.472	0.478	0.478	0.478	0.477
Root MSE	27.4	27.4	27.2	27.2	27.2	27.2

To be continued on next page.

Table 3.9 – *continued from previous page*

Regression	(7)	(8)	(9)	(10)	(11)	(12)
W_{IND} (p-value)	0.229	0.226	0.243	0.240	0.239	0.167
W_{SIZE} (p-value)	—	—	—	—	—	0.236
$W_{\beta_f=\beta_m}$(p-value)	0.872	0.889	0.685	0.687	0.718	0.970
Hansen J	1.30	1.32	0.96	0.95	0.97	1.17
(df)	(3)	(3)	(3)	(3)	(3)	(3)
p-value	0.729	0.726	0.810	0.814	0.808	0.760

Notes: ∗ ∗ ∗, ∗∗, and ∗ indicate significance on a 1%, 5%, and 10% level, respectively (standard errors robust to heteroskedasticity in parentheses). Number of firms: 1,319. Instruments: CONT_RD, RANGE, PATENT, CLIENT, and SCIENCE. Regression (12) includes size dummies, and Suits' method is used to calculate the overall constant and the 3 size dummies. See also the notes of Table 3.7.

different types of process innovations may be one explanation as to why there is no clear empirical evidence of a robust (negative or positive) effect of process innovations on employment. The aims associated with the introduction of new production technologies (and, thus, the composition of process innovations in the sample under consideration) may, for instance, differ according to the level of economic activity or to different industries.[60]

Employment changes might be influenced by many other economic factors. Besides the technological progress and the industry structure, wages, investment, or firm size[61] might be important in explaining employment growth. Labour supply factors like preferences for leisure or the qualification level of the labour supply may also have an influence on the employment. Due to data limitations I cannot control for the latter ones. But, firm size (proxied by three different size classes according to employment in the base year 1998) and investment were controlled for in the last columns of Tables 3.9 and 3.10. Firm size, however, as well as the investment variable turned out to be not significant.[62]

---

[60] König, Licht, and Buscher (1995) found a significant positive effect of process innovations for the boom period 1990-1992 while Blechinger and Pfeiffer (1999) reported a significant negative effect for the recession period 1993-1995.

[61] According to Gibrat's law, firms grow (in terms of employment or sales) proportionally and independently of their size, see Gibrat (1934). In contrast to that, Jovanovic (1982), for instance, stressed the importance of managerial efficiency and learning by doing and developed a model in which surviving young and small firms grow faster than older and larger ones.

[62] The theoretical considerations in section 3.2 have shown that the degree of competition might also affect employment effects. I have experimented with a market concentration index (Herfindahl-Hirschmann index on a 3-digit NACE level); this variable, however, also turned out to be insignificant in all regressions. One expla-

Table 3.10: Employment Effects of Different Types of Product and Process Innovations for Service Firms, 1998-2000 (Extended Model)

Extended Model: $l - (g_1 - \tilde{\pi}_1) = \alpha_0 + \alpha_c\,d_c + \alpha_{nc}\,d_{nc} + \beta_m\,g_{2m} + \beta_f\,g_{2f} + v$

Regression	(7)	(8)	(9)	(10)	(11)	(12)
Constant	-7.682 **	-7.498 **	-7.796 **	-7.776 **	-7.730 **	-8.924 *
	(3.006)	(2.928)	(3.212)	(3.219)	(3.202)	(4.606)
PROC	0.411	—	—	—	—	—
	(3.995)					
COST	—	1.810	—	—	—	—
		(3.202)				
OTHER_PROC	—	-1.596	—	—	—	—
		(5.606)				
PROC_ONLY	—	—	2.746	—	—	—
			(3.152)			
COST_ONLY	—	—	—	2.500	2.495	2.780
				(3.399)	(3.393)	(3.946)
OTHER_PROC_ ONLY	—	—	—	2.411	2.403	2.712
				(4.664)	(4.656)	(5.027)
COST&PROD	—	—	—	—	2.291	—
					(4.012)	
SALES_FIRM	0.948 **	0.941 **	0.939 **	0.941 **	0.919 **	0.957 **
	(0.470)	(0.448)	(0.410)	(0.409)	(0.407)	(0.415)
SALES_MARK	0.953 **	0.952 **	0.971 **	0.969 **	0.960 **	0.979 **
	(0.449)	(0.449)	(0.454)	(0.454)	(0.450)	(0.431)
SIZE: 10-49	—	—	—	—	—	0.850
						(2.793)
SIZE: 50-499	—	—	—	—	—	3.378
						(2.246)
SIZE: 500+	—	—	—	—	—	-4.228
						(4.518)
INVEST	—	—	—	—	—	-0.006
						(0.005)
Adj. R^2	0.394	0.395	0.392	0.391	0.394	0.389
Root MSE	34.0	34.0	34.1	34.1	34.0	34.1
W_{IND}(p-value)	0.020	0.023	0.019	0.019	0.018	0.019
W_{SIZE} (p-value)	—	—	—	—	—	0.243

To be continued on next page.

Table 3.10 – *continued from previous page*

Regression	(7)	(8)	(9)	(10)	(11)	(12)
$W_{\beta_f=\beta_m}$ (p-value)	0.996	0.991	0.970	0.974	0.961	0.979
Hansen J	0.11	0.10	0.11	0.11	0.12	0.18
(df)	(2)	(2)	(2)	(2)	(2)	(2)
p-value	0.949	0.950	0.945	0.945	0.943	0.916

Notes: ***, **, and * indicate significance on a 1%, 5%, and 10% level, respectively (standard errors robust to heteroskedasticity in parentheses). Number of firms: 849. Instruments: CONT_RD, PATENT, CLIENT, and SCIENCE. Regression (12) includes size dummies, and Suits' method is used to calculate the overall constant and the 3 size dummies. See also the notes of Table 3.8.

Eq. (3.15) was derived under the assumption of constant factor prices. Table 3.11 shows some further robustness checks of the basic model by relaxing this assumption and controlling for changes in average labour costs. The sample had to be remarkably reduced for this exercise because the labour cost growth rate could only be constructed by merging the German innovation surveys of 2001 and 1999, and the intersection of firms came to 55% in manufacturing and 30% in services.[63] The negative sign of the estimator associated with the labour costs variable is what one would expect (see Blechinger et al., 1998; Smolny, 1998) while the coefficients associated with the innovation variables are little affected. The coefficient of the sales growth due to new products has slightly declined in manufacturing and has decreased to a larger extent in services; however, this seemed to be the result of the reduced sample itself.

3.5.4 Decomposition of Employment Growth

Based on the basic model estimation, the following decomposition holds for each firm (see Harrison et al., 2005):

$$l = \widehat{\alpha}_0 + \widehat{\alpha}_1 d + [1 - I(g_2 > 0)](g_1 - \widetilde{\pi}_1)$$
$$+ I(g_2 > 0)(g_1 - \widetilde{\pi}_1 + \widehat{\beta} g_2) + \widehat{u}, \tag{3.17}$$

where $I(\cdot)$ denotes the indicator function. The first term shows the change in employment due to productivity gains which are not attributable to own

nation for this result is presumably the fact that the index is often an insufficient indicator of firms' market power, in particular because innovation activities might change the innovator's market power.

[63] The core CIS questionnaire did not provide information on labour cost. The latter is an additional information in the German data set.

Table 3.11: Effects of Innovations and Labour Costs on Employment, 1998-2000 (Reduced Sample)

Basic Model: $l - (g_1 - \tilde{\pi}_1) = \alpha_0 + \alpha_1 d + \beta g_2 + v$

	Manufacturing			Services		
Regression	(1)	(2)	(3)	(4)	(5)	(6)
Constant	-6.162***	-6.020***	-5.484***	-7.696***	-1.857	-2.197
	(1.449)	(1.501)	(1.502)	(2.685)	(5.033)	(4.569)
PROC_ONLY	-6.475**	-5.893*	-6.169*	2.628	-7.252	-9.412*
	(2.857)	(3.249)	(3.212)	(2.986)	(5.587)	(4.903)
SALES_	0.984***	0.981***	0.977***	0.958***	0.843***	0.857***
NEWPD	(0.063)	(0.072)	(0.071)	(0.076)	(0.217)	(0.195)
INVEST	-0.013	-0.027	-0.028	-0.006	0.009	0.003
	(0.039)	(0.036)	(0.035)	(0.005)	(0.017)	(0.014)
LAB_COSTS	—	—	-0.091**	—	—	-0.296***
			(0.045)			(0.070)
Adj. R^2	0.480	0.473	0.476	0.393	0.519	0.564
Root MSE	27.2	23.6	23.5	34.1	22.7	21.6
W_{IND} (p-value)	0.228	0.085	0.072	0.012	0.020	0.008
W_β (p-value)	0.797	0.795	0.751	0.580	0.471	0.463
Hansen J	1.15	0.72	0.71	0.14	2.55	2.71
(df)	(4)	(4)	(4)	(3)	(3)	(3)
p-value	0.887	0.949	0.951	0.987	0.467	0.439
No. of firms	1,319	701	701	849	257	257

Notes: ∗∗∗, ∗∗, and ∗ indicate significance on a 1%, 5%, and 10% level, respectively (standard errors robust to heteroskedasticity in parentheses). Instruments: CONT_RD, RANGE (only in manufacturing), PATENT, CLIENT, and SCIENCE. For the definition of W_{IND}, W_β, and J, see Table 3.7.

process innovations in the respective period but to organisational changes, sales of less productive firm components, acquisitions of higher productive firms, improvements in human capital endowment, learning or spill-over effects etc. Notice that incremental changes in the production process are likewise counted here since they are not covered by the definition of process innovation (see section 2.1.2). This term is referred to as a general productivity trend. The second term presents the net employment contribution made by process innovations related to the production of old products. Here, net contribution is understood as the result of displacement effects brought about by process innovations and the compensatory demand effects owing to cost and price reductions. The third component registers so-called general output effects seen in the production of the old product for non-product innovators. That is, the third component accounts for changes in employment growth due to shifting demand for the existing product. This shift in demand can be the result of cyclical impacts, rivals' product innovations, changes in consumers' preferences etc. Finally, the fourth term summarises the net contribution of product innovations on employment for product innovators. In this case, this effect constitutes the result of increases in demand for the new product and possible shifts in demand for the old one. $\widehat{u}$ is the residual term. In the case of the extended model, the enlargement and interpretation of the decomposition is straightforward:

$$l = \widehat{\alpha}_0 + \widehat{\alpha}_c \, d_c + \widehat{\alpha}_{nc} \, d_{nc} + [1 - I(g_2 > 0)] \, (g_1 - \widetilde{\pi}_1)$$
$$+ I(g_2 > 0)(g_1 - \widetilde{\pi}_1 + \widehat{\beta_m} \, g_{2m} + \widehat{\beta_f} \, g_{2f}) + \widehat{u}. \tag{3.18}$$

A dissection of the average employment growth can be obtained by inserting the average shares of innovators from the sample, the average price growth rates, and the estimated coefficients into the equation.[64] Table 3.12 separately displays the results of the employment growth component dissection for both the manufacturing and the service sector. As an advance disclaimer, it should be mentioned that this decomposition presents the average effect of innovation activities on the employment growth of firms which survived, i.e. were active in the market at the beginning and end of the phase. Since no information on newly founded or withdrawing firms enter the analysis, macroeconomic conclusions are limited.

It is apparent that employment growth in manufacturing primarily results from product innovations. In the period 1998-2000, general productivity gains, process innovations, and output effects related to old products would have led to an overall decrease in employment of 2%. This deterioration of labour was, however, more than compensated for by product innovations, even considering the fact that new products replace previously offered goods by product innovators to some extent. The net effect of product innovation is about 7.5%. The observed employment growth was, thus, mostly based on the introduction of new products. Looking at the extended model, one can infer that the contribution of firm novelties to employment growth is higher than that of market novelties. Given that the estimated coefficients for both kinds of product innovations are very similar, this result is mainly driven by the different means of the sales growth rates which in part also reflect the fact that market novelties are less common than firm novelties across product innovating firms. The net impact of process innovations on employment growth

---

[64] This is equal to calculate separately the four terms and the residual for each firm and then take the average of each term. Note that the mean of $\widehat{u}$ is zero by construction.

Table 3.12: Decomposition of Average Employment Growth, 1998-2000[a]

	Manufacturing		Services	
	Basic Model	Exten-ded Model	Basic Model	Exten-ded Model
Employment Growth (%)	**5.9**	**5.9**	**10.2**	**10.2**
Decomposed into:				
Productivity trend in production of old pro-ducts[b]	-6.9	-6.9	-3.6	-3.5
Net contribution of process innovations	-0.7	—	0.3	—
Net contribution of rationalisation innovations	—	-0.6	—	0.1
Net contribution of other process innovations	—	-0.1	—	0.1
Output growth of old products	6.0	6.0	5.4	5.4
Net contribution of product innovations	7.5	7.5	8.2	8.1
thereof:				
output reduction of old products	-8.8	-8.8	-7.4	-7.4
output increase of new products	16.4	—	15.6	—
output increase of market novelties	—	5.6	—	6.3
output increase of firm novelties	—	10.8	—	9.3

Notes: [a] Decomposition is based on Tables 3.4, 3.5 and on regressions (6) in Tables 3.7 and 3.8 in the basic model as well as on regressions (10) in Tables 3.9 and 3.10 in the extended model. The sum of decomposition values may slightly differ from employment growth because of rounding.
[b] Productivity trend is the weighted sum of industry dummy values and, hence, differs from the constant of the regression.

is negative in manufacturing, but is of secondary importance when observed quantitatively (-0.7%). However, it should be noticed that using PROC_ONLY the significance of process innovations may be slightly underestimated. But as mentioned above, with the data at hand it is not possible to distinguish which process innovations of product innovators relate to the old and which to the new products.

The general picture in the service sector is similar, however, with some interesting differences. Most obviously, based on the estimates, the general productivity trend in the production of old products in the service sector is merely about half of that in manufacturing. On the other hand and similarly to manufacturing, product innovations contribute the most to employment growth, with the absolute value being higher for services (8.2% in the basic model). Their relative influence, however, is weaker than in manufacturing. In other words, in the service sector general productivity effects, process in-novations, and demand effects related to old products positively contributed

to employment growth, that is led overall to a labour expansion. As in manufacturing, firm novelties contribute more to employment growth than market
novelties. All in all, the net effect of process innovations is negligible in the
service sector.

3.5.5 Sensitivity Analysis

The estimates of the employment effects attributable to innovations in the
previous section were based on the period 1998-2000, a period that was characterised by a boom phase in Germany. Since the employment effects may
vary with the cyclical circumstances faced by firms, the results presented so
far may not be representative of average firm-level effects at other stages of
the business cycle. In phases of cyclical upsurge, more pronounced demand effects expected to lead to stronger employment growth are possible; especially
since production capacities are already utilised more heavily in such periods.
During recessions, product innovations are accordingly expected to have less
of an effect on employment since demand effects tend to be weaker and firms
are already struggling with excess capacity. Additionally, unfavourable demand development may reduce both the firms' willingness to take risks and
incentives to introduce product innovations; this in turn can also reduce employment effects. Due to data limitations, I cannot control for firms' capacity
utilisations or demand expectations when estimating employment effects. To
check the robustness of results, employment effects from the period 1998-2000
will, therefore, be compared with those from 2000-2002.

As mentioned above, the period 1998-2000 was characterised by a boom
while the German economy underwent a significant cyclical slump in the years
2000-2002. This fact also mirrors in Table 3.13 which displays the average employment and nominal revenue growth rates for firms in the manufacturing and
the service sector in the period 2000-2002. As was to be expected due to cyclical progression, the average (and median) employment and revenue growth
rates in both groups reach levels significantly lower than those recorded in the
years 1998-2000. But in both phases, the average rise in employment in the
service sector is approximately twice the size of manufacturing. Nominal sales
growth is also greater in services in both periods. However, if price development is taken into account, both industry groups show a similar real annual
revenue growth rate of around 2.5% in this period.[65] It can also be diagnosed
that in both industries employment and sales development progress is again
much more favourably in innovative firms – especially in those introducing
new products.

Despite the cyclically adverse circumstances seen between 2000 and 2002,
product innovators in manufacturing were able to realise a similarly high

---

[65] In the period 2000-2002, prices mounted on average by 1.8% in the manufacturing
sample and 3.2% in the service sample. The same price information as in section
3.5.1 was used.

Table 3.13: Employment and Sales Growth Rates for Innovators and Non-Innovators, 2000-2002

	Firm Type		Employ- ment Growth		Sales Growth		Sales Growth – Old Products		Sales Growth – New Products	
	No.	%	mean	med	mean	med	mean	med	mean	med
Manufacturing										
NON-INNO	578	38.3	-0.8	-0.2	1.9	-1.8	1.9	-1.8	—	—
PROC_ONLY	101	6.7	3.3	0.0	8.0	2.2	8.0	2.2	—	—
PROD	831	55.0	5.3	0.0	9.9	4.2	-23.9	-19.5	33.7	21.8
thereof:										
PD_ONLY	365	24.2	5.5	0.0	8.6	4.2	-24.4	-20.1	33.0	21.7
PD&PC	466	30.9	5.1	1.0	10.9	4.1	-23.5	-18.9	34.3	22.2
Total	1,510	100.0	2.8	0.0	6.7	2.1	-11.9	-10.7	18.6	4.7
Services										
NON-INNO	348	55.2	2.2	0.0	3.9	0.0	3.9	0.0	—	—
PROC_ONLY	41	6.5	2.1	0.0	7.3	1.8	7.3	1.8	—	—
PROD	241	38.3	9.9	5.1	14.5	8.6	-19.1	-14.4	33.6	21.6
thereof:										
PD_ONLY	101	16.0	7.6	3.8	13.1	6.4	-16.5	-11.5	29.6	16.0
PD&PC	140	22.2	11.6	7.3	15.4	10.1	-21.0	-18.3	36.4	25.6
Total	630	100.0	5.2	0.0	8.1	3.5	-4.7	-3.2	12.8	0.0

Note: For lack of space PROD_ONLY is abbreviated as PD_ONLY and PROD&-PROC as PD&PC.

revenue growth rate as in the earlier period by means of new products (33% compared to 34% in 1998-2000). In the service sector, however, cyclical factors seem to have an effect. For product innovators revenue growth attributable to new products came in at around 33.5% in the recession period 2000-2002, about 8 percentage points below the corresponding figure from the boom phase. Still, one must note that the revenue generated by product innovators with old goods decreases considerably; this again indicates that new products largely replace older ones. This decline in old-product revenue is much more pronounced in both industry groups during the recession, suggesting that firms thin out their product ranges to a greater extent in such periods and, most notably, that innovative products have a better chance of surviving in the marketplace.

Table 3.14 shows the estimation results of the basic model for different treatments of process innovations; the interpretation, however, is based largely on the preferred regressions (3) and (6). As can be seen, product innovations have stimulated employment growth in both industry groups. In manufacturing the coefficient of sales growth attributable to new products is slightly lower at around 0.93 in the recession period but is still not significantly different from one. In the service sector, product innovations had a positive effect on employment demand as well. However, their impact was less pronounced in the recession period. The coefficient fell from 0.96 in the period 1998-2000 to 0.86 in the period 2000-2002. This decline is statistically significant and tends to confirm the initial posits, at least for the service sector, that in recessive cyclical phases, weaker employment effects of product innovations can be expected.

In the period 1998-2000, the labour productivity growth not attributable to the firm's process innovations of that period stood between 3.2% and 3.8% per year in manufacturing, depending on the estimation. For 2000-2002, average annual productivity growth fell sharply to around 0.35%. In addition to the fact that the productivity effects which the firms were able to realise from the aforementioned changes (organisational changes etc.) were probably less significant, these figures may reveal that a number of firms produce goods in cyclically sketchy phases merely for the sake of the activity (without attaining or accounting for the respective revenue), saving their employees for better times rather than downsizing immediately. If this is the case, fluctuations in the capacity utilisation of the production factor labour might be reflected in the coefficient of the constant.

In the service sector, average productivity growth not attributable to process innovations comes in at 3-4% per year in the period 1998-2000. In the recessive phase, this figure drops to zero; the coefficient is actually positive but statistically not significantly different from zero. However, a decline in labour productivity in the service sector can also be a statistical effect. Employment is measured here in full-time positions while part-time employees are represented by halves of these. If the average number of hours per part-time employee lowers over time, however, employment growth measured in full-time equivalents will be overestimated and labour productivity, thus, underestimated. Such developments involving decreasing number of hours per part-time position are definitely plausible in the German service sector in the observation period since marginally employed individuals (occupying "€400-jobs") were being utilised as part-time labour to an increasing extent.

The results observed on the influence of process innovations prove to be quite mixed. In manufacturing, process innovations contributed to a decline in employment in both periods although the effect is less pronounced (and no longer significant) in the period 2000-2002. The fact that the net employment effect registers lower in the period 2000-2002 may also be related to increased pricing pressure felt by firms in cyclically difficult times: Firms tend to pass cost reductions directly to their customers during such phases. However, the service sector presents a very different picture. The coefficient of the PROC_ONLY variable was positive in the period 1998-2000 and negative in

Table 3.14: Effects of Innovations on Employment, 2000-2002

Basic Model: $l - (g_1 - \tilde{\pi}_1) = \alpha_0 + \alpha_1\,d + \beta\,g_2 + v$

Regression	Manufacturing			Services		
	(1)	(2)	(3)	(4)	(5)	(6)
Constant	-0.759	-0.678	-0.678	1.688	2.031	2.347*
	(1.307)	(1.424)	(1.391)	(1.368)	(1.398)	(1.399)
PROC	-1.663	—	—	2.468	—	—
	(1.961)			(2.639)		
PROC_ONLY	—	-2.304	-2.287	—	-4.289	-4.605
		(3.551)	(3.534)		(3.241)	(3.238)
PROC&PROD	—	-1.407	—	—	5.878*	—
		(2.550)			(3.330)	
SALES_ NEWPD	0.961***	0.954***	0.929***	0.828***	0.777***	0.855***
	(0.070)	(0.086)	(0.062)	(0.079)	(0.088)	(0.070)
Adj. R^2	0.288	0.291	0.303	0.404	0.407	0.404
Root MSE	30.7	30.6	30.4	26.7	26.6	26.7
W_{IND} (p-value)	0.065	0.062	0.060	—	—	—
W_β (p-value)	0.577	0.594	0.254	0.031	0.011	0.040
Hansen J	4.71	4.75	4.59	7.52	7.09	6.65
(df)	(4)	(4)	(4)	(4)	(4)	(4)
p-value	0.319	0.315	0.332	0.111	0.131	0.156
No. of firms	1,510	1,510	1,510	630	630	630

Notes: $***$, $**$, and $*$ indicate significance on a 1%, 5%, and 10% level, respectively (standard errors robust to heteroskedasticity in parentheses). Instruments: CONT_RD, RANGE, CLIENT, SCIENCE, and a dummy variable indicating whether the firm has introduced at least one market novelty. Industry dummies were left out in the service sector since the null hypothesis that they are jointly equal to zero could not be rejected [corresponding p-values of a Wald test (regression): 0.692 (4), 0.538 (5) and 0.786 (6)].

the second period. However, both coefficients were not significantly different from zero.

Finally, Table 3.15 displays the results of the employment growth component dissection for both time periods. While in the period 1998-2000, general productivity effects, process innovations, and output effects related to old products would have led to an overall employment downsizing of 2%, these effects more or less cancelled each other out in the period 2000-2002 (-0.4%). Both phases' employment growth was, thus, based mostly on the introduction

Table 3.15: Decomposition of Average Employment Growth – A
Comparison in Time Between 1998-2000 and 2000-2002[a]

	1998-2000	2000-2002
Manufacturing		
Employment Growth (%)	**5.9**	**2.8**
Productivity trend in production of old products[b]	-7.5	-0.6
Net contribution of process innovations	-0.6	-0.2
Output growth of old products	6.0	0.4
Net contribution of product innovations	8.0	3.2
Services		
Employment Growth (%)	**10.2**	**5.2**
Productivity trend in production of old products[b]	-3.0	2.3
Net contribution of process innovations	0.1	-0.3
Output growth of old products	5.4	0.8
Net contribution of product innovations	7.6	2.3

Notes: [a] Decomposition for 2000-2002 is based on Table 3.13 and regressions (3) and (6) in Tables 3.14. The sum of decomposition values may slightly differ from employment growth because of rounding.
[b] Productivity trend is the weighted sum of industry dummy values and, hence, differs from the constant of the regression.

of new products. In the service sector, product innovations also contribute the most to employment growth although their influence is, once again, relatively weaker than in manufacturing. That is, here, general productivity effects, process innovations, and demand effects related to old products led to overall labour expansion though to varying degrees in the respective cyclical phases. The net impact of process innovations is negative in nearly every case but is once again of secondary importance when observed quantitatively.

3.6 International Comparison Between France, Spain, UK and Germany*

In the last two decades, the European economic integration and globalisation has made great progress leading to a rise in both active (through growing export orientation) and passive (through growing import competition) international competition of domestic firms. For France, Spain, the UK, and

---

* This section mainly summarises results of the joint paper "Does Innovation stimulate employment? A Firm-Level Analysis Using Comparable Micro Data From Four European Countries" with Rupert Harrison, Jordi Jaumandreu and Jacques Mairesse, see Harrison et al. (2005).

Germany, the countries under consideration in this section, this is impressively confirmed by the development of the average annual growth rate in exports or imports since 1992, the year which marked the completion of the internal European market. This can be gathered from Table 3.16, which also depicts some other macroeconomic characteristics of the four countries. Taking the development of the GDP in this period into account, the share of trade as percentage of GDP mounted remarkably by 4.9 percentage points in the UK, 6.7 in France, 8.9 in Germany, and even 13 percentage points in Spain. Thus, in 2000, the share of trade had become alike in the four countries, ranging between 28% in France and nearly 34% in Germany. Stronger international competition means that market structures of national markets become more homogenous and that national characteristics are likely to diminish. But despite this progress, firms in these countries still operate, at least partly, in different economic and institutional environments, which is especially true for the service sector. Apart from the obvious difference in the size of the (national) home markets, institutional arrangements, for example, in the labour market or innovation policy still differ across countries. Furthermore, dominantly acquired positions in one or another market, possibly due to scale economies, previous sunk investments, or technological advantages and spill-overs, tend to persist over time despite globalisation (see Abramovsky, Jaumandreu, Kremp, and Peters, 2004). As mentioned above, differences in national market structures might have an impact to which extent firms pass on cost reductions due to process innovations to their customers and, thus, on the amount of compensating effects.

However, cross-country comparisons of firm-level employment effects caused by innovations are rarely available in the literature, Blechinger et al. (1998) being one exception. Moreover, the existing national studies widely vary in terms of the methodology and the data set used, impeding comparisons of such effects across countries. Blechinger et al. investigated the impact of innovation on employment in several European countries using CIS 1 data. However, due to legal protection rights, they could not lean themselves on the original firm-level data but on a micro-aggregated database provided by Eurostat.[66] In contrast, this section compares employment effects of innovation activities between the four countries France, Spain, the UK, and Germany using original firm-level data. As already mentioned, the CIS data are internationally harmonised, and we apply the same econometric model as well as the same estimation method to achieve common ground for comparison of the results. Due to legal restrictions in the usage of the data, we were not allowed to pool all observations into a single sample.

In what follows, subsection 3.6.1 briefly describes the data set and depicts main features of the innovation activities in the four countries observed. The econometric results are shown and discussed in subsection 3.6.2.

---

[66] Furthermore, some countries had to be excluded from the analysis, like the UK, Portugal, Greece, or in part Spain and the Netherlands.

Table 3.16: Macroeconomic Characteristics of France, Germany, Spain, and the UK

	FRA	GER	SPA	UK
Population in 2000 (in million)	58.896	82.160	40.171	58.655
Population growth rate in 2000 (in %)	0.47	0.17	0.82	0.21
Number of enterprises in 2000, manufacturing[a]	24,512	49,519	44,605	44,990
Number of enterprises in 2000, services[a,b]	16,998	65,855	26,695	43,630
GDP in 2000[c] (in billion US $)	1532.5	2042.8	811.3	1485.1
GDP per capita in 2000 (in US $)	25,293	24,851	20,317	25,322
Average annual growth rate in real GDP, 1995-2000 (in %)	2.6	1.8	3.7	3.1
Average annual growth rate in labour productivity, 1995-2000[d] (in %)	1.4	1.2	0.8	1.7
Average annual growth rate in multi-factor productivity, 1995-2000[e] (in %)	1.47	1.02	n.a.	0.99
Share of trade in GDP in 2000[f] (in %)	27.9	33.6	31.2	29.1
Increase in share of trade in GDP, 1992-2000 (in percentage points)	6.7	8.9	13.0	4.9
Average annual growth rate in nominal exports in goods, 1992-2000 (in %)	3.1	3.1	7.2	5.4
Average annual growth rate in nominal imports in goods, 1992-2000 (in %)	3.1	2.5	5.5	5.5
Trade balance in goods in 2000 (in billion US $)	-8.5	54.8	-39.5	-55.7
Trade balance in services in 2000 (in billion US $)	19.8	-55.0	22.4	20.5
Standardised unemployment rate in 2000[g] (in %)	9.1	7.7	11.3	5.4
Long-term unemployment in 2000[h] (in %)	42.6	51.5	47.6	28.0
Government debt in 2000[i] (in %)	66.2	60.9	67.3	45.9

Notes: [a] With 10 or more employees; in France: 20 or more. [b] Included services: 51, 60-67, 72, 73, 74.2, 74.3. [c] Current prices and purchasing power parities. [d] The growth of labour productivity is obtained by dividing the growth of value added at constant prices by the growth of the labour force. [e] The rate of multi-factor productivity growth is the part of GDP growth which is not explained by the weighted average of the rates of growth of capital and labour inputs. [f] Average of imports and exports (of both goods and services) at current prices as a percentage of GDP. [g] The unemployment rate is defined as the number of unemployed persons as a percentage of the civilian labour force, where unemployed persons are defined as those who report that they are without work, that they are available for work, and that they have taken active steps to find work in the last 4 weeks (according to ILO guidelines). [h] Long-term unemployment is here measured as those who have been unemployed for 12 months or more as a percentage of the total number of persons unemployed. [i] Gross financial liabilities as a percentage of GDP.
Source: OECD (2005b); Eurostat (2004); own calculations.

3.6.1 Data and Descriptive Analysis

In 2001, CIS 3 were conducted in the (at that time) 15 European Union (EU) member states as well as Norway. Under the general coordination of Eurostat, the statistical office of the EU, the surveys were carried out by national authorities. The questionnaire – including definitions – is widely harmonised across countries[67] and includes some core as well as some optional questions. Beyond the questionnaires, statistical survey methods as well as data mining and analytical methods are coordinated by Eurostat.

Table 3.17 summarises the main methodological characteristics of the surveys in each of the four countries. Abramovsky et al. (2004) described the four data sets and their comparability in more detail. They conclude that CIS 3 is a EU-wide harmonised statistic although some differences in the wording or institutional framework for some questions remain across countries, which imply that very specific comparisons must be made with care.

The target population in CIS 3 encompasses enterprises with 10 or more employees. In France, however, it covers only firms with 20 or more employees in manufacturing (not in services), complicating comparisons between the four countries. In each of the countries the survey is based on a stratified random sample applying disproportional drawing probabilities by size class and sector (and region in UK and Germany). One remarkable difference concerns participation in the survey which is voluntary for firms in Germany and the UK while it is compulsory in the other two countries. This fact results in considerably varying net samples, with Germany at the bottom.[68] Nonetheless, all samples are broadly representative by strata.

Details on the actual sample size and average firm size by sector in each country can be found in Tables 3.18 and 3.19. Below, the selection criteria as well as the variable definitions correspond to those set out in section 3.5. The average firm size differs widely across the four samples. The high value for manufacturing in France is likely to be the result of the higher cut-off point (20 employees). In manufacturing, the average German firm size is twice as high compared to Spain and 1.5 times higher than in the UK. The ratios are quite similar regarding these countries' total firm population although the samples' average firm sizes are higher as a result of the disproportionate drawing probabilities (see Abramovsky et al., 2004; Eurostat, 2004).

The breakdown of the sample by sector further reveals the well-known differences in sector specialisation which can also be found in total firm population. Germany has a comparatively large share of firms in machinery, electrical engineering (including medical, precision, and optical instruments), plastic/rubber, and metals. Spain shows relatively high shares in food, textile and

---

[67] Of course, slight differences cannot be completely ruled out due to the translation of the English questionnaire into national languages.

[68] However, remember that a non-response analyses have been carried out in Germany in order to control for a response bias, see section 2.1.1.

Table 3.17: Characteristics of CIS3 in France, Germany, Spain, and the UK

	FRA	GER	SPA	UK
Managing national authority	INSEE: trade and services; SESSI: manufacturing; Ministry of Research: R&D firms, banks and insurances; SCEES: food industry[a]	ZEW, on behalf of the Ministry of Education and Research	INE (Instituto Nacional de Estadistica)	DTI (Department of Trade and Industry)
Participation	compulsory	voluntary	compulsory	voluntary
Target population (number of employees)	20 for manufacturing, 10 elsewhere	5	10	10
Frame population[b]	Business Register	Credit reform database	Official INE register of firms (DIRCE)	Interdepartmental Business Register (IDBR)
Covered sectors[c]	C, D, E, G, I, J, K	C, D, E, F, G, I, J, K, O (only 90)	C, D, E, F, G, H, I, J, K, N,O	C, D, E, F, G (except 50, 52), I, J, K
Stratification	Size, sectors	Size, sectors, region	Size, sectors	Size, sectors, region
Gross sample[d]	9,620	20,717	n.a.	19,602
Net sample	7,836	4,611	11,778	8,172
Response rate	82	22	n.a.	42
Non-response[e]	no	yes	no	yes

Notes: [a] INSEE (Institut National de la Statistique et des Etudes Economiques), SESSI (Industrial Statistics Bureau of the Ministry of Industry), SCEES (Ministry of Agriculture).
[b] A business register did not exit in Germany, Creditreform is the largest German credit rating agency.
[c] According to NACE classification: C (mining and quarrying), D (manufacturing), E (electricity, gas and water supply), F (construction), G (wholesale, retail trade, repair of motor vehicles), H (hotels), I (transport, storage and communication), J (financial intermediation), K (real estate, renting and business activities), N (health and social work), O (other community, social and personal service activities).
[d] In France, the sampling rate varies by industry.
[e] Size of the non-response sample in Germany: 4,000.
Source: Abramovsky et al. (2004).

glass/ceramics, and furniture/recycling. The UK is rather strongly represented in transport, chemicals, and wood/paper while France shows comparatively high firm numbers in food, textile, chemicals, and metals. In total, Germany has a larger weight of high technology sectors, defined by machinery, vehicles, electrical engineering, and chemicals, followed by the UK, France, and Spain.

Table 3.18: Number of Firms, by Country and Sector

	NACE	Number of firms							
		FRA		GER		SPA		UK	
		No.	%	No.	%	No.	%	No.	%
Manufacturing									
Food	15-16	893	19.3	113	8.6	502	11.0	179	7.2
Textile	17-19	571	12.3	77	5.8	668	14.7	143	5.7
Wood	20-22	420	9.1	112	8.5	629	13.8	355	14.2
Chemicals	23-24	381	8.2	92	7.0	297	6.5	82	3.3
Plastic/rubber	25	279	6.0	116	8.8	199	4.4	130	5.2
Glass/ceramics	26	163	3.5	78	5.9	332	7.3	52	2.1
Metal	27-28	617	13.3	227	17.2	610	13.4	358	14.4
Machinery	29	425	9.2	184	14.0	286	6.3	202	8.1
Electrical	30-33	460	9.9	214	16.2	370	8.1	398	15.9
Vehicles	34-35	197	4.3	53	4.0	252	5.6	262	10.5
Furniture/recycling	36-37	225	4.9	53	4.0	403	8.9	332	13.3
Total		4,631	100.0	1,319	100.0	4,548	100.0	2,493	100.0
Services									
Wholesale	51	743	44.9	204	24.0	406	22.1	743	41.4
Transport	60-63	—	—	204	24.0	341	18.5	464	25.9
Post/telecomm.	64	31	1.9	26	3.1	76	4.1	64	3.6
Banks/insurances	65-67	251	15.2	97	11.4	128	7.0	328	13.3
Computers	72	211	12.8	80	9.4	180	9.8	79	4.4
R&D	73	64	3.9	75	8.8	72	3.9	34	1.9
Technical services	74.2-74.3	353	21.4	163	19.2	636	34.6	172	9.6
Total		1,653	100.0	849	100.0	1,839	100.0	1,794	100.0

Source: Harrison et al. (2005).

As market incentives to innovate as well as technological opportunities for developing new products and processes are typically larger in high technology sectors, one may expect the highest share of innovative firms in Germany and the lowest one in Spain. However, this is only partially confirmed by the data. Table 3.20 presents descriptive statistics for manufacturing from the four countries. For each variable the sample in each country is once again split into three sub-samples according to whether the firm reports that it has

Table 3.19: Average Firm Size, by Country and Sector

	NACE	Average Firm Size[a]			
		FRA	GER	SPA	UK
Manufacturing					
Food	15-16	282	149	150	303
Textile	17-19	124	219	78	148
Wood	20-22	234	358	87	144
Chemicals	23-24	483	330	213	364
Plastic/rubber	25	396	148	105	131
Glass/ceramics	26	415	247	141	260
Metal	27-28	258	153	110	67
Machinery	29	302	291	150	178
Electrical	30-33	540	482	157	197
Vehicles	34-35	1,164	340	367	224
Furniture/recycling	36-37	217	253	66	132
Total		345	276	132	172
Services					
Wholesale	51	62	410	146	124
Transport	60-63	—	1,272	373	291
Post/telecommunication	64	102	220	191	586
Banks/insurances	65-67	1,044	808	527	282
Computers	72	81	95	151	238
R&D	73	168	91	68	337
Technical services	74.2-74.3	129	56	301	135
Total		233	531	268	215

Note: [a] Average firm size is measured by the average number of employees in year 2000.
Source: Harrison et al. (2005).

not introduced any innovations, has introduced only process innovations, or has introduced product innovations. The table shows that in the samples innovators represent between about 60% of the firms in Germany and 40% in the UK. Innovators that only introduce process innovations generally constitute up to one in four of all innovators.

Unlike the share of innovators, the average employment growth rate is lowest in Germany and particularly high in Spain. But the general employment picture is similar across all four countries: The employment growth of innovators is consistently higher than the employment growth of non-innovators across the four countries, with the employment growth of product innovators slightly higher than firms that only introduce process innovations. Productivity gains tend also to be higher in the innovating firms with the exception of

Spain, where there is only little difference in average productivity growth between innovators and non-innovators. Notice that the increase in employment of innovative firms is higher despite their larger labour productivity gains. This suggests that compensation effects resulting from the growth of output dominate displacement effects of innovation at the firm level.

The average increase in sales over the period 1998-2000 is high in all countries, reflecting both the expansionary phase of the industrial cycle and the fact that these are samples of continuing firms. Average sales growth is particularly high for Spain, even when deflated with the corresponding highest rate of price increase, but the Spanish economy was experiencing high overall growth at the time (see also Table 3.16). Average industry price increases are negligible at that time in the UK and very low in Germany.

Sales growth is consistently higher for innovators than non-innovators, with no systematic difference between firms that only introduce process innovations and those that introduce product innovations. For product innovators, sales of new products are a very important component of total sales growth: sales in 2000 of new or significantly improved products introduced during the 1998-2000 period amount to more than one third of sales of the old products in 1998 for the German, Spanish, and UK firms and nearly 20% for the French firms. Sales of new products appear to partly replace sales of old products although the extent of cannibalisation varies across countries and is markedly lower in France than in the other countries.[69] The proportion of sales of new products that are accounted for by products that are new to the market (as opposed to simply new to the firm) is almost one half for France, about one third for Germany and Spain, and only one quarter for the UK.

Table 3.21 reports the same information for firms in the service sector. The proportion of innovators is lower in all countries than in manufacturing but relatively high in Germany and particularly low in the UK and Spain. The proportion of innovators that only introduce process innovations is slightly lower than in manufacturing for all the countries.

In all countries employment growth is somewhat higher for innovators and, compared to manufacturing, it is remarkably higher for product innovators than for firms that only introduce process innovations. This suggests that demand increases associated with new products play an important role in employment creation in service sectors.

The growth of nominal sales during the period is very high, but notice that average price increases are now significant for all countries as well. As with employment growth, sales growth is higher for product innovators but not particularly for firms that only introduce process innovations. The productivity growth of innovators is, however, sometimes higher (France, Spain)

---

[69] We should note that the fact that average growth in sales of unchanged products is negative for product innovators does not necessarily imply cannibalisation of old products by new products. For example, it is possible that firms whose traditional markets are declining are more likely to introduce product innovations.

Table 3.20: Manufacturing Firms in France, Germany, Spain, and the UK: Innovation Status, Employment, Sales, Productivity, and Price Growth, 1998-2000

	FRA	GER	SPA	UK
No. of firms	4,631	1,319	4,548	2,493
Innovation Status (%)				
NON_INNO	47.7	41.5	55.4	60.5
PROC_ONLY	7.1	10.2	12.2	11.0
PROD[a]	45.2	48.4	32.4	28.5
of which: PROD&PROC	24.3	27.4	20.0	14.2
Employment Growth (%)				
All firms	8.3	5.9	14.2	6.7
NON_INNO	7.0	2.4	12.6	5.6
PROC_ONLY	7.5	6.0	16.2	8.0
PROD	9.8	8.9	16.2	8.5
Sales Growth (%)				
All firms	13.0	15.2	23.2	12.3
NON_INNO[b]	11.0	10.8	21.7	10.8
PROC_ONLY[b]	13.4	21.7	23.6	16.3
PROD	15.0	17.5	25.7	13.9
thereof:				
due to old products	-2.3	-17.0	-13.7	-21.5
due to new products	17.3	34.5	39.4	35.4
of which: new to the market	8.2	13.1	13.8	9.1
Productivity Growth (%)				
All firms	4.7	9.3	9.0	5.6
NON_INNO	4.0	8.4	9.1	5.2
PROC_ONLY	5.9	15.7	7.4	8.3
PROD	7.5	8.7	9.5	5.4
Prices Growth[c] (%)				
NON_INNO	2.5	1.1	4.0	0.1
PROC_ONLY	3.1	2.4	4.2	-0.2
PROD	2.4	1.3	3.7	-0.4

Notes: [a] Product innovators only as well as process and product innovators.
[b] By definition, sales growth is due to old products for non-innovators and process innovators only.
[c] Prices computed for a set of industries and assigned to firms according to their activity. For details, see section 3.6.2.
Source: Harrison et al. (2005).

Table 3.21: Service Firms in France, Germany, Spain, and the UK: Innovation Status, Employment, Sales, Productivity, and Price Growth, 1998-2000

	FRA	GER	SPA	UK
No. of firms	1,653	849	1,839	1,794
Innovation Status (%)				
NON_INNO	60.2	51.4	69.1	73.2
PROC_ONLY	8.5	9.3	9.4	7.0
PROD[b]	31.3	39.3	21.5	19.8
of which PROD&PROC	17.2	21.7	11.9	8.1
Employment Growth (%)				
All firms	15.5	10.2	25.9	16.1
NON_INNO	14.2	5.9	24.8	13.8
PROC_ONLY	9.9	6.1	24.5	18.6
PROD	19.4	16.9	30.1	23.7
Sales Growth (%)				
All firms	18.4	18.5	32.3	22.7
NON_INNO[c]	16.3	14.4	30.9	21.2
PROC_ONLY[c]	16.1	11.2	30.9	24.1
PROD	23.1	25.6	37.8	28.2
thereof:				
due to old products	-3.2	-15.9	-8.9	-14.1
due to new products	26.3	41.5	46.7	42.2
of which: new to the market	9.8	16.4	19.2	11.1
Productivity Growth (%)				
All firms	4.7	9.3	9.0	5.6
NON_INNO	2.1	8.5	6.1	7.4
PROC_ONLY	6.2	5.1	6.4	5.5
PROD	3.7	8.7	7.7	4.5
Prices Growth[c] (%)				
NON_INNO	1.8	5.0	7.3	2.3
PROC_ONLY	1.8	4.7	7.3	1.0
PROD	1.8	3.0	7.3	3.0

Notes: [a] Product innovators only as well as process and product innovators.
[b] By definition, sales growth is due to old products for non-innovators and process innovators only.
[c] Prices computed for a set of industries and assigned to firms according to their activity. For details, see section 3.6.2.
Source: Harrison et al. (2005).

and sometimes equal or lower (Germany, UK) than productivity growth of non-innovators.

For product innovators, sales of new products are as large a part of total sales growth as in manufacturing although there appears to be slightly less cannibalisation of old products by new products. As in manufacturing, the proportion of sales growth due to market novelties is higher in Germany and Spain than in France and the UK.

3.6.2 Empirical Results

Table 3.22 presents the results for firms in manufacturing, where we leave out process innovations for the moment. In all cases the dependent variable is, again, the employment growth minus the growth of sales due to the un-changed products. As discussed above, we control for changes in the prices of old products by deducting an industry price growth index from the nominal sales growth of unchanged products. Unfortunately, while the CIS data are harmonised across the four countries, the availability of disaggregated price indices varies between the countries to a certain extent.[70]

Panel A presents simple OLS results. Remember that the estimated co-efficient on SALES_NEWPD is an estimate of the relative efficiency of the production process for new products compared with that for old ones. The fact that the coefficient is significantly less than one for all countries suggests that new products are produced more efficiently than old products. However, as discussed above, any endogeneity due to unobserved price changes is likely to produce a downwards bias in this coefficient, overstating the efficiency in-creases associated with new products.

Panel B, thus, applies the two-stage least squares approach, taking SALES_ NEWPD as endogenous. In order to preserve comparability across countries, the choice of instruments is restricted to variables that are present in the common questionnaire. We start our international comparison by taking only a single instrument in all countries, i.e. the equation is exactly identified. The instrument that we use is the degree of impact of innovation on the in-crease in the range of goods and services produced as reported by the firm (INCRANGE). The variable is coded 0 if innovation is not relevant for the

---

[70] Computation of PRICE: France: computed at the 2.5-digit level using the Na-tional Accounts value-added deflators, both for manufacturing and the service sector. Germany: computed from producer price indices on a 3-digit level for manufacturing published by the German statistical office. In a few cases no 3-digit level information was available, and corresponding 2-digit indices are used. Seven different price indices are used for services (producer price indices or different components from the consumer price index). Spain: computed from 88 industry series for manufacturing, coming from the "Indices de precios industriales" elab-orated by the INE and from the services component of the Consumer Price Index. UK: computed at the 4-digit level for manufacturing using ONS output deflators and at the 1.5-digit level for services using OECD output deflators.

Table 3.22: Effects of Product Innovations on Employment in Manufacturing Firms in France, Germany, Spain, and the UK, 1998-2000

Basic Model: $l - (g_1 - \tilde{\pi}_1) = \alpha_0 + \beta\, g_2 + v$

	FRA	GER	Spain	UK
	\multicolumn{4}{c}{Panel A: OLS}			
Constant	-1.87***	-5.63***	-3.58***	-3.28***
	(0.57)	(1.11)	(0.67)	(0.81)
SALES_NEWPD	0.77***	0.88***	0.86***	0.80***
	(0.05)	(0.06)	(0.03)	(0.06)
RMSE	28.02	27.25	35.97	30.44
	\multicolumn{4}{c}{Panel B: IV with one instrument}			
Constant	-3.60***	-7.43***	-5.88***	-5.22***
	(0.58)	(1.30)	(0.84)	(0.85)
SALES_NEWPD	0.98***	1.00***	1.02***	0.99***
	(0.06)	(0.07)	(0.04)	(0.05)
RMSE	28.21	27.34	36.28	30.84
	\multicolumn{4}{c}{Panel C: IV with more instruments}			
Constant	-3.51***	-6.90***	-5.83***	-5.20***
	(0.74)	(1.25)	(0.83)	(0.85)
SALES_NEWPD	0.97***	0.97***	1.02***	0.99***
	(0.06)	(0.06)	(0.04)	(0.05)
RMSE	28.19	27.23	36.27	30.83
Hansen J	1.77	3.20	0.45	1.72
(df)	(2)	(2)	(2)	(2)
No. of firms	4,631	1,319	4,548	2,493

Notes: $***$, $**$, and $*$ indicate significance on a 1%, 5%, and 10% level, respectively (standard errors robust to heteroskedasticity in parentheses). RMSE denotes the root mean squared error. All regressions include 10 industry dummies, and Suits' method is used to calculate the overall constant (see section 3.5.3). Unique instrument used in regression B is INCRANGE. Instruments used in regression C are INCRANGE, CLIENT, and CONT_RD. Hansen J reports the test statistic of a test of overidentifying restrictions. Critical value for a probability error of $\alpha = 0.05$: $\chi^2_{0.95}(2) = 5.99$.
Source: Harrison et al. (2005).

range of goods and services produced, 1 if the impact of innovation on the range is low, and 2 if it is medium or 3 if it is high.[71] Other related questions ask about the impact of innovation on market share or product quality, so the INCRANGE variable could be interpreted as a measure of the extent to which the firm's innovation is associated with horizontal as opposed to vertical product differentiation. As a result we expect the instrument to be uncorrelated with changes in the price of new products compared to old products. In addition, while innovation activity itself may not be exogenous with respect to employment growth, it seems plausible that the *effects* of innovation on the range of products produced might be. The variable is positively and significantly correlated with the endogenous variable but there remain concerns about the true exogeneity of the instrument.[72] We attempt to investigate this in Panel C by testing the validity of overidentifying restrictions in an overidentified specification.

The IV estimates of the coefficient of SALES_NEWPD in Panel B are, as expected, higher than the OLS estimates, consistent with a downwards bias due to unobserved price changes. All of the IV estimates are now extremely close to one, so there is no evidence that new products are produced with higher efficiency than old products in each of the four countries. That is, there is no evidence of employment displacement effects associated with product innovation. From the constant term we get an estimate of average productivity growth (over 2 years) in production of the old products that varies between about 3.6% in France and 7.4% in Germany.

In Panel C we attempt to test the validity of the instrument using an overidentified specification. We use CLIENT and CONT_RD as additional instruments. The important point is that in all countries the results are extremely robust to the inclusion of the new instruments (compare Panel B to Panel C), and the test of overidentifying restrictions does not reject at conventional levels. Nevertheless, the test does have some power for rejection: Different subsets of potential instruments from a broader list, including QUALITY, MARKET, RD_INTENS, and INNO_INTENS, were invariably rejected as valid instruments in at least one country.

In Table 3.23 we extend the basic specification in Panel B of Table 3.22 by allowing process innovations to affect productivity growth. Panel A only considers the process innovations of firms that do not introduce new products

---

[71] In contrast, RANGE in section 3.5 was defined as a 0/1 variable. However, this does only marginally affect results . We have further experimented with a more flexible form of this variable but this step variable appears to fit the data remarkably well with very little evidence of any non-linear effect in the reduced-form equation.

[72] In France, Germany, Spain, and the UK, the R^2 statistics obtained in the first-stage reduced-form regressions are 0.39, 0.20, 0.35, and 0.28, respectively. The coefficients on INCRANGE are equal to 5.3, 10.5, 11.2, and 14.5, respectively, with t-statistics of 30.8, 15.8, 26.9, and 16.0.

since in this case we can be sure that the process innovation relates to the old product. The coefficient is negative and significant for Germany and the UK indicating a displacement of labour in production of the old product after allowing for any pass through of productivity improvements in lower prices.[73] In both cases the size of the coefficient is similar to that of the constant suggesting that process innovation is associated with about a doubling in the rate of productivity growth in production of the old product. The coefficient is negative but insignificant for France and positive but insignificant for Spain. As discussed above, the Spanish result is a little surprising and could be due to larger pass-through of any productivity improvements in prices or alternatively to reactive process innovation in response to negative productivity growth shocks.

In Panels B and C we introduce the process innovations of firms that introduce product innovations as well. Since we do not know whether these process innovations refer to the production of the old or the new products, we try both alternatives. In Panel B we assume that all the process innovations of product innovators refer to the production of the old product by including the dummy variable PROC&PROD while in Panel C we assume that they all refer to production of the new product.

The coefficient on PROC&PROD in Panel B is negative and insignificant for Germany and Spain but positive and marginally significant for France and the UK, apparently suggesting that the process innovations of product innovators are associated with employment growth in production of the old product after allowing for any price pass-through. However, in both cases the coefficient on SALES_NEWPD is reduced from about one to 0.9, suggesting a problem of multicollinearity.[74]

Thus, an alternative hypothesis is that process innovations of product innovators are, in fact, associated with the production of a new product, and this is tested in Panel C, where we introduce an interaction between the PROC&PROD dummy and SALES_NEWPD. This allows the β coefficients to be different for firms that introduce process innovations as well. The results closely correspond to those in Panel B with insignificant negative coefficients on the interaction for Germany and Spain and positive and marginally significant coefficients for France and the UK, suggesting that new products are associated with smaller productivity increases (or larger productivity decreases) for firms that also introduce process innovations. One possible interpretation of this result for France and the UK is that new products that are associated

---

[73] We tested for the endogeneity of PROC_ONLY using the overidentifying restrictions provided by the additional instruments in Panel C of Table 3.22 (CONT_RD and CLIENT). We were not able to reject the hypothesis that the variable was exogenous though this may be partly due to the relatively low explanatory power of the instruments in predicting process innovation.

[74] Note that the standard error of SALES_NEWPD is about 50% higher in France in panel B than in panel A and roughly 40% in the UK.

Table 3.23: Effects of Innovations on Employment in Manufacturing Firms in France, Germany, Spain, and the UK, 1998-2000

Model: $l - (g_1 - \tilde{\pi}_1) = \alpha_0 + \alpha_1\, d_1 + \beta_0\, g_2 + \beta_1\, d_2\, g_2 + v$

	FRA	GER	Spain	UK
	Panel A			
Constant	-3.52***	-6.95***	-6.11***	-4.69***
	(0.78)	(1.36)	(0.90)	(0.88)
PROC_ONLY	-1.31	-6.19**	2.46	-3.85**
	(1.57)	(2.92)	(1.78)	(1.87)
SALES_NEWPD	0.98***	1.01***	1.02***	0.98***
	(0.06)	(0.07)	(0.04)	(0.05)
RMSE	28.21	27.31	36.25	30.74
	Panel B			
Constant	-3.51***	-6.96***	-6.14***	-4.73***
	(0.78)	(1.37)	(0.91)	(0.88)
PROC_ONLY	-1.26	-6.20**	2.47	-3.84**
	(1.56)	(2.92)	(1.79)	(1.87)
PROC&PROD	2.59*	-1.98	-1.49	5.51**
	(1.43)	(2.80)	(2.64)	(2.55)
SALES_NEWPD	0.90***	1.04***	1.05***	0.90***
	(0.09)	(0.07)	(0.07)	(0.07)
RMSE	28.07	27.46	36.35	30.40
	Panel C			
Constant	-3.50***	-6.97***	-6.12***	-4.62***
	(0.78)	(1.37)	(0.90)	(0.88)
PROC_ONLY	-1.32	-6.18**	2.47	-3.88**
	(1.57)	(2.92)	(1.78)	(1.87)
SALES_NEWPD	0.90***	1.03***	1.03***	0.89***
	(0.09)	(0.08)	(0.06)	(0.07)
SALES_NEWPD × PROC	0.14*	-0.04	-0.02*	0.16**
	(0.08)	(0.07)	(0.06)	(0.08)
RMSE	28.20	27.27	36.26	30.47
No. of firms	4,631	1,319	4,548	2,493

Notes: ***, **, and * indicate significance on a 1%, 5%, and 10% level, respectively (standard errors robust to heteroskedasticity in parentheses). Unique instrument used in regressions A and B is INCRANGE. Instruments used in regression C are INCRANGE and INCRANGE interacted with PROC. See also the notes of Table 3.22.
Source: Harrison et al. (2005).

with less productive production technologies tend to induce process innovations in order to reduce production costs.

However, given the available data, we are not able to distinguish between the alternative hypotheses embodied in Panels B and C, so the truth must be presumed somewhere in between, with some process innovations being associated with old products and some with new products. For this reason the preferred specification is that in Panel A, where we can be sure that the process innovations of firms that do not introduce new products relate to the old product.

Tables 3.24 and 3.25 present equivalent results for firms in the service sector. Besides the aforementioned concerns that product and process innovations are harder to distinguish in the service sector, the following specific differences should be noted. Firstly, we only use a single price deflator for all service activities in Spain; the deflators used for France, Germany, and the UK are at a higher level of aggregation than those used in the manufacturing specification. Secondly, the proportion of innovating firms is lower than in manufacturing, particularly in Spain and the UK. Despite these caveats, the results raise up some interesting differences.

As with manufacturing the coefficient on SALES_NEWPD is less than one in the OLS case (particularly for Germany) but rises to become insignificantly different from one for all countries once the variable is instrumented (see Table 3.24). Thus, we cannot reject the hypothesis that on average new products are manufactured with the same productivity as the old ones although some indication is present that new products are made with higher productivity in Germany and lower productivity in France. As with manufacturing the results are extremely robust to introducing more instruments, and the overidentifying restrictions are not rejected. Average productivity growth in production of the old product, as revealed by the constant term, is higher than in manufacturing for France, lower in Germany and Spain, and about the same in the UK.

Table 3.25 introduces the effects of process innovation as before. None of the coefficients on PROC_ONLY is significant in Panel A, suggesting no net effect after any price pass-through of process innovation. The same is true for both process innovation variables in Panel B. In Panel C, the only significant result is the negative interaction term for Spain, suggesting that new products are associated with larger productivity increases (or smaller productivity decreases) for product innovators that also introduce process innovations. There is very little evidence in these results of significant employment displacement effects associated with process innovation in services although it is difficult to draw strong conclusions given the concerns discussed above.

Table 3.26 presents an international comparison of the employment growth decomposition explored in section 3.5.4. Before discussing the results of the decomposition, let us briefly comment on its interpretation. Firstly, given that many of the estimated coefficients are similar across countries, differences in the results of the decomposition across countries will often be driven by differences in the average values of the variables. Nevertheless, the decomposition

Table 3.24: Effects of Product Innovations on Employment in Service
Firms in France, Germany, Spain, and the UK, 1998-2000

Basic Model: $l - (g_1 - \tilde{\pi}_1) = \alpha_0 + \beta\, g_2 + v$

	FRA	GER	Spain	UK
	Panel A: OLS			
Constant	-2.13	-0.31	-3.04	-3.53 **
	(1.95)	(2.66)	(2.01)	(1.48)
SALES_NEWPD	0.85 ***	0.75 ***	0.92 ***	0.89 ***
	(0.07)	(0.06)	(0.05)	(0.06)
RMSE	44.49	33.42	43.32	37.94
	Panel B: IV with one instrument			
Constant	-5.32 **	-3.29	-4.06 *	-5.12 ***
	(2.42)	(3.00)	(2.21)	(1.53)
SALES_NEWPD	1.15 ***	0.93 ***	0.99 ***	1.04 ***
	(0.13)	(0.08)	(0.08)	(0.06)
RMSE	45.09	33.68	43.37	38.01
	Panel C: IV with more instruments			
Constant	-5.08 **	-3.59	-3.95 *	-5.05 ***
	(2.36)	(2.96)	(2.20)	(1.53)
SALES_NEWPD	1.13 ***	0.94 ***	0.98 ***	1.03 ***
	(0.13)	(0.08)	(0.08)	(0.06)
RMSE	45.02	33.80	43.36	37.99
Hansen J	0.41	1.09	0.35	3.55
(df)	(2)	(2)	(2)	(2)
No. of firms	1,653	849	1,839	1,794

Notes: ∗ ∗ ∗, ∗∗, and ∗ indicate significance on a 1%, 5%, and 10% level, respectively (standard errors robust to heteroskedasticity in parentheses). RMSE denotes the root mean squared error. All regressions include 12 industry dummies, and Suits' method is used to calculate the overall constant (see section 3.5.3). Unique instrument used in regression B is INCRANGE. Instruments used in regression C are INCRANGE, CLIENT, and CONT_RD. J reports the test statistic of a test of overidentifying restrictions. Critical value for a probability error of $\alpha = 0.05$: $\chi^2_{0.95}(2) = 5.99$.
Source: Harrison et al. (2005).

Table 3.25: Effects of Innovations on Employment in Service Firms in France, Germany, Spain, and the UK, 1998-2000

Model: $l - (g_1 - \tilde{\pi}_1) = \alpha_0 + \alpha_1 d_1 + \beta_0 g_2 + \beta_1 d_2 g_2 + v$

	FRA	GER	Spain	UK
		Panel A		
Constant	-5.25**	-3.36	-4.04*	-5.51***
	(2.48)	(3.05)	(2.25)	(1.61)
PROC_ONLY	-1.45	1.54	-0.38	3.21
	(3.47)	(3.07)	(3.37)	(3.54)
SALES_NEWPD	1.16***	0.92***	0.99***	1.05***
	(0.13)	(0.08)	(0.08)	(0.06)
RMSE	45.11	33.66	43.37	38.02
		Panel B		
Constant	-4.96**	-3.39	-3.82*	-5.45***
	(2.44)	(3.04)	(2.20)	(1.62)
PROC_ONLY	-1.63	1.56	-0.46	3.10
	(3.47)	(3.06)	(3.36)	(3.53)
PROC&PROD	-3.81	1.80	-6.52	-6.26
	(5.55)	(4.26)	(6.72)	(4.96)
SALES_NEWPD	1.23***	0.90***	1.07***	1.10***
	(0.18)	(0.11)	(0.14)	(0.09)
RMSE	45.36	33.53	43.51	38.19
		Panel C		
Constant	-5.24**	-3.23	4.07*	-5.61***
	(2.48)	(3.05)	(2.24)	(1.62)
PROC_ONLY	-1.45	1.46	-0.32	3.25
	(3.47)	(3.07)	(3.37)	(3.53)
SALES_NEWPD	1.18***	0.86***	1.13***	1.10***
	(0.17)	(0.11)	(0.12)	(0.10)
SALES_NEWPD × PROC	-0.04	0.09	-0.23*	-0.10
	(0.20)	(0.10)	(0.12)	(0.11)
RMSE	45.11	33.76	43.25	38.07
No. of firms	1,653	849	1,839	1,794

Notes: ***, **, and * indicate significance on a 1%, 5%, and 10% level, respectively (standard errors robust to heteroskedasticity in parentheses). Unique instrument used in regressions A and B is INCRANGE. Instruments used in regression C are INCRANGE and INCRANGE interacted with PROC. See also the notes of Table 3.24.

Source: Harrison et al. (2005).

would not be possible without the estimated coefficients. Secondly, the results are based on an expansionary period for all four countries and so may not be representative of average firm-level effects at other stages of the cycle.[75] Finally, recall the limitations of the estimation results which have been stressed above. In particular, process innovation effects are not separately identified from the effects of associated price changes, and firm-level compensation effects do not distinguish between pure market expansion and business-stealing. Furthermore, we are describing the average employment growth of a sample of continuing firms. Entering and exiting firms should be included to obtain a more complete picture of aggregate employment effects.

Table 3.26: Decomposition of Employment Growth – An International Comparison for Manufacturing and Services, 1998-2000[a]

	FRA	GER	SPA	UK
Manufacturing				
Employment Growth (%)	**8.3**	**5.9**	**14.2**	**6.7**
Decomposed into:				
Productivity trend in production of old products[b]	-1.9	-7.5	-5.7	-5.0
Net contribution of process innovations	-0.1	-0.6	0.3	-0.4
Output growth of old products	4.8	6.0	12.2	8.3
Net contribution of product innovations	5.5	8.0	7.4	3.9
Services				
Employment Growth (%)	**15.5**	**10.2**	**25.9**	**16.1**
Decomposed into:				
Productivity trend in production of old products[b]	-2.3	-3.0	1.0	-5.0
Net contribution of process innovations	-0.1	0.1	-0.0	0.2
Output growth of old products	9.9	5.4	18.5	15.5
Net contribution of product innovations	8.0	7.6	6.5	5.4

Notes: [a] Decomposition is based on Tables 3.20, 3.21, and regressions A in Tables 3.23 and 3.25. The sum of decomposition values may slightly differ from employment growth because of rounding.
[b] Productivity trend is the weighted sum of industry dummy values and, hence, differs from the constant of the regression.
Source: Harrison et al. (2005).

In manufacturing, incremental productivity improvements in the production of existing products are an important source of reductions in employ-

---

[75] For Germany, it was shown that the main results are quite robust to the business cycle, see section 3.5.5.

ment requirements for a given level of output. The effect is smallest in France (-1.9% over 2 years) and largest in Germany (-7.5% over 2 years). However, growth in output of existing products over this expansionary period more than compensates the productivity effect in all countries except Germany.

Individual process innovations account for only a small employment change in all countries, generally resulting in a small net displacement effect. This is partly due to measuring process innovation effects in net terms after any price pass-through but also because the number of firms that introduce only process innovations is small. Employment reductions resulting from process innovations may be important for individual firms but they amount to only a small fraction of overall employment changes.

In contrast, product innovations play an important role in stimulating firm-level employment growth. The decomposition shows that the effect of new product sales, even net of the substitution for old products, is sizeable in all countries. It implies an average firm-level employment increase over the period ranging from 3.9% in the UK to 8.0% in Germany.

Overall, the importance of innovation in stimulating firm-level employment growth becomes clear when the different sources of employment change are compared. In Germany, existing products would have led to a decrease in employment during the period as the combined effect of general productivity gains, process innovations, and output growth is negative. The whole average firm-level employment increase can be attributed to product innovation. Even in Spain and the UK, where increases in sales of existing products are responsible for a large proportion of net employment growth, product innovation was, on average, more important than the net effect of growth in sales of existing products.

The results for service sector firms are somewhat different. Average within-firm employment growth is almost twice as much as in manufacturing during the period and more than double in the UK. On average, product innovation accounts for a smaller, but still non-negligible, proportion of total employment growth than in manufacturing. In Spain and the UK, the main source of firm-level employment growth is growth in production of old products, with a small counterbalancing effect of trend productivity increases only in the UK. In France, the contribution of product innovation is roughly the same as the net contribution of growth in sales of existing products. Total employment growth is lower in Germany, and growth in production of new products accounts for a larger share of employment growth than in the other countries.

3.7 Summary and Discussion of Results

The relationship between employment and innovation is a research topic that raises a lot of policy interest and that has been lively discussed for a long time. From a theoretical point of view, product as well as process innovations can lead to a reduction or an expansion of employment. Using the same multi-product approach recently proposed by Jaumandreu (2003) and Harrison et al. (2005), this chapter investigated to what extent employment growth in the German manufacturing and service sector between 1998-2002 can be explained by output growth of existing products, output of newly introduced products, and the productivity growth both attributable and not attributable to process innovation. In a second step, I contributed to the literature by analysing different types of both product and process innovations according to the theoretical considerations that their employment effects may differ. Finally, an international comparison between the four major European countries France, Spain, the UK, and Germany was performed.

With regard to the five questions raised in the introduction of this chapter, the following facts can be recorded: Firstly, the econometric results confirm that successful product innovations have a positive impact on gross employment in the innovating firm during the period 1998-2000. Furthermore, there is no evidence of labour displacement effects associated with product innovation, and the results provide evidence that gross employment does grow one-for-one with the sales growth accounted for by new products. The impact tends to be larger in manufacturing than in service firms although the difference is statistically not significant. That is, an increase in the success of product innovations (measured in terms of sales growth due to new products) by 1% lead to an increase in gross employment by 1%. At the same time, new products can displace existing ones within the innovating firm to a considerable extent which leads to downsizing. But, the decomposition of employment growth provides evidence that the net effect is positive and that product innovations have been the major driver of employment growth in the period under consideration. This result turns out to be very robust with respect to different specifications, the business cycle, and methods used. Various specification tests further show that the preferred instrumental variable estimation is appropriate and does not suffer from endogenous or weak instruments, which could heavily bias the complete results.

Secondly, the estimation results indicate that new jobs are not only created in firms that have positioned themselves on the cutting edge by launching products that are new to the market but also in firms which successfully pursue product imitation strategies. Moreover, the coefficients of both indicators of product innovation success are not significantly different. This holds for manufacturing and service firms. Hence, this result contradicts the hypothesis that employment effects depend on the degree of product novelty.

Thirdly, the impact of process innovations on employment growth turns out to be variable. In manufacturing firms, results indicate that process innovations are labour-saving. That is, labour displacement effects outweigh compensation effects, leading to a fall in employment. One surprising result is that this negative effect turns out to be significant in the boom period 1998-2000 but not in the recession period 2000-2002. But, as expected, the estimation results also reveal that not all process innovations are associated with labour reduction. Jobs are merely deteriorated through rationalisation innovations but not as a consequence of other process innovations, e.g., as those intended to improve product quality. In the service sector, however, a different picture emerges. Here, process innovations are not responsible for a significant downsizing in labour in both periods. Various reasons could explain this difference between manufacturing and service. The first explanation is related to the specific nature of services and their production. The provision of services is typically strongly geared towards customer preferences, and clearly structured production processes are often lacking, complicating the distinction between new and existing products (services) and processes. If this is true, this could imply that a part of the effects of new processes is attributed to product innovations. This could explain why the coefficient of this variable is a bit lower than in manufacturing (assuming process innovations have, likewise, a negative impact in the service sector). An alternative explanation might be that service firms are, on average, smaller than manufacturing firms and have, thus, less market power which forces them to pass on efficiency gains derived from innovations to customers to a larger extent. Unfortunately, with the data at hand, it is not possible to distinguish between these alternative explanations. All in all, the decomposition of the employment growth provides evidence that the net effect of process innovation is only small in both manufacturing and the service sector.

Finally, from an international perspective the econometric results for the employment effects of product innovations are very similar to those found for Spain, the UK, and France, thus, supporting a discernible international pattern in the firm-level association between innovation and employment. The higher average employment growth rates in France, Spain, and the UK can be largely explained by higher output growth rates in existing products. While in Germany employment growth can be solely (manufacturing) or for the most part (services) attributed to the introduction of new products, it is likewise the output growth in existing products which substantially contributes to a raise in employment in the other three countries. This effect is most striking in Spain, and might be explained by the strong economic upswing taking place as a result of Spain's efforts to catch up with the European standard. However, the empirical analysis reveals different impacts of process innovations across the four European countries. For example, no evidence has been found for a net displacement effect of process innovation in Spanish manufacturing, possibly due to a greater pass-through of productivity improvements in lower prices.

The results highlight the importance of innovation activities in stimulating employment in Germany. For the sake of completeness, however, some limitations of the study and hints on future research should be addressed. Firstly, the potential employment effects of innovations may even be underestimated for the boom period 1998-2000 because a growing number of firms reported for that period that they could not meet their demand for qualified personnel (see Ebling, Gottschalk, Janz, and Niggemann, 2000).

Secondly, this study focusses on the nexus between innovation and employment at the firm level while neglecting the wider consequences. Therefore, only limited macroeconomic conclusions can be drawn. On the industry or an aggregate level, technological change may be associated with further impacts on firms' labour demand, which are beyond the scope of the present study. Theoretically, the total effect at the industry level can be calculated as the sum of the effects of all continuing firms and those effects of entering and exiting firms. However, in attempting to do this, one would be faced with two main problems (see Harrison et al., 2005): The first problem is that firm-level compensation effects that have been estimated do not explicitly distinguish between pure market expansion and business stealing. Due to data restriction, I cannot explicitly model the demand side. If innovation results in business stealing rather than market expansion, the aggregate effect will be generally smaller (either less positive or more negative) than the firm-level effect. But notice, that a firm's change of output growth in existing products may be partly due to innovation activities of its competitors and, thus, embodies business-stealing effects by rivals, even if I do not know their identity or observe them in the sample. The second problem relates to the fact that the sample is constituted of continuing firms only; thus, employment creation or job destruction due to entering and withdrawing firms is not taken into account. Firm entry and exit is closely related to innovation activities. For instance, firm entry often goes hand-in-hand with the introduction of a new product while firms which cannot keep pace with the technological progress of their competitors have to leave the market. For Germany, the development of the number of firm foundations and firm exits between 1998 and 2002 give rise to the supposition that the net employment effect was positive between 1998 and 2000 but negative in the second period (see Rammer and Metzger, 2003; Rammer, 2004).

Thirdly, the empirical analysis show that, on average, total employment growth is higher in firms introducing new products, and admittedly the effect of process innovation comes up negative in some cases but turns out to be rather small. However, these results leave it open whether the employment consequences are more distressing in certain groups of workers. Indeed, the literature presents evidence that at least the introduction of new information and communication technologies have induced a change in the skill structure in favour of high-skilled employees in the German service sector in the second half of the 1990s; see Kaiser (2000; 2001) and Falk and Seim (2000; 2001). These studies are limited to the service sector, focus only on a particular kind of technological change, and use input indicators to measure it. One task for future research is, therefore, to extend the multi-product framework and model the employment effects differentiated by labour skills.

Fourthly, I consider a 3-year period to analyse the impact of innovation activities on labour, and admittedly, I cannot observe the point in time in which the innovation is introduced. One might ask whether this is enough to assess the entire employment consequences. While it is sensible to assume that displacement effects of process or product innovations will not be lagging much to the time of their introduction, compensation effects especially of process innovations may appear with a certain delay (see Franz, 2006). Given that this assumption is true, this would imply that I may even overestimate the negative, respectively underestimate the presumably positive employment impact of process innovations. Estimating the time period in which compensation effects of product innovations arise is further complicated by the fact that the amount and sustainability of such compensation effects, resulting from demand increases, depend on the competition and the way and delay with which competitors react. A full assessment of long-term employment effects would require a panel data analysis which is on the agenda of future research.

In the fifth place, one drawback of the data at hand is that I cannot observe and control for firm-level price changes. Instead, different types of deflators were used at the 3- and 2-digit level. However, this might be not sensitive enough for some industries, especially for the service sector, but had to be the procedure of choice here.

Finally, I do not model the firm's choice to innovate or not. The possible simultaneous determination of innovation and employment might induce an additional endogeneity problem in the estimation.

Appendix B

Table 3.27: Sample by Industry

Industry	Nace	Total		NON_INNO		PROC_ONLY		PROD_ONLY		PROD&PROC	
		No.	%[a]	No.	%[b]	No.	%[b]	No.	%[b]	No.	%[b]
Manufacturing											
Food	15-16	113	8.6	72	63.7	7	6.2	13	11.5	21	18.6
Textile	17-19	77	5.8	48	62.3	7	9.1	16	20.8	6	7.8
Wood	20-22	112	8.5	58	51.8	21	18.8	11	9.8	22	19.6
Chemicals	23-24	92	7.0	28	30.4	10	10.9	21	22.8	33	35.9
Plastic	25	116	8.8	39	33.6	10	8.6	28	24.1	39	33.6
Glass	26	78	5.9	39	50.0	4	5.1	14	18.0	21	26.9
Metals	27-28	227	17.2	113	49.8	40	17.6	23	10.1	51	22.5
Machinery	29	184	14.0	58	31.5	14	7.6	55	29.9	57	31.0
Electrical eng.[c]	30-33	214	16.2	46	21.5	9	4.2	75	35.1	84	39.3
Vehicles	34-35	53	4.0	21	39.6	4	7.6	11	20.8	17	32.1
Furniture	36-37	53	4.0	25	47.2	8	15.1	10	18.9	10	18.9
Total		**1,319**	**100**	**547**	**41.5**	**134**	**10.2**	**277**	**21.0**	**361**	**27.4**
Services											
Wholesale	51	204	24.0	131	64.2	16	7.8	28	13.7	29	14.2
Transport	60-63	204	24.0	143	70.1	20	9.8	18	8.8	23	11.3
Post/telecom-munication	64	26	3.1	19	73.1	1	3.9	2	7.7	4	15.4
Bank/insurance	65-67	97	11.4	36	37.1	10	10.3	12	12.4	39	40.2
Computer	72	80	9.4	16	20.0	4	5.0	33	41.3	27	33.8
R&D	73	75	8.8	15	20.0	8	10.7	20	26.7	32	42.7
Technical ser-vices	74.2-74.3	163	19.2	76	46.6	20	12.3	37	22.7	30	18.4
Total		**849**	**100**	**436**	**51.4**	**79**	**9.3**	**150**	**17.7**	**184**	**21.7**

Notes: [a] As percentage share of total firms in manufacturing and services, respectively.

[b] As percentage share of firms in the relevant branch of industry.

[c] Electrical eng. denotes electrical engineering (including medical, precision, and optical instruments).

Table 3.28: Sample by Size Class

Size Class	Total		NON_ INNO		PROC_ ONLY		PROD_ ONLY		PROD& PROC	
	No.	%[a]	No.	%[b]	No.	%[b]	No.	%[b]	No.	%[b]
Manufacturing										
10-19	193	14.6	115	59.6	18	9.3	35	18.1	25	13.0
20-49	321	24.3	177	55.1	30	9.4	63	19.6	51	15.9
50-99	244	18.5	109	44.7	23	9.4	53	21.7	59	24.2
100-199	198	15.0	74	37.7	25	12.6	44	22.2	55	27.8
200-499	221	16.8	47	21.3	25	11.3	54	24.4	95	43.0
500-999	91	6.9	17	18.7	10	11.0	18	19.8	46	50.6
1000+	51	3.9	8	15.7	3	5.9	10	19.6	30	58.8
Total	**1,319**	**100**	**547**	**41.5**	**134**	**10.2**	**277**	**21.0**	**361**	**27.4**
Services										
10-19	266	31.3	159	59.8	21	7.9	48	18.1	38	14.3
20-49	257	30.3	153	59.5	20	7.9	46	17.9	38	14.8
50-99	127	15.0	59	46.5	18	14.2	21	16.5	29	22.8
100-199	87	10.3	35	40.2	7	8.1	15	17.2	30	34.5
200-499	46	5.4	18	39.1	5	10.9	8	17.4	15	32.6
500-999	33	3.9	7	21.2	5	15.2	8	24.2	13	39.4
1000+	33	3.9	5	15.2	3	9.1	4	12.1	21	63.4
Total	**849**	**100**	**436**	**51.4**	**79**	**9.3**	**150**	**17.7**	**184**	**21.7**

Notes: [a] As percentage share of total firms in manufacturing and services, respectively.

[b] As percentage share of firms in the relevant branch of industry.

Table 3.29: Descriptive Statistics of Instrumental Variables

	Unit	Manufacturing				Services			
		Total sample		Innovative sample[a]		Total sample		Innovative sample[a]	
Variables		mean	s.d.	mean	s.d.	mean	s.d.	mean	s.d.
Quantitative									
SHARE_MARK	%	−		8.5	14.9	−		9.3	16.2
INNO_INTENS	%	−		6.3	8.8	−		10.7	20.2
RD_INTENS	%	−		2.7	4.9	−		6.0	14.1
EXP_INTENS	%	21.8	24.5	26.3	25.4	5.9	15.9	7.9	17.9
Qualitative									
CONT_RD	[0/1]	0.385	0.489	0.612	0.486	0.259	0.438	0.484	0.500
PATENT	[0/1]	0.265	0.444	0.399	0.490	0.099	0.300	0.182	0.386
RANGE	[0/1]	0.489	0.500	0.785	0.411	0.395	0.389	0.763	0.426
QUALITY	[0/1]	0.522	0.499	0.838	0.368	0.432	0.496	0.816	0.388
MARKET	[0/1]	0.449	0.498	0.720	0.449	0.328	0.470	0.617	0.487
CLIENT	[0/1]	0.468	0.499	0.732	0.443	0.336	0.473	0.608	0.489
SCIENCE	[0/1]	0.077	0.266	0.120	0.325	0.067	0.250	0.131	0.338

Note: [a] Innovative firms are defined as firms with product and/or process innovations.

Table 3.30: First-Step Estimation Results

	Manufacturing			Services		
Endog. Var.	SALES_ NEWPD	SALES_ FIRM	SALES_ MARK	SALES_ NEWPD	SALES_ FIRM	SALES_ MARK
Regr.	(6)	(10)	(10)	(6)	(10)	(10)
Const	0.168 (2.467)	-0.178 (1.704)	0.345 (1.788)	2.521 (2.298)	0.947 (1.656)	1.503 (1.550)
PROC_ ONLY	-18.053*** (2.395)	—	—	-18.186*** (3.749)	—	—
COST_ ONLY	—	-11.805*** (1.930)	-6.000*** (2.026)	—	-11.691*** (3.694)	-7.324** (3.457)
OTHER_ PROC_ ONLY	—	-12.690*** (2.880)	-5.949** (3.023)	—	-10.947*** (3.789)	-6.796* (3.546)
CONT_ RD	10.482*** (1.952)	3.689*** (1.348)	6.797*** (1.415)	15.231*** (3.145)	9.205*** (2.268)	6.057*** (2.123)
RANGE	11.922*** (1.928)	9.992*** (1.332)	1.936 (1.398)	—	—	—
CLIENT	7.597*** (1.937)	5.350*** (1.338)	2.244* (1.404)	9.897*** (2.673)	5.301*** (1.927)	4.632*** (1.804)
SCIENCE	7.418*** (2.782)	6.033*** (1.921)	1.381 (2.016)	15.437*** (4.920)	13.284*** (3.546)	2.151 (3.318)
PATENT	2.055 (1.873)	-1.626 (1.293)	3.679*** (1.357)	20.677*** (4.465)	4.539 (3.219)	16.119*** (3.012)
Adj. R^2	0.27	0.23	0.10	0.26	0.19	0.13
Partial R^2	0.199	0.169	0.075	0.154	0.089	0.093
Shea R^2	0.199	0.051	0.023	0.154	0.021	0.022
Partial F	83.74	55.14	30.10	20.10	20.48	21.42
p-value	0.000	0.000	0.000	0.000	0.000	0.000

Notes: ***, **, and * indicate significance on a 1%, 5%, and 10% level, respectively. Industry dummies are included in all regressions. 'Regr.' refers to the regression number in Tables 3.7 and 3.9 for manufacturing as well as to the regression number in Tables 3.8 and 3.10 for services. Partial F is the F-statistic of the partialled-out reduced-form regression. Under the null hypothesis, F asymptotically follows a $\chi^2(5)$ and $\chi^2(4)$ distribution in manufacturing and services, respectively. Partial R^2 reports the R^2 of the partialled-out reduced-form regression. Shea R^2 denotes Shea's Partial R^2 for two endogenous variables.

Table 3.31: Robustness of Estimation Results: Instrumental Variable vs General Method of Moments Estimation

Basic Model: $l - (g_1 - \tilde{\pi}_1) = \alpha_0 + \alpha_1 d + \beta g_2 + v$

Method	Manufacturing		Services	
	IV	GMM	IV	GMM
Constant	-6.433***	-6.573***	-7.870***	-7.877***
	(1.336)	(1.325)	(2.695)	(2.682)
PROC_ONLY	-6.684**	-6.780**	2.792	2.816
	(2.910)	(2.882)	(2.989)	(2.981)
SALES_NEWPD	0.980***	0.985***	0.955***	0.952***
	(0.063)	(0.062)	(0.075)	(0.073)
Adj. R^2	0.480	0.480	0.394	0.395
Root MSE	27.2	27.2	34.0	34.0
W_{IND} (p-value)	0.238	0.231	0.013	0.013
W_β (p-value)	0.747	0.812	0.547	0.517
PH_{all} (p-value)	0.745	—	1.000	—
PH_{lev} (p-value)	0.120	—	0.714	—
Hansen J	1.08	1.08	0.12	0.12
(df)	(4)	(4)	(3)	(3)
p-value	0.897	0.897	0.990	0.990
No. of firms	1,319	1,319	849	849

Notes: * * *, **, and * indicate significance on a 1%, 5%, and 10% level, respectively (standard errors robust to heteroskedasticity in parentheses). Instruments: CONT_RD, RANGE (only in manufacturing), PATENT, CLIENT, and SCIENCE. Regressions include industry dummies, and Suits' method is used to calculate the overall constant (see section 3.5.3). The Wald test statistic W_{IND} tests for the null hypothesis that the industry dummies are jointly equal to zero. Under H_0, it is asymptotically $\chi^2(10)$ distributed in manufacturing and $\chi^2(6)$ in services. W_β is the Wald test statistic of the test $H_0 : \beta = 1$ and is asymptotically $\chi^2(1)$ distributed under H_0. PH_{all} and PH_{lev} test the null hypothesis of homoskedasticity. $PH_{all} \sim \chi^2(91)$ and $PH_{lev} \sim \chi^2(16)$ under H_0 in manufacturing and $PH_{all} \sim \chi^2(48)$ and $PH_{lev} \sim \chi^2(11)$ in services. Here, only the corresponding p-values are reported. J reports the test statistic of a test of overidentifying restrictions. Under H_0, J follows a $\chi^2(m)$ distribution with m as the number of overidentifying restrictions.

4

Productivity Effects of Innovation Activities*

4.1 Introduction

Understanding and quantifying the driving factors behind productivity and productivity growth, and in particular the role of innovation activities in this context, has been of major interest in the field of empirical economics for several decades.[76] This can be explained by the fact that innovation is widely believed to be a key long-term driving force for competitiveness and growth of firms and national economies as a whole. Recent years have even seen a surge of studies on productivity, in particular at the firm level. This is in part due to new theoretical underpinnings from the endogenous growth theory, which emphasises that economic growth is positively correlated with investments in research (see Romer, 1986; 1990) and human capital (Lucas, 1988). Another reason is the increasing availability of comprehensive micro databases. However, as was set out in section 1.2, quantifying the importance of innovation for productivity is a challenging task and, despite a large number of empirical studies, innovation research has only been partly successful (see Griliches, 1995; Bartelsman and Doms, 2000).

One reason for this conclusion lies in the difficulties of adequately measuring innovation. For a long time, the empirical literature has focussed on input-oriented innovation indicators. The majority of these studies used the production function approach as a theoretical backbone, including R&D-based measures as an additional input factor. But it is a well-known fact that R&D is not the only way for an enterprise to introduce new products and processes. Furthermore, it is presumably not the input of innovation activities but rather their outcome that exercises influence over firm performance (see,

---

* This chapter largely draws on Peters (2005b).

[76] Furthermore, there is a related group of studies focussing on the description of cross-sectional distributions of productivity across firms in an industry and its evolution over time (see, e.g., Nelson, 1981; Baily, Hulten, and Campbell, 1992; Bartelsman and Dhrymes, 1998).

e.g., Blundell, Griffith, and van Reenen, 1993; Llorca Vivero, 2002). R&D or more general innovation expenditure translate into product as well as process innovations, both affecting productivity via different channels. However, the traditional approach treats the innovation process itself, i.e. the link between the resources devoted to the innovation process and their outcome, as a black box. Patents have been seen as an option to get over this shortcoming. But patent-based indicators have been heavily criticised as being a poor indicator of innovative output.[77] Another problem in quantifying the impact of innovation on productivity at the firm level relates to the fact that only some of the firms are engaged in R&D or, more generally, in innovation activities, and the sample of innovative firms is unlikely to be random. It is well-known that a restriction to the selected (innovative) sample may induce biased estimates (Heckman, 1979).

A huge step forward was taken by Crépon et al. (1998) who addressed several of these deficiencies. They developed an empirical model, known as the CDM model in the literature, which was the first to connect innovation input, innovation output, and productivity. Crépon et al. estimated their model for French manufacturing firms, and a growing number of studies for other countries followed this line of research. This field of literature has considerably benefited from the adoption of the Oslo Manual and the release of new internationally harmonised innovation survey data (CIS). The model allows us to look more thoroughly into the *black box* of the innovation process at firm level. Not only the relationship between innovation input and productivity will be analysed but also some light is shed on the process in between. By allowing the innovation process to be modelled in more detail and by using the rich CIS data, a step forward in the search for identification of the contribution of innovation to productivity is possible (van Leeuwen, 2002).

A flaw of previous studies is that they only incorporate an equation for product innovations as output of the innovation activity while the input measure (R&D or innovation expenditure) is related to both product and process innovations. Yet, firms may experience labour productivity increases due to both kinds of innovations. Up to now, most of the studies ignored this problem. Only recently, a few studies tried to address this problem by incorporating a discrete indicator for process innovations to control for this problem (see Mairesse and Mohnen, 2005; Parisi, Schiantarelli, and Sembenelli, 2006; Griffith, Huergo, Mairesse, and Peters, 2006).[78] In contrast to innovation surveys in other European countries, the German innovation surveys include a quan-

---

[77] See the discussion of the role of patents in measuring innovation output in section 1.2.

[78] Llorca Vivero (2002) examined the impact of process innovations on productivity growth using the number of product and process innovations. However, he did not analyse the whole innovation input, output, and productivity relationship.

titative output indicator for process innovations as well.[79] While the success of product innovations is measured as the share of sales due to new or significantly improved products, the success of process innovations is measured as the share of cost reduction in unit costs due to new or significantly improved processes. These output indicators can be interpreted as sales- and cost-weighted innovation counts, respectively.

The objective of this study is to enlarge the CDM model by specifying separate knowledge production functions for product and process innovation output and to study the impact of both kinds of outcome on labour productivity. The main research questions addressed in this chapter are whether different factors are crucial to the success of process innovations compared to product innovations and whether firms are, on average, more successful in increasing their labour productivity by means of product or process innovations. To analyse these questions, I use panel data for German manufacturing firms covering the period 2000-2003.

The remainder of this chapter is organised as follows. Section 4.2 reviews the related literature. The empirical model and the estimation method used are presented in section 4.3. Section 4.4 describes the underlying data set. The empirical implementation and estimation strategy employed in the empirical analysis are set out in section 4.5. Section 4.6 puts a descriptive analysis of the data; section 4.7 presents the econometric results. Section 4.8 draws some conclusions about the relationship between innovation input, innovation success, and labour productivity.

4.2 Literature Review

This section first briefly summarises important empirical findings concerning the determinants of innovation input and innovation output. It then reviews some main empirical results regarding the link between innovation and productivity.

4.2.1 Innovation Input

Two important determinants explaining innovation activities go back to Schumpeter (1942), who stated that large firms in concentrated markets have an advantage in innovation. Hence, firm size and market structure are usually taken into account in empirical studies. The first Schumpeter hypothesis claims that, as firm size increases, innovation activities increase more than

---

[79] This output indicator is likewise based on the recommendations of the Oslo Manual. Note that within the context of the current revision of the Oslo Manual one major aspect is the further development of output indicators for process innovations.

proportionally.[80] There are several explanations as to why the incentive to innovate should increase with firm size. Firstly, larger firms may have easier access to capital markets to finance risky innovation projects because size and market power can increase the availability and stability of internal funds. Secondly, there may be economies of scale in the R&D production function. Thirdly, large parts of the innovation outlays, in particular for R&D activities, are fixed costs and are spread over a higher sales volume in large firms. And fourthly, innovation activities are complementary to other activities, particularly management activities, which are more developed in larger firms.[81] A survey of empirical studies testing the Schumpeter hypotheses can be found in Cohen and Levin (1989), Cohen (1995), Cohen and Klepper (1996) or, more recently, in Klette and Kortum (2004) and Ahn (2002). As reported in these surveys, size has been found to be a highly significant determinant of firms' likelihood to engage in innovation. However, regarding the innovation intensity, the results are mixed. Cohen and Klepper (1996) summarise as *stylised fact 2* that among R&D performers R&D rises monotonically with firm size, implying that the R&D intensity (measured, e.g., in terms of R&D expenditure to turnover or R&D personnel per employee) is independent of firm size (see, e.g., Cohen, Levin, and Mowery, 1987; Crépon et al., 1998). Contrariwise, more recent studies have found evidence for a non-linear U-shaped relationship (see, e.g., Bound, Cummins, Griliches, Hall, and Jaffe, 1984; Felder, Licht, Nerlinger, and Stahl, 1996).[82]

The second Schumpeter hypothesis states that ex ante product market power stimulates innovation activities because it increases monopoly rents from innovation and reduces the uncertainty associated with excessive rivalry that tends to reduce the incentive to innovate. Furthermore, the possession of market power increases firms' profits, which provide firms with internal funds necessary to innovate. The negative relationship between product market competition and innovation was also formalised in early endogenous growth models (see Romer, 1990; Aghion and Howitt, 1992). The empirical evidence so far is inconclusive. Many studies pointed to a positive relationship between market concentration and R&D (or negative relationship between competition and R&D) although these results were sensitive to the inclusion of industry effects (see, e.g., Scott, 1984; Levin, Cohen, and Mowery, 1985). On the other hand, Blundell, Griffith, and van Reenen (1999) or Geroski (1995) ascertained a positive relationship between product market competition and innovation.

---

[80] Schumpeter himself only pointed to the qualitative difference between small and large firms. Nonetheless, the empirical literature has interpreted his claim as a more than proportionate relationship (Cohen, 1995).

[81] But then, excessive bureaucratic control may impede innovation activities in large firms (Cohen and Levin, 1989).

[82] Of course, comparisons must be made with care since the studies differ in their samples of firms and industries, measures of innovation and firm size, econometric methods, and their time periods.

In a recent work Aghion, Bloom, Blundell, Griffith, and Howitt (2005) argued in favour of and found evidence for an inverted-U relationship between competition and innovation. They emphasised that innovation incentives do not depend upon post-innovation rents per se but more upon the difference between post-innovation and pre-innovation rents. Their model predicts that for low initial levels of competition an escape-competition effect dominates (i.e. competition increases the incremental profits from innovating, and, thereby, encourages innovation investments) whereas the Schumpeterian effect tends to dominate at higher levels of competition.

The modern innovation literature stresses that there are additional firm-level determinants other than firm size and market structure. Cohen (1995) distinguished between *firm* and *industry or market* characteristics. Firm characteristics which have been found to explain innovation activities are:

- Degree of internationalisation: There are at least three hypothesised mechanisms on how internationalisation stimulates innovation activities.[83] The first one is a learning-by-export hypothesis. That is, globally engaged firms can make use of more knowledge from abroad for their own innovation activities, knowledge which is usually not available to non-exporters or at least difficult to reach. This includes knowledge from sources like foreign customers, suppliers, competitors, or universities. In case of a multinational group, a firm can also learn from the intra-firm worldwide pool of information (see Criscuolo, Haskel, and Slaughter, 2005). Second, it is argued that internationally operating firms are exposed to a more intense competition and are, therefore, forced to improve their products and processes faster than firms which operates only on domestic markets.[84] Third, opening up of foreign markets will enlarge profits stemming from innovation activities and, thus, enforce innovation (see Ebling and Janz, 1999).

- Availability of financial resources: The importance of internal funds to finance innovation projects was already stressed by Schumpeter. Due to adverse selection and moral hazard problems (see Stiglitz and Weiss, 1981), firms are usually forced to finance innovation projects by means of internal funds. The majority of empirical studies have found that firm's cash flow as a measure of internal financial capability is associated with higher levels of R&D intensity (see Mueller, 1967; Himmelberg and Petersen, 1994; Cohen, 1995; and the references cited therein). In a recent study Bond, Harhoff, and van Reenen (2003) compared the impact of financial constraints for British and German firms. They reported mixed results in a sense that financial constraints are significant in Britain and affect the decision to engage in R&D rather than the level of R&D spending by firms.

---

[83] Note that the causality may also run from innovation to export. The technology gap trade theory by Krugman (1979) or the life-cycle theory by Vernon (1966) states that innovation is the driving force behind export activities.

[84] However, in open economies domestic firms also face competition via imports from foreign companies (see Bernard and Wagner, 1997).

On the other hand, there is no significant effect of cash flow for German firms. Finally, Kukuk and Stadler (2001) investigated the effect of financial constraints on the timing of innovation. They showed that German service firms being financially constrained are less likely to plan innovation activities.

- Technological or innovative capabilities: Dosi (1988: 1156) defines innovative capabilities as "different degrees of technological accumulation and different efficiencies in the innovative search process". Related to these two components of innovative capabilities, Cohen (1995) argued that there are two strands of literature. One strand focusses on differences in firms' areas of technological expertise which leads them to pursue different innovation strategies and activities and, hence, also different innovation inputs (see, e.g., Cohen and Klepper 1992a; 1992b). The other strand characterises firms as pursuing similar innovation activities but some firms are more successful than others in either generating or profiting from innovation. These differences in the productivity/innovation performance of R&D are traced back to firm-specific organisational or procedural capabilities (see Nelson, 1991; Henderson, 1993; Teece, 1986).

- Degree of diversification: Nelson (1959) stressed that more diversified firms possess more opportunities for exploiting new knowledge and complementarities among their diversified activities (economies of scope in innovation). Thus, more diversified firms tend to be more innovative. This hypothesis has been empirically confirmed, for instance, by Crépon et al. (1998).

- Corporate governance structure: One argument stressed by the principal agency theory is that managers prefer to carry out less risky investment – innovation projects are usually associated with a relatively high risk – than owners because managers are more closely related to the company. They will be threatened with the loss of their job if the investment fails while owners can spread their risk by diversification strategies (see Jensen and Meckling, 1976; Easterbrook, 1984). On the other hand, the manager's income (as well as prestige) is often related to the firm's realised profit or turnover. Managers may, therefore, have a higher incentive to do innovation activities and to invest more in innovation projects as innovations are expected to exert a positive impact on firm performance (see, e.g., Czarnitzki and Kraft 2004a; 2004b).

- Ownership structure: The firm's ownership structure may also have an impact on the incentive to conduct innovation activities. Enterprises which are part of a conglomerate may have easier access to external capital to finance innovation activities in a world of capital market imperfections. But some authors have stressed that foreign-owned firms are less engaged in innovation activities. One argument in favour of a negative link is that R&D plays a crucial role in the long-term strategic planning of a company, and managers wish to maintain direct control over such activities. Therefore, R&D activities usually take place at or in close proximity to the companies' headquarters (Howell, 1984).[85] So far, empirical evidence is inconclusive. The studies by Harris (1991) and Bishop and Wiseman (1999) reported that foreign ownership had a negative impact upon innovation while Love, Ashcroft, and Dunlop (1996) or Love and Roper (2001) found evidence for a positive relationship.

As mentioned above, market or industry characteristics – alone or in combination with firm-specific features – may be important for innovation activities. In this context technological opportunities (Cohen and Levinthal, 1989), incoming spill-overs, and effective appropriability conditions for innovation activities are emphasised (e.g., Spence, 1984; Becker and Peters, 2000). Effective appropriability conditions are important in that they allow innovators to receive the returns on their innovation activities and, thus, for their success. As a result, they also increase the incentives for and amount of innovation activities, as was shown by Spence in a theoretical model. On the other hand, strong appropriability conditions for current innovators might prevent other firms from further innovating. The concept of technological opportunities can be summarised by the fact that the prevailing technological dynamics in some industries (basic inventions, spill-over potentials of new technologies) spur innovation more strongly than in other industries. Nelson (1988) showed in a theoretical model that improved technological opportunities increase the incentive to invest in R&D.

4.2.2 Innovation Output

The literature has also pointed towards several factors explaining the success of product innovations. These determinants can be classified as follows:

- Innovation effort: The majority of studies corroborate that R&D or innovation expenditure positively affects product innovation success (see Crépon et al., 1998; Lööf and Heshmati, 2002; Janz, Lööf, and Peters, 2004).[86]
- Internal knowledge: Internal knowledge encompasses firms' innovative capabilities as well as absorptive capacities. The importance of innovative capabilities on innovation performance was already explored in the previous section. Absorptive capacities describe the "ability to identify, assimilate and exploit knowledge from the environment" (Cohen and Levinthal, 1989: 569). A positive impact of internal knowledge has been reported, for instance, in the studies by Love and Roper (2001) for German firms or Klomp and van Leeuwen (2001) for Dutch enterprises.

---

[85] Kleinknecht and Poot (1992) have linked this argument into a product life cycle approach. They argue that early stages of a cycle are associated with considerable R&D activities which are, therefore, carried out close to the headquarters while less R&D activities are necessary in later stages for incremental product or process modifications and can, hence, be decentralised.

[86] An exception is the study of Lööf, Heshmati, Asplund, and Naas (2003) which finds a positive impact for Swedish firms but not for Finnish and Norwegian firms.

- External knowledge: Hagedoorn (2002) pointed out that industries and technologies have undergone major changes in recent years. The uncertainty and complexity of innovation processes have increased, the costs for the development of new products and processes have risen, and product life cycles have shortened. These changes have intensified the need for external knowledge. External knowledge can be transmitted in the course of formal cooperation projects[87] but also in a rather informal way by sourcing the know-how of external partners. Knowledge sources can be split up according to the type of partner into academic sources and industrial sources (customers, suppliers, or competitors). The industrial sources can further be divided into upstream sources (suppliers) and downstream sources (customers). Klomp and van Leeuwen (2001) found that firms which are involved in innovation cooperations demonstrate a significantly higher share of sales due to new products. Von Hippel (1988) showed that network relationships, particularly with customers, stimulate innovation success. This finding is supported by Gemünden, Heydebreck, and Herden (1992), who have ascertained that firms that do not use external knowledge are less capable of innovation. Similarly, Klomp and van Leeuwen found evidence that sourcing knowledge from industrial sources positively affects innovation success. Crépon et al. (1998) found a significant impact of customers and competitors on the share of sales with new products.
- Other factors: Czarnitzki and Kraft (2004a; 2004b) analysed the impact of the corporate governance structure on the success of new products. Their results indicate that manager-led firms tend to be more successful than owner-led enterprises.

To the best of my knowledge, empirical evidence for factors explaining the (direct) success of process innovations is still lacking.

4.2.3 Productivity

There is an enormous amount of work examining the factors underlying productivity and productivity growth. In addition to innovation, the importance of human capital in determining productivity in particular has been extensively examined. Other factors relate to investments in information and communication technologies (ICT, see Lichtenberg, 1995; Brynjolfsson and Hitt, 1996; or Hempell, 2004), organisational practices, alone or in combination with ICT (see Brynjolfsson and Hitt, 2000; Bertschek and Kaiser, 2004), ownership (see, e.g., Lichtenberg and Siegel, 1990), managerial abilities and management practices (e.g., Bloom, Sadun, and van Reenen, 2007), regulation (e.g., Olley and Pakes, 1996), and export activities.[88] Summarising the findings of this

---

[87] One of the main incentives to collaborate on innovation projects is to get access to external knowledge (Cassiman and Veugelers, 2002).

[88] The majority of previous empirical studies confirm a positive correlation between productivity and exports at the firm level. Recent studies mainly fo-

large field of literature is beyond the scope of this section. Hence, I refer to the above-mentioned studies and the references cited therein. An overview can further be found in Bartelsman and Doms (2000). I will merely concentrate on studies investigating the relationship between innovation and productivity.

The majority of studies have used a Cobb-Douglas production function as their theoretical framework, augmented by knowledge capital K as an additional input:[89]

$$Q = AL^\alpha C^\beta M^\delta K^\gamma e^u. \tag{4.1}$$

Q denotes the output; L, C, and M are the conventional input factors labour, physical capital, and material. A is a constant that covers other factors which systematically affect output. The error term u captures unsystematic productivity shocks. α, β, γ, and δ can be interpreted as (partial) output elasticities of the corresponding input factors. The knowledge capital was usually measured by an R&D capital stock in this level formulation (e.g., Griliches, 1986; Griliches and Mairesse, 1983; 1984).

Taking logs, eq. (4.1) can be written as (where small letters denote corresponding log values):

$$q = a + \alpha l + \beta c + \delta m + \gamma k + u. \tag{4.2}$$

Many authors have assumed constant returns to scale in conventional input factors, i.e. $\alpha + \beta + \delta = 1$, and have rewritten eq. (4.2) as:

$$q - l = a + (\alpha + \beta + \delta - 1)l + \beta(c - l) + \delta(m - l) + \gamma k + u. \tag{4.3}$$

An alternative formulation rests on corresponding growth rates. Under the assumption that the depreciation of knowledge capital is zero, it can be shown that the above equation becomes (see Mairesse and Sassenou, 1991):

$$\Delta(q - l) = (\alpha + \beta + \delta - 1)\Delta l + \beta\Delta(c - l) + \delta\Delta(m - l) + \varrho r + \Delta u. \tag{4.4}$$

---

cus on the direction of causality. The "learning-by-exporting" hypothesis states that exporting firms may profit from technological knowledge and expertise available on foreign markets, resulting in a positive productivity effect (see Evenson and Westphal, 1995). However, recent studies by and large confirm the hypothesis of self-selection, that is best-performing domestic firms self-select into export markets (see, e.g., Bernard and Jensen, 1999; Arnold and Hussinger, 2005; De Loecker, 2004). This implies that there is a causal link from productivity to exporting whereas no evidence of the opposite direction was found.

[89] In time series analyses, the function usually includes the term $e^{\lambda t}$, where t denotes time and λ measures the rate of disembodied technical change.

r denotes R&D investments per output; $\varrho = \gamma(Q/K)$ is the gross rate of return on R&D. This formulation was used, for instance, by Griliches (1986) or Link (1981).[90]

A large number of studies have documented a positive relationship between R&D and productivity. Griliches and Lichtenberg (1984) found that process-related R&D contributes more to productivity growth than product-related R&D.[91] The estimated output elasticity of R&D capital ranges between 0.06 and 0.2, whereas the estimated rate of return mostly varies between 0.2 and 0.5. Surveys by Mairesse and Sassenou (1991) and Griliches (1998) provide a useful overview. Despite significant positive effects, Griliches (1995) argued that the estimated coefficients are not large enough to account for much of the productivity development in the US.[92] One reason might be that the role of R&D is underestimated because spill-over effects of R&D are neglected. Moreover, few of these studies correct for potential selection bias, accounting for non-R&D performers and for simultaneity bias, recognising the stochastic nature of R&D itself. Moreover, these studies generally do not take any information on the innovation output into account (Mairesse and Mohnen, 2005).

Crépon et al. (1998) addressed these problems and proposed and estimated a model, which describes the relationship between R&D input, innovation output, and productivity. Lööf and Heshmati (2002) were the first to slightly modify the CDM model by using innovation input rather than R&D input.[93] The general structure of the CDM approach can be interpreted as a three-step model consisting of four equations. In the first step, firms decide whether to engage in R&D activities or not and on the amount of money to invest in R&D. Given the firm's decision to invest in R&D projects, the second step defines the knowledge production function in the spirit of Pakes and Griliches (1984), in which innovation output results from innovation input and other factors. In a third step, the augmented Cobb-Douglas production function describes the effect of innovative output on productivity.

There is a growing number of national as well as cross-country firm-level studies on the innovation-productivity link using CIS data and versions of the CDM. Table 4.1 summarises the main studies, the data used, the set-up, the

---

[90] Instead of R&D investments knowledge capital has also been approximated by R&D employment, then labour is measured as non-R&D personnel (see Hall and Mairesse, 1995).

[91] Results further show that basic research has a greater effect on productivity than applied research. The same is true of company-financed compared to publicly-funded R&D (Griliches, 1986).

[92] His statement was based on the observation that the R&D intensity had fallen from 4.2 to 3.1 in the US from 1968 to 1975. Based on an average estimated rate of return of 0.4, the estimated decline in total productivity was 0.44%. The actual decline in productivity, however, was 2%. That is, R&D could only explain about 20% of the development.

[93] For the distinction between the two concepts, see section 2.1.

Table 4.1: Empirical Studies Based on the CDM Model

Authors	Data	Endogenous Variables[a]	Estimation Method	Results	Remarks
Crépon et al. (1998)	French manufacturing, firm level, cross-section 1986-1990.	I: R&D stock/emp, O: number of patents, share of sales due to new products (ordinal), P: labour productivity (level)	Simultaneous ALS estimation.	Innovation output rises with research input. Positive correlation between innovation output and productivity.	Sample restricted to innovative firms, correction for R&D selection bias.
Lööf and Heshmati (2001)	Swedish manufacturing, firm level, cross-section 1994-1996.	I: innovation expend/emp, O: sales due to new products/emp, sales due to market novelties/emp, P: labour productivity (level, growth).	Separate estimation; 1: Generalised Tobit (FIML), 2 and 3: 2SLS with correction for selection bias.	Innovation output increases with innovation input (though not for market novelties), and productivity rises with innovation output.	Sample included all firms, correction for innovation selection bias. Allowing for feedback effects from productivity to innovation output.
Lööf et al. (2003)	Manufacturing in Sweden (S), Norway (N), Finland (F), firm level, cross-section 1994-1996.	I: innovation expend/emp, O: sales due to new products/emp, sales due to market novelties/emp, P: labour productivity (level, growth).	Separate estimation; 1: Generalised Tobit (FIML), 2 and 3: 3SLS.	Output increases with innovation input in S (only for new products) but not in F and N. Productivity rises with innovation output in N and S but not in F.	Sample included all firms, correction for innovation selection bias. Feedback effects from productivity to innovation output in N but not in S and F.

To be continued on next page.

Table 4.1 – *continued from previous page*

Authors	Data	Endogenous Variables	Estimation Method	Results	Remarks
Klomp and van Leeuwen (2001)	Dutch manufacturing, firm level, cross-section 1994-1996.	I: innovation expend/emp, O: share of sales due to new products, P: sales growth, employment growth.	Separate estimations; 1: OLS or Heckman, 2: OLS or Heckman (also joint estimation of 1 and 2: FIML), 3: OLS or FIML.	Modest impact of input on output. Product innovations positively contribute to sales growth but negatively to employment growth.	Sample included product and process innovators.
van Leeuwen and Klomp (2006)	Dutch manufacturing, firm level, cross-section 1994-1996.	I: innovation expend/emp, R&D expend/emp, O: share of sales due to new products, P: value added, revenue function.	Separate estimations; 1: Generalised Tobit (FIML) 2 and 3: 3SLS or FIML. Joint estimation (FIML).	Positive impact of innovation input on output. No impact of product innovations on value added; positive impact on revenue function.	Sample included product and process innovators. Results on innovation output are sensitive to the method used.
Janz, Lööf, and Peters (2004)	Swedish and German knowledge-intensive manufacturing firms, cross-section 1998-2000.	I: innovation expend/emp, O: sales due to new products/emp, P: labour productivity (level).	Two-step estimation; 1: Generalised Tobit (FIML), 2 and 3: 2SLS with correction for selection bias. Pooled estimation.	Output increases with innovation input. Positive impact of innovation output on productivity. Both elasticities are not significantly different between both countries.	Sample included all firms, correction for innovation selection bias. Allowing for feedback effects from productivity to innovation output.

To be continued on next page.

Table 4.1 – *continued from previous page*

Authors	Data	Endogenous Variables	Estimation Method	Results	Remarks
Criscuolo and Haskel (2003)	UK manufacturing, firm level, 2 cross-sections (1994-1996, 1998-2000).	I: R&D expend/emp, O: share of sales due to new products and to market novelties, novel and non-novel process innovation (0/1), P: TFP growth.	Separate estimation; 1: Tobit, 2: Tobit, 3: OLS.	R&D positively affects all types of innovation output. New products do not boost productivity, weak positive evidence for market novelties. Non-novel process innovations do not contribute to productivity, negative effect of novel process innovations.	Sample included all firms.
Mairesse and Mohnen (2005)	French manufacturing, cross-section 1994-1996.	I: R&D expend/emp, O: share of sales due to new products, process innovation (0/1), P: labour productivity (level).	Simultaneous ALS estimation.	R&D positively affects both types of innovation output. Process innovations do not significantly boost productivity but product innovations do.	Sample included innovative firms, correction for continuous R&D selection bias.
Jefferson, Huamao, Xiaojing, and Xiaoyun (2006)	Chinese manufacturing, large and medium-sized firms, 3 cross-sections 1997, 1998, 1999.	I: innovation expend/sales (1998), O: share of sales due to new products (1999), P: labour productivity (1999), profit.	Separate estimation; 1: OLS, IV, 2: OLS, IV, 3: OLS, IV (sales instrumented in each equation).	Input positively affects innovation output (decreases with firm size). Innovation output has a positive impact on productivity and profits.	Sample included only innovative firms with positive profits, no correction for innovation selection bias. No consideration of censoring in the output variable.

To be continued on next page.

Table 4.1 – *continued from previous page*

Authors	Data	Endogenous Variables	Estimation Method	Results	Remarks
Parisi et al. (2006)	Italian manufacturing, firm level, panel data with T=2 (periods 1992-1994, 1995-1997).	O: process innovation (0/1), product innovation (0/1) (both: 1995-1997), P: labour productivity growth (1994-1997), TFP Tornquist index.	Separate estimation; 1: Logit, RE Logit and Cond. Logit, 2: IV.	R&D has a positive impact on product innovations but not on process innovations. Positive effect of process innovation on productivity but no impact of product innovations. No significant differences between high- and low-tech or small and medium-sized firms.	Productivity estimation based on a single cross-section. Sample included all firms, no correction for selection bias.
Griffith et al. (2006)	France (F), Germany (G), Spain (S), and UK, firm level, manufacturing, cross-section 1998-2000.	I: R&D expend/emp, O: process innovation (0/1), product innovation (0/1), P: labour productivity (level).	Separate estimation; 1: Generalised Tobit (FIML), 2: Probit, 3: 2SLS.	R&D positively affects both types of innovation: Effects on product innovation are very similar for G, S, and the UK, somewhat higher for F. Effects on process innovation are similar for G, S, and F, somewhat lower for the UK. Product innovation has a positive impact on productivity in all countries except in G. Process innovation is only significant for F.	Sample included all firms, correction for R&D selection bias.

Notes: [a)] I: Innovation input, O: innovation output, P: productivity. "emp" and "expend" denotes number of employees and expenditure, respectively.

estimation method used, and their main results. The majority of studies corroborate that innovation input significantly boosts innovation output, an exception is the study by Lööf et al. (2003). The results, however, are more mixed with respect to productivity effects of innovation output. Product innovations are often found to be positively correlated with productivity levels (see Crépon et al., 1998; Lööf and Heshmati, 2002; Lööf et al., 2003; Mairesse and Mohnen, 2005; Jefferson et al., 2006; Griffith et al., 2006) and productivity growth (see Lööf and Heshmati, 2002, and the results for Sweden and Norway by Lööf et al., 2003). However, Criscuolo and Haskel (2003), Parisi et al. (2006) or Lööf et al. (2003) for Finland could not confirm a positive impact of product innovation outcome on productivity growth. A rather inconclusive picture emerges when one looks at the few studies which have considered process innovations. While Parisi et al. ascertained that process innovations increase productivity, Mairesse and Mohnen could not find any impact and Criscuolo and Haskel even detected a negative effect on productivity.

4.3 Econometric Model

This study will rely on the modified version of the CDM approach proposed by Lööf and Heshmati (2002). But, it will enlarge the model by introducing a second knowledge production function for the outcome of process innovations.

In attempting to investigate the nexus between innovation input, output, and productivity, I have to take the fact into consideration that not all firms become involved in innovation activities and that it is fair to presume that the innovative sample is not a random sample of all firms. It is well-known that in this case, a restriction to the selected (innovative) sample would imply biased estimates (see Heckman, 1976; 1979). As a result, a selection equation ascertaining whether a firm is working on innovation activities is modelled in the first stage. Let y_{1i}^* be a latent (unobserved) endogenous variable measuring the propensity to innovate:[94]

$$y_{1i}^* = x_{1i}\beta_{1i} + \varepsilon_{1i} \qquad i = 1, \ldots, N. \tag{4.5}$$

The propensity to innovate depends on some observable explanatory variables summarised in the k-dimensional row vector x_{1i} and on unobservable variables summarised in the idiosyncratic error ε_{1i}. N is the number of firms. The latent variable can be interpreted as a decision criterion, such as the expected present value of a firm's profit accruing to innovations. If y_{1i}^* is larger than a constant threshold (without any loss of generality, I assume zero), I observe that firm i engages in innovation activities. y_{1i} is the observed binary en-

---

[94] The following convention holds: Variables with a star characterise latent variables; all other variables are observable (except the residuals).

dogenous variable, taking the value 0 for non-innovative and 1 for innovative firms:

$$y_{1i} = \begin{cases} 1 & \text{if} \quad y_{1i}^* > 0 \\ 0 & \text{if} \quad y_{1i}^* \leq 0. \end{cases} \qquad (4.6)$$

On the condition that firm i has decided to invest in innovation projects ($y_{1i} = 1$), one can observe the amount of resources devoted to such projects denoted as y_{2i} and explained by the following equation:

$$y_{2i} = x_{2i}\beta_2 + \varepsilon_{2i}. \qquad (4.7)$$

Likewise, conditional on the fact that firm i has decided to invest in innovation projects, eq. (4.8) and (4.9) describe the transformation process from innovation input to product innovation output (y_{3i}) and process innovation output (y_{4i}). Unfortunately, the data at hand does not allow me to separate between innovation budgets for new products and for new processes. Pakes and Griliches (1984) called this transformation the knowledge production. However, not all innovative firms introduce both new products and new processes. But, only on the condition that firm i launched at least one new product, one can measure the success of this activity. The same holds for the success of rationalisation innovations. The fact that both variables are censored is taken into account at the second stage by specifying two Tobit models to explain the success of new products and processes, respectively:

$$y_{3i} = \begin{cases} y_{3i}^* = \alpha_1\, y_{2i} + x_{3i}\,\beta_3 + \varepsilon_{3i} & \text{if} \quad y_{3i}^* > 0 \\ 0 & \text{if} \quad y_{3i}^* \leq 0 \end{cases} \qquad (4.8)$$

and

$$y_{4i} = \begin{cases} y_{4i}^* = \alpha_2\, y_{2i} + x_{4i}\,\beta_4 + \varepsilon_{4i} & \text{if} \quad y_{4i}^* > 0 \\ 0 & \text{if} \quad y_{4i}^* \leq 0. \end{cases} \qquad (4.9)$$

Like the majority of empirical studies I use an augmented Cobb-Douglas production function at the third stage. Eq. (4.10) is the log-transformed production function and describes the link between productivity y_{5i} and knowledge capital, proxied by product and process innovation output, as well as some other explanatory variables x_{5i}:

$$y_{5i} = \alpha_3\, y_{3i} + \alpha_4\, y_{4i} + x_{5i}\beta_5 + \varepsilon_{5i}. \qquad (4.10)$$

The α's, β's, and γ's are the unknown parameter vectors. x_{1i}, x_{2i}, x_{3i}, x_{4i}, and x_{5i} are vectors of various exogenous variables explaining the decision to innovate, innovation input, innovation output, and productivity. The inverse Mills ratio (Heckman, 1979) is included in x_{3i}, x_{4i}, and x_{5i} to correct for a possible selection bias. The specification of the model will be explored in more detail in section 4.5.

ε_{1i} and ε_{2i} are bivariate normal with zero mean, variances $\sigma_1^2 = 1$, and σ_2^2 and correlation coefficient ρ. ε_{3i}, ε_{4i}, and ε_{5i} are $i.i.d.$ drawings from a normal distribution with $N\left(0, \sigma_j^2\right)$ for $j = 3, 4, 5.$[95] ε_{2i}, ε_{3i}, ε_{4i}, and ε_{5i} are mutually uncorrelated. In other words, I assume a recursive structure in model equations (4.7)-(4.10) and do not allow for feedback effects. Innovation input explains the success of new products as well as processes, and the two outputs of the innovative activities are endogenous in the productivity equation. For estimation purposes I, therefore, apply a three-step estimation procedure. In the first step the generalised Tobit model (eq. (4.6) and (4.7)) is estimated by full maximum-likelihood techniques. In the second step the two innovation output equations are separately estimated applying instrumental variable Tobit estimators, using the predicted value of the input variable as instrument (see Maddala, 1983). In the last step the productivity equation is estimated by two-stage least squares (2SLS) using the predicted values from the second step.

4.4 Data Set

The underlying data set comes from the Mannheim Innovation Panel (MIP), which was described in more detail in chapter 2. Previous CDM studies mainly used cross-sectional CIS data. In this context there are three main deficiencies associated with this kind of cross-sectional data. Firstly, the innovation input variable (innovation expenditure) is a flow variable and not a stock measure. Secondly, it is only observed in the same year in which one observes innovation output. This means that the lag between the investment in innovation and the occurrence of the innovation is ignored, along with a possible lag between the introduction of a new product and its market acceptance or of a new process and its cost-saving effects. Thirdly, in addition to the endogeneity problems already explored in the previous section, some of the variables (e.g., exports or public funding), which are used to explain firm's innovation input and output, are also only observed contemporarily. But they are likely to be determined simultaneously and, hence, suffer from endogeneity problems.

To overcome the first drawback, panel data with a sufficient long-time dimension would be necessary to construct a firm's innovation input stock. Since the MIP is a highly unbalanced panel, I am not able to follow this strategy.[96] However, I try to address the second and third deficiency by imposing a more sensible time structure on the model. To reduce endogeneity

---

[95] $i.i.d.$ means *independent and identically distributed.*

[96] Crépon et al. (1998) used additional information from the French R&D survey to build up an R&D stock. However, they ascertained that in cross-sectional

problems of explanatory variables resulting from simultaneity, I fall back on corresponding lagged values. I further use the lagged innovation expenditure to explain current product and process innovation output. Admittedly, this approach does not completely solve the second problem as, for instance, the product innovation output is measured as the sales share in one year due to new products introduced within the previous 3-year period.[97]

In order to be able to account for the last two points, I merged the cross-sections of the years 2000, 2001, and 2002.[98] In the following, I first explain the decision to invest in innovation activities in the year 2001 mainly by means of explanatory variables relating to the year 2000. In the second stage, the innovation input of the year 2001 is linked to the innovation output of the year 2002 which in turn is related to the productivity level of the year 2002 or the productivity growth between 2002 and 2003.[99] A similar approach was also taken by Jefferson et al. (2006). The empirical specification along with the time structure will be set out in more detail in the following section. Although a real panel data analysis would be preferable, I decided not to follow this course due to the model complexity and the fact that many variables potentially explaining innovation expenditure and output are not available for all years.

For the analysis, I restrict the sample to firms for which information is available for all three cross-sections and which are assigned to manufacturing industries. In addition, a few outliers were eliminated,[100] and firms with incomplete data for relevant variables were dropped for estimation purposes. The resulting sample consists of 879 manufacturing firms. Table 4.9 in Appendix C provides an overview of the industries and their distribution across the total sample and both non-innovative and innovative sample. Table 4.10 contains corresponding information on the distribution by size class.

---

analyses the results did not significantly change when using the flow instead of the stock measure. The explanation is that in cross-sections the flow variable is a good proxy for the stock variable. See Griliches and Mairesse (1984) or Hall (1990) for the construction of a knowledge capital stock using R&D expenditure and patents.

[97] Since the Oslo Manual focusses on the whole of the firm's innovation behaviour (subject approach) and not on a specific innovation project (object approach), it is not possible to directly assign the innovation expenditure to a specific innovation output.

[98] These cross-sections correspond to the surveys 2001, 2002, and 2003.

[99] Note that this requires additional merging of the 2003 cross-section which leads to a reduction of the sample.

[100] Only those firms whose labour productivity ranges between the 1st and 99th percentile are taken into account.

4.5 Empirical Implementation

Potential factors explaining innovation input, innovation output, and productivity, and the empirical implementation of each equation will be explored in the following subsections. Note that the specification of each equation requires some a priori assumptions (exclusion restrictions) in order to be able to estimate and identify the model. The assumptions seems to be quite sensible from an economic point of view, however, they are not really testable (see Crépon et al., 1998).

4.5.1 Innovation Input

In this analysis an innovative firm is defined as a firm that has positive innovation expenditure in the year 2001 ($INNOSEL_{01}$). The innovation input ($INPUT_{01}$) is measured by the log of innovation expenditure per employee. A complete list of all variables and their definitions can be found in Table 4.11 in Appendix C.

In accordance with the Schumpeterian tradition, I include firm size and market structure as explanatory variables. Firm size is measured by the log number of employees ($SIZE_{00}$); the market structure is captured by the Herfindahl-Hirschmann index ($HERFIN_{00}$) measured on a 3-digit NACE level. One problem in this context is the potential endogeneity of both variables. Innovation activities often aim to change firm size and existing market structures. Thus, there might be a feedback effect from innovation to firm size and market concentration. I try to solve this problem by relating both variables to the previous year 2000. According to Schumpeter a positive effect of both variables is expected.

As mentioned in section 4.2.1, the innovation literature emphasises that certain firm characteristics, like the degree of product diversification, the degree of internationalisation, the availability of financial resources and technological capabilities, are of crucial importance for explaining innovation activities. Like many other empirical studies, I use the export intensity ($EXPORT_{00}$) to account for the degree to which a firm is exposed to international competition. The hypothesis is that the more a firm is exposed to international competition, the higher the innovation effort is. The availability of financial resources is proxied by an index of creditworthiness ($RATING_{00}$). The hypothesis is that $RATING_{00}$ negatively affects the propensity to innovate since the index ranges from 1 (best rating) to 6 (worst rating). Thus, a higher value of $RATING_{00}$ implies that less external funding is available and that it is more costly due to higher interest rates, making fewer innovation projects profitable. Although the data set does not contain a direct measure for internal financial resources like profit or cash flow, both enter the index of creditworthiness. Thus, $RATING_{00}$ reflects internal financial capabilities to a certain extent as well. As the data set does not contain information on product diversification, I cannot take this hypothesis into account.

Technological capabilities are proxied by the share of employees with a university degree ($HIGH_{00}$), the amount of training expenditure per employee ($TRAIN_{00}$), and the firm age (AGE_{01}). One problem that arises is the fact that particularly R&D personnel demonstrate high qualification levels. Hence, carrying out innovation activities may have an impact on the share of high-skilled employees. Similarly, part of the training expenditure might be incurred in the context of innovation projects. To avoid problems of endogeneity and double counting, I include the lagged values of HIGH and TRAIN. I expect that higher technological capabilities increase the incentive to innovate and the innovation intensity.

The estimation also controls for the corporate governance structure by distinguishing between public limited companies (PLC, *Aktiengesellschaften*), private limited liability companies (LTD, *GmbH* or *GmbH & Co. KG*) and private partnerships (PRIVPART, *Personengesellschaften*, i.e. *Einzelunternehmen, Gesellschaft bürgerlichen Rechts, offene Handelsgellschaften, OHG,* or *Kommanditgesellschaften, KG*). The legal form of the company might be important for two reasons: Firstly, in private partnerships there is usually no split between management and ownership function.[101] Secondly, liability rules differ according to the legal form and might have impact on getting external funding. In addition, firm-specific variables reflecting location (EAST), whether the firm received public funding in the previous period (PUBLIC), whether the firm is part of an enterprise group (GROUP), and whether the group's headquarter is located abroad (FOREIGN) are included. On the one hand, enterprises which are part of a conglomerate may have easier access to external capital in a world of capital market imperfections, and I would, therefore, hypothesise a positive relationship. But clearly, GROUP may also capture other effects of the companies' organisational structure on innovative activities. As mentioned in section 4.2, I expect foreign ownership to have a negative impact.

As mentioned above, market or industry characteristics like technological opportunities, spill-overs, and effective appropriability conditions – alone or in combination with firm-specific features – may be important for innovation activities. All three concepts are very complex and cannot be readily observed since managers can hardly be surveyed to give reasonable direct estimates of them. The variables measuring appropriability and incoming spill-overs are designed in accordance with Cassiman and Veugelers (2002). In other words, I distinguish between the importance of legal (patents, design patterns, trademarks, copyrights) and strategic appropriability conditions (secrecy, complexity of design, time-lead), called $LEGAL_{98-00}$ and $STRAT_{98-00}$. Incoming spill-overs ($SPILL_{98-00}$) are measured by the importance of professional conferences, meetings, and journals as well as exhibitions and fairs as sources of innovation. Technological opportunities are proxied by the impor-

---

[101] Note that according to the German Commercial Code (Art. 164 HGB), the limited partner cannot exert management functions in a limited partnership (KG).

tance of science-based information sources (universities, public or commercial research institutes) on the one hand and private sources (customers, suppliers, competitors) on the other (see Felder et al., 1996).[102] All five variables are measured on a 2-digit Nace level.

While Crépon et al. (1998) used the same set of variables explaining the decision to conduct R&D and the amount of R&D investment, I will follow Lööf and Heshmati (2002) and only allow a partial overlap of the vectors x_{1i} and x_{2i}. This ensures that the identification does not solely rely on functional form assumptions. In particular, I include $SIZE_{00}$, $RATING_{00}$, and AGE_{00} in the selection equation but exclude them from the input equation. Excluding SIZE corresponds to stylised fact 2 by Cohen and Klepper (1996) (see section 4.2.1). Furthermore, these exclusion restrictions seem to be justified due to the fact that all three variables turned out to be far from significant in the input equation when using a specification with x_{1i} and x_{2i} being equal.[103] However, they are not really testable.

4.5.2 Innovation Output

The success of product innovations (PD_OUT_{02}) is measured by the sales in the year 2002 stemming from new products launched in the previous 3 years. Process innovation output (PC_OUT_{02}) is defined as cost savings in 2002 due to new processes introduced in the period 2000-2002. Both innovation output variables are scaled by number of employees. Both innovation output equations are specified as a function of the lagged innovation input.

A flaw of previous empirical studies is that most data sets do not allow to distinguish whether firms undertake specific activities, for instance, the use of external knowledge, in the course of the development of new products or of new processes. A major advantage of the data at hand is that it contains separate information on relevant variables for both kinds of innovation activities. Hence, the analysis explicitly distinguishes between innovative capabilities to develop new products and new processes. Firms may have in-house capabilities for one activity but not necessarily for both. $PD\_INHOUSE_{00-02}$ is a

---

[102] Based on CIS 1 data, Felder et al. used a third variable, the importance of low technological opportunities, as a hampering factor. However, this information is not available for 2000.

[103] In a first step I used a specification in which the explanatory variables x_{1i} matched x_{2i} and the Heckman two-step estimator. In this model specification the parameters of the input equation are identified because the inverse Mills ratio is a non-linear function of the variables included in the selection equation. However, the non-linearity of the inverse Mills ratio arises from the assumption of normality in the selection equation. The assumption of normality was, therefore, tested and not rejected. In this specification $SIZE_{00}$, $RATING_{00}$, and AGE_{00} turned out to be insignificant in the input equation but not in the selection equation. I also experimented with squared terms to allow for potential non-linearities but this did not alter the results.

dummy variable indicating that the new products have mainly been developed inside the firm in the period 2000-2002. A positive impact on innovation success is expected. Similarly, $PC\_INHOUSE_{00-02}$ equals one if process innovations have mainly been developed in-house.[104] The data set also allows to split up knowledge sourcing by innovation activities. In each equation I include a set of five dummy variables indicating that customers, suppliers, competitors, science, or laws and regulations have been a major source of product and process innovations, respectively (PD_CUST_{00-02}, PD_SUPP_{00-02}, PD_COMP_{00-02}, PD_SCIEN_{00-02}, and PD_REG_{00-02} in the product innovation equation as well as PC_CUST etc. in the process innovation equation). In case of product innovations, the importance of industrial sources (relative to the industry average) is, furthermore, applied as an indicator for the importance of incoming knowledge spill-overs ($INSPILL_{00-02}$). Innovation output is further modelled as a function of $COOP_{00-02}$, indicating that the firm has entered innovation cooperations. Unfortunately, I cannot distinguish whether the cooperation was related to product or process innovation activities or indeed to both.

The 2002 cross-section does not contain information about appropriability conditions or technological opportunities in the same way that the 2000 cross-section does. Hence, industry dummies are intended to account for both effects. Furthermore, the innovation success is specified as a function of firm size ($SIZE_{01}$) and, in case of product innovation, also of market concentration ($HERFIN_{01}$). Finally, both equations control for location ($EAST_{02}$) and ownership ($GROUP_{02}$).

4.5.3 Productivity

The final relationship is the productivity equation (4.10). Productivity is measured in terms of labour productivity, which is proxied by turnover per employee. The level of labour productivity in the year 2002 ($PROD_{02}$) as well as the growth rate of labour productivity between 2002 and 2003 ($\Delta PROD_{03}$) have been analysed.

In addition to knowledge capital, which is proxied here by both innovation output variables, the productivity equation controls for input variations in material ($MATERIAL_{02}$) and physical capital ($CAPITAL_{02}$). Although productivity is measured in intensity form, firm size ($SIZE_{02}$) is additionally included in the set of explanatory variables. This allows me to test for the hypothesis of constant returns to scale which corresponds to a zero coefficient of $SIZE_{02}$ (see section 4.2.3). The basic specification further controls for industry characteristics and location ($EAST_{02}$). In an extended specification I further consider differences in the human capital endowment ($HIGH_{01}$) and

---

[104] Most empirical studies include a dummy variable for permanent R&D activities to measure innovative capabilities. The variables used here encompass innovative capabilities in a broader sense.

the export intensity ($EXPORT_{01}$). Both variables enter the equation with lagged values to reduce potential endogeneity.

Table 4.2 summarises the structure of the model (note that time indices are omitted for ease of representation). The estimation strategy used formally guaranties the identification of the parameters.

4.6 Descriptive Analysis

Before turning to the econometric results, I first provide a brief descriptive analysis of the data. Nearly 60% of the firms sampled were engaged in innovation activities in the year 2001. Table 4.3 summarises the main characteristics of innovative and non-innovative firms. First of all, it turns out that the average labour productivity is about 13% higher in innovative than in non-innovative firms. The mean difference test indicates that this difference is statistically significant at the 1% level. However, average labour productivity growth does not significantly differ between the two groups. Moreover, innovative firms are typically larger and older than their non-innovative counterparts, and they show a significantly better performance with regard to their creditworthiness. They are likewise more exposed to international competition and demonstrate an export intensity of 26% which is nearly twice as large as that of non-innovative firms.[105] The average share of highly skilled employees is also nearly two times greater among the the innovative firms (14.1%) than among the non-innovators (8.0%). On the other hand, and perhaps somewhat surprisingly, innovative firms do not spend more money on training their employees to increase their knowledge base. Nonetheless, the main conclusion drawn from Table 4.3 is that the group of innovative firms is quite different from the non-innovator group. This supports the supposition that selectivity might be a problem and should be taken into account.

Looking at the core innovation indicators in Table 4.4, one can see that, on average, innovation budgets amount to 6.7% of turnover in innovative firms. The median is clearly lower at 3.8%. On the output side, process innovators experience a reduction of 5% in unit costs and on average about 26% of product innovators' sales originate from new products.

Another important aspect that emerges from Table 4.4 is the fact that only 7 out of 10 innovative firms launch new products (read: demonstrate product innovation output figures). Process innovations are less prevalent, with 45% of all innovative firms recording at least one such innovation.[106] The introduction of new production technologies may be motivated by several different factors as was already set out in chapter 2. In this sample two out

---

[105] One cannot draw any conclusions from this figure regarding the causality between innovation and export activity; see also the explanations in section 4.2.1.

[106] Note that a fairly large percentage of firms with positive innovation effort in 2001 had not yet been successful innovators in 2002 (21%).

Table 4.2: Estimation Strategy

Variable	INNOSEL	INPUT	PD_OUT	PC_OUT	PROD
INPUT	−	−	x	x	−
PD_OUT	−	−	−	−	x
PC_OUT	−	−	−	−	x
SIZE	x	−	x	x	x
HERFIN	x	x	x	−	−
RATING	x	−	−	−	−
EXPORT	x	x	−	−	(x)
PUBLIC	x	x	−	−	−
Ownership:					
GROUP	x	x	x	x	(x)
FOREIGN	x	x	−	−	−
PLC	x	x	−	−	−
LTD	x	x	−	−	−
Internal Innovative Capabilities:					
HIGH	x	x	−	−	(x)
TRAIN	x	x	−	−	−
AGE	x	−	−	−	−
PD_INHOUSE	−	−	x	−	−
PC_INHOUSE	−	−	−	x	−
External Knowledge:					
COOP	−	−	x	x	−
PD_CUST etc.	−	−	x	−	−
PC_CUST etc.	−	−	−	x	−
INSPILL	−	−	x	−	−
SPILL (ind)	x	x	−	−	−
Appropriability:					
LEGAL (ind)	x	x	−	−	−
STRAT (ind)	x	x	−	−	−
Technological Opportunities:					
TECHOPP1 (ind)	x	x	−	−	−
TECHOPP2 (ind)	x	x	−	−	−
CAPITAL	−	−	−	−	x
MATERIAL	−	−	−	−	x
EAST	x	x	x	x	x
IND	x	x	x	x	x

Notes: For ease of presentation time indices are not reported. "ind" means that the variable is measured on a 2-digit NACE industry level. (x) indicates that the variable is only used in the extended specification.

Table 4.3: Characteristics of Non-Innovative and Innovative Firms

	Unit	Non-Innovative Firms			Innovative Firms			Mean Diff.[a]
		med	mean	s.d.	med	mean	s.d.	t-stat
$PROD_{02}$[b]	1000 €	97.8	130.8	100.2	122.3	148.3	102.9	-2.516**
$\Delta PROD_{03}$[c]	%	1.1	2.0	18.9	3.0	2.5	19.7	-0.352
$SIZE_{00}$	No. empl.	44.0	141.4	266.0	126.0	1,865.6	15,197.5	-2.591***
$SIZE_{01}$	No. empl.	42.0	147.9	297.3	121.5	1,783.5	14,582.4	-2.562**
$SIZE_{02}$	No. empl.	41.0	142.5	272.2	124.0	1,593.7	13,675.5	-2.424**
$HERFIN_{00}$	[0-100]	1.4	3.2	5.2	2.0	4.2	6.4	-4.305***
$HERFIN_{01}$	[0-100]	1.1	2.5	4.1	1.4	3.9	6.7	-5.815***
AGE_{01}	years	13.0	18.5	15.3	13.0	21.7	22.9	-2.498**
$CAPITAL_{02}$	1000 €	48.1	56.4	57.9	48.1	63.8	70.5	-1.706*
$MATERIAL_{02}$	1000 €	38.6	66.8	77.5	52.1	73.9	79.8	-1.317
$TRAIN_{00}$	1000 €	0.1	0.4	2.4	0.2	0.5	1.1	-0.312
$RATING_{00}$	[1-6]	2.1	2.2	0.7	2.0	2.1	0.7	3.092***
$EXPORT_{00}$	[0-1]	0.017	0.134	0.212	0.182	0.256	0.255	-7.705***
$EXPORT_{01}$	[0-1]	0.027	0.140	0.253	0.203	0.261	0.253	-7.492***
$HIGH_{00}$	[0-1]	0.051	0.085	0.105	0.182	0.143	0.142	-7.048***
$HIGH_{01}$	[0-1]	0.050	0.080	0.099	0.100	0.141	0.144	-7.377***
$EAST_{02}$	[0/1]		0.331	0.471		0.322	0.468	0.270
$GROUP_{01}$	[0/1]		0.235	0.425		0.450	0.498	-6.863***
$GROUP_{02}$	[0/1]		0.359	0.480		0.594	0.492	-7.067***
$FOREIGN_{01}$	[0/1]		0.672	0.251		0.094	0.292	-1.446
PLC_{01}	[0/1]		0.017	0.129		0.056	0.229	-3.195***
LTD_{01}	[0/1]		0.118	0.323		0.071	0.257	2.287**
$PRIVPART_{01}$	[0/1]		0.863	0.345		0.872	0.335	-0.381
$PUBLIC_{98-00}$	[0/1]		0.072	0.260		0.370	0.483	-11.764***
No. of firms			357			522		
% of total obs			41.6			59.4		

Notes: [a] ***, **, and * indicate significance on a 1%, 5%, and 10% level in a two-tailed t-test on equal means in both groups (the variances are allowed to be unequal between both groups).
[b] Values shown for PROD as well as for SIZE, AGE, CAPITAL, MATERIAL, and TRAIN are not log-transformed. For estimation purposes, however, a log-transformation of these variables is used to take the skewness of the distribution into account.
[c] Reduced sample of 602 observations.

Table 4.4: Innovation Characteristics of Innovative Firms

	Unit	Innovative Firms mean	med	PD mean	PC mean
Innovation intensity$_{01}$	%	6.7	3.8	7.2	7.3
INPUT$_{01}$	1000 €	8.0	4.7	9.3	9.2
Product innovators$_{02}$	[0/1]	70.5	—	—	—
Share of sales with new products$_{02}$	%	18.7	10.0	26.4	—
PD_OUT$_{02}$	1000 €	26.9	13.9	38.2	—
PD_INHOUSE$_{00\text{-}02}$	[0/1]	53.6	—	76.1	—
PD_CUST$_{00\text{-}02}$	[0/1]	33.9	—	48.1	—
PD_SUPP$_{00\text{-}02}$	[0/1]	9.8	—	13.9	—
PD_COMP$_{00\text{-}02}$	[0/1]	14.9	—	21.2	—
PD_SCIEN$_{00\text{-}02}$	[0/1]	4.6	—	6.5	—
PD_REG$_{00\text{-}02}$	[0/1]	10.3	—	14.7	—
Process innovators$_{02}$	[0/1]	44.9	—	—	—
Cost-reducing process innovators$_{02}$	[0/1]	30.8	—	—	69.1
Cost savings$_{02}$	%	2.2	0.0	—	5.0
PC_OUT$_{02}$	1000 €	2.8	0.0	—	6.3
PC_INHOUSE$_{00\text{-}02}$	[0/1]	26.2	—	—	58.8
PC_CUST$_{00\text{-}02}$	[0/1]	6.0	—	—	13.3
PC_SUPP$_{00\text{-}02}$	[0/1]	3.8	—	—	8.6
PC_COMP$_{00\text{-}02}$	[0/1]	2.7	—	—	6.0
PC_SCIEN$_{00\text{-}02}$	[0/1]	0.8	—	—	1.7
PC_REG$_{00\text{-}02}$	[0/1]	2.1	—	—	4.7
COOP$_{00\text{-}02}$	[0/1]	29.3	—	37.8	41.2

Notes: PD and PC denote product and process innovators. For binary variables the median value is not shown; the mean value is represented as percentage share of innovative firms.

of three process innovators – 30% of all innovative firms – introduce new technologies to rationalise processes. Therefore, a censoring problem occurs and has to be considered of in the estimation of the output equations.

Nearly every third innovative firm has entered innovation cooperations to get access to external knowledge, the share being nearly the same for product and process innovators. However, interesting differences in innovative capabilities and external knowledge sourcing emerge for both kind of innovation activities. About 76% of the product innovators develop their new products mainly in-house whereas not quite 60% of the process innovators demonstrate comparable abilities for the development of new production technologies. This can be explained by the fact that, to a certain extent, firms realise process innovations by buying new machines which have been developed by other firms. At the same time, product innovators use all types of external knowledge sources more often.

4.7 Econometric Analysis

Misspecification of the likelihood function, in particular concerning homoskedasticity and normality, might lead to inconsistent estimators in the probit model.[107] Hence, before interpreting the results, I start by separately testing the assumptions of normality and homoskedasticity in the selection equation using appropriate Lagrange multiplier (LM) tests based on the first-stage probit estimation (see Verbeek, 2000). To test for the existence of heteroskedasticity, I assume that heteroskedasticity is modelled by the 11 industry dummies and 8 size class dummies.[108] With p-values of 0.572 and 0.637, the LM tests indicate that both hypotheses cannot be rejected. Hence, there are no indications that the selection equation is misspecified.

Table 4.5 reports the results of the generalised Tobit estimation; the coefficients are depicted in the columns two and four while the columns three and five present the marginal effects. The likelihood ratio test on whether $\rho = 0$ rejects the null hypothesis, and hence, selectivity has to be taken into account. As expected and in line with other empirical findings, the decision to innovate is heavily dependent on firm size. An increase in firm size by 1% steps up the probability of innovating by roughly 0.06 percentage points.[109] But remember, as already diagnosed in section 4.5, I do not find any significant impact of firm size on the innovation input. Regarding the second Schumpeterian determinant, the opposite conclusion can be drawn. That is, market structure, measured in terms of the market concentration index, turns out to be insignificant in the selection equation. But, on the condition that a firm has decided to engage in innovation, firms in more concentrated markets spend significantly more money on innovation projects.[110]

A second important finding is that innovative capabilities, proxied by the share of highly skilled employees and the amount of training expenditure, have

---

[107] Under certain assumptions the pseudo maximum likelihood method leads to consistent estimates even in case of misspecification, see, e.g., Ruud (1986).

[108] Results do not qualitatively change if I allow heteroskedasticity to depend on industry or size alone.

[109] As an illustration, this implies that based on a sample mean of 1,165 employees, an increase by 100 employees raises the probability of innovating by 0.451 percentage points. Furthermore, I also include the square of size but no evidence for a non-linear relationship was found.

[110] Scherer (1967) found evidence for an inverse U-shaped relationship. I tested for this hypothesis by running an additional regression including the square of HERFIN as well. However, this hypothesis was not confirmed in this analysis.

Table 4.5: Estimation Results: Innovation Input

	Selection Equation INNOSEL$_{01}$		Input Equation INPUT$_{01}$	
	coeff. (s.e.)	marg. eff. (s.e.)	coeff. (s.e.)	marg. eff. (s.e.)
const	-0.486 (0.514)	—	-5.602*** (0.448)	—
SIZE$_{00}$	0.149*** (0.046)	0.056*** (0.017)	—	—
HERFIN$_{00}$	-0.064 (0.088)	-0.024 (0.033)	0.013** (0.006)	0.014** (0.006)
RATING$_{00}$	-0.041 (0.072)	-0.015 (0.027)	—	—
EXPORT$_{00}$	0.499** (0.246)	0.188** (0.093)	0.567** (0.269)	0.512* (0.269)
PUBLIC$_{98-00}$	1.015*** (0.144)	0.330*** (0.037)	0.441*** (0.124)	0.343** (0.123)
GROUP$_{01}$	0.188 (0.124)	0.070 (0.046)	-0.140 (0.141)	-0.161 (0.141)
FOREIGN$_{01}$	-0.138 (0.185)	-0.053 (0.072)	0.333* (0.181)	0.348* (0.181)
PLC$_{01}$	-0.157 (0.282)	-0.060 (0.110)	0.418** (0.192)	0.436** (0.192)
PRIVPART$_{01}$	0.072 (0.172)	0.027 (0.063)	-0.020 (0237)	-0.028 (0.237)
HIGH$_{00}$	1.290*** (0.466)	0.485*** (0.175)	1.912*** (0.476)	1.770*** (0.478)
TRAIN$_{00}$	0.093*** (0.024)	0.035*** (0.009)	0.140*** (0.040)	0.130*** (0.040)
AGE$_{01}$	0.010 (0.075)	0.004 (0.028)	—	—
LEGAL$_{98-00}$	2.233 (2.177)	0.840 (0.818)	3.967 (2.788)	3.721 (2.760)
STRAT$_{98-00}$	-1.410 (1.298)	-0.531 (0.488)	-3.890** (1.756)	-3.734** (1.749)

To be continued on next page.

Table 4.5 – *continued from previous page*

	Selection Equation INNOSEL$_{01}$		Input Equation INPUT$_{01}$	
TECHOPP1$_{98\text{-}00}$	0.683 (1.424)	0.257 (1.536)	-1.400 (1.749)	-1.471 (1.738)
TECHOPP2$_{98\text{-}00}$	-0.693 (2.295)	-0.261 (0.864)	2.260 (2.415)	2.337 (2.370)
SPILL$_{98\text{-}00}$	1.995 (1.619)	0.751 (0.609)	2.622 (2.308)	2.402 (2.278)
EAST$_{01}$	-0.142 (0.120)	-0.054 (0.046)	-0.267* (0.139)	-0.251 (0.140)
IND	yes	yes	yes	yes
ρ	—		0.153 (0.059)	—
σ_2	—		1.294 (0.051)	—
λ	—		0.198 (0.078)	—
W_{IND} (p-value)	0.666		0.000	
W_ρ (p-value)	—		0.010	
W_{all} (p-value)	—		0.000	
ln L			-1344.5	
Pseudo R^2	0.204		—	
LM_{norm}(p-value)	0.572		—	
LM_{het}(p-value)	0.637		—	
Total obs	879		522	
Censored obs	357		–	
Uncensored obs	522		–	

Notes: ***, **, and * indicate significance on a 1%, 5%, and 10% level, respectively (standard errors robust to heteroskedasticity in parentheses). Marginal effects (at the sample means) for the probability of conducting innovation activities and for the expected value of the innovation input conditional on being selected are reported. Note that $\lambda = \rho\sigma_2$. W_{IND} tests for the null hypothesis that the industry dummies are jointly equal to zero. Pseudo R^2 measures the pseudo R^2 of the first-step probit estimates of the selection equation. LM_{norm} and LM_{het} report p-values of tests for normality and heteroskedasticity in the first-step probit estimates. $LM_{norm} = 1.117 \sim \chi^2(2)$ under the null hypothesis of normality. $LM_{het} = 16.307 \sim \chi^2(19)$ under the null hypothesis of homoskedasticity. W_ρ is a Wald test of independence of the selection and innovation input equation (equivalent test for $\rho = 0$). The test statistic $W_\rho = 8.85$ has a $\chi^2(1)$ distribution. W_{all} is a Wald test of overall significance of the input equation. $W_{all} = 175.5$ and follows $\chi^2(21)$ distribution.

a crucial influence on both the decision to engage in innovation activities and the innovation input. For example, a 1% increase in the share of highly skilled personnel raises the probability of innovating by about 0.5 percentage points and the innovation input by roughly 1.2% (conditional on being innovative).

The results further provide evidence that the probability of being an innovator and the innovation input are increasing functions of the lagged export intensity proxying the degree of internationalisation. Moreover, firms which receive public funding in the previous period exhibit a higher propensity to innovate and a higher innovation input than innovators without previous financial support.

Conversely, none of the variables controlling for various aspects of ownership have a significant impact on the firms' likelihood to innovate. But, conditional on being innovative, foreign-owned firms as well as public limited companies spend more money on innovation activities. The variable reflecting the availability of financial resources demonstrates the expected negative sign but is not significant.

Industry levels of technological opportunities and incoming spill-overs are expected to increase the incentive to innovate and to induce higher innovation input. However, the results do not corroborate these hypotheses. But admittedly, this may be due to the fact that these concepts are extremely complex and not easy to operationalise in empirical studies. The effects of appropriability conditions are mixed. Firms belonging to industries in which strategic appropriability conditions are more important tend to make lower budgets available for innovation projects. Contrarily, legal protection methods do not significantly enter either of the equations.

Table 4.6 depicts the estimation results of the knowledge production functions. Both equations have been separately estimated using IV Tobit estimators. To account for the fact that the instrument itself, that is the predicted innovation input, is not exogenous but an estimated variable, standard errors have been calculated using the bootstrap method (based on 50 replications).

Product innovation output is significantly determined by innovation input. This result is in line with other empirical findings. The estimated elasticity of product innovation output with respect to innovation input is somewhat higher compared to figures reported by Lööf and Heshmati (2002). However, it is similar to the value found for knowledge-intensive German manufacturing firms for the period 1998-2000 by Janz, Lööf, and Peters (2004). Furthermore, it turns out that taking account of the endogeneity of the innovation input leads to a significant rise in the estimated elasticity as is shown in Table 4.7. Conversely, the results provide only weak evidence of a positive impact of innovation input on process innovation output. Innovation input is significant at the 10% level when endogeneity is ignored (see Table 4.7). However, this effect vanishes when taking endogeneity into consideration and using IV methods.

Whereas the incentive to innovate depends, to a large extent, on firm size, no direct firm-size effect can be detected in the context of product and process innovation output. The results further show that firms in ex ante higher con-

Table 4.6: Estimation Results: Product and Process Innovation Output

	Product Innovation Output		Process Innovation Output	
	PD_OUT_{02}		PC_OUT_{02}	
	coeff. (s.e.)	marg. eff. (s.e.)	coeff. (s.e.)	marg. eff. (s.e.)
const	-0.774 (1.080)	—	-3.476 ** (1.713)	—
$INPUT_{01}$	0.573 *** (0.188)	0.570 *** (0.187)	0.299 (0.284)	0.277 (0.263)
$SIZE_{01}$	0.052 (0.052)	0.052 (0.052)	0.076 (0.067)	0.070 (0.062)
$HERFIN_{01}$	-0.016 *** (0.006)	-0.016 *** (0.010)	—	—
$PD/PC\_INHOUSE_{00-02}$	0.321 ** (0.152)	0.319 ** (0.151)	0.068 (0.184)	0.063 (0.170)
$COOP_{00-02}$	-0.005 (0.139)	-0.005 (0.138)	-0.067 (0.174)	-0.062 (0.160)
PD/PC_CUST_{00-02}	0.251 (0.204)	0.250 (0.202)	0.247 (0.297)	0.232 (0.284)
PD/PC_SUPP_{00-02}	-0.094 (0.188)	-0.090 (0.187)	0.277 (0.407)	0.260 (0.388)
PD/PC_COMP_{00-02}	-0.213 (0.191)	-0.211 (0.190)	1.076 *** (0.391)	1.044 *** (0.385)
PD/PC_SCIEN_{00-02}	-0.240 (0.246)	-0.238 (0.243)	-0.072 (0.774)	-0.067 (0.652)
PD/PC_REG_{00-02}	-0.019 (0.171)	-0.019 (0.170)	-0.294 (0.608)	-0.264 (0.531)
$INSPILL_{00-02}$	0.388 *** (0.096)	0.386 *** (0.094)	—	—
$GROUP_{02}$	0.057 (0.149)	0.056 (0.148)	0.297 * (0.180)	0.273 * (0.163)
$EAST_{02}$	0.091 (0.142)	0.091 (0.141)	-0.445 ** (0.205)	-0.405 ** (0.184)
MILLS	0.068 (0.292)	0.067 (0.290)	0.076 (0.456)	0.070 (0.394)
IND	yes	yes	yes	yes

To be continued on next page.

Table 4.6 – *continued from previous page*

	Product Innovation Output	Process Innovation Output
	PD_OUT$_{02}$	PC_OUT$_{02}$
σ	0.969	0.879
	(0.050)	(0.065)
W_{IND} (p-value)	0.022	0.560
W_{α}	5.05	1.23
(df)	(1)	(1)
p-value	0.025	0.268
W_{all}	173.0	65.1
(df)	(25)	(23)
p-value	0.000	0.000
ln L	-1356.1	-1060.0
Total obs	522	522
Censored obs	159	362
Uncensored obs	363	160

Notes: ∗ ∗ ∗, ∗∗, and ∗ indicate significance on a 1%, 5%, and 10% level, respectively. Bootstrapped standard errors are in parentheses (50 replications are used on the whole estimation procedure). Marginal effects (at the sample means) for the expected value of the dependent variable conditional on being uncensored are reported. PD/PC_CUST means that the variable PD_CUST was included in the product innovation output equation, and PC_CUST was included in case of process innovation output. Analogous applies for the other variables. W_{IND} tests for the null hypothesis that the industry dummies are jointly equal to zero. W_{α} is a Wald test of the exogeneity of INPUT and has a $\chi^2(1)$ distribution. W_{all} is a Wald test of the overall significance of the explanatory variables and follows a $\chi^2(m)$ distribution, where m is number of explanatory variables.

centrated markets achieve significantly lower sales with new products. One explanation might be that firms in less competitive markets are less aware of consumer preferences which leads to a lower acceptance rate of the new product and, hence, to a lower innovation success.

Another substantial finding concerns internal and external knowledge. In this area, very different factors seem to be crucial for the success of product and process innovations. While product innovators that develop their new products mainly in-house enjoy significantly higher innovative sales compared to other firms, a similar regularity is not present for process innovation outcomes.[111] This may be explained by the fact that process innovations are often

---

[111] The coefficient of PC_INHOUSE is significant in the usual Tobit regression but the effect vanishes when endogoneity of the innovation input is taken into account.

Table 4.7: Sensitivity Analysis: Tobit vs IV-Tobit Estimation

Assumption	Without Endogeneity:		With Endogeneity:	
Method	Tobit		IV-Tobit	
	coeff. (s.e.)	marg. eff. (s.e.)	coeff. (s.e.)	marg. eff. (s.e.)
Product innovation output:				
INPUT$_{01}$	0.244 *** (0.086)	0.186 *** (0.065)	0.573 ** (0.188)	0.570 *** (0.187)
Process innovation output:				
INPUT$_{01}$	0.168 * (0.104)	0.044 * (0.027)	0.299 (0.284)	0.277 (0.262)

Notes: $***$, $**$, and $*$ indicate significance on a 1%, 5%, and 10% level, respectively. Bootstrapped standard errors are in parentheses (50 replications are used on the whole estimation procedure). Marginal effects (at the sample means) for the expected value of the dependent variable conditional on being uncensored are reported.

realised through buying machines that are completely developed outside the firm. Additionally, the results show that process innovations which heavily rely on knowledge from competitors are more successful. It seems likely that this knowledge sourcing implies picking and imitating more efficient technologies from the rivals. Hence, this seems to be a promising strategy in case of process innovations. A positive impact can also be found for process innovations which are mainly based on knowledge from suppliers although the effect is not significant. In the case of product innovations, the dummy variables for whether a firm has used a specific innovation source are not significant. However, it turns out that the importance of incoming knowledge spill-overs generated by market sources (measured relative to the industry average) significantly affects innovation success.[112]

Table 4.8 displays the results relating to the impact of innovation output on the level of labour productivity. Table 4.12 in Appendix C also reports results for labour productivity growth. Regression (1) of Table 4.8 assumes that both types of knowledge capital are exogenous. Regressions (2) and (3) allow innovation output to be endogenous using the predicted values of stage 2 as

---

[112] Since the spill-over variable is based on the importance of knowledge sources in terms of sales, this variable might be endogenous. However, the results in the productivity equation are quite robust to the inclusion or exclusion of this variable in the product output equation.

instruments. Another source of bias might be the fact that profit-maximising firms simultaneously determine factor inputs and output. Firms will presumably react to productivity shocks at a point in time early enough so as to adjust input decisions (Arnold, 2005). This implies that the input factors are correlated with the error term of the productivity equation. One remedy might be the IV or GMM method. Therefore, regressions (4) and (5) additionally instrument MATERIAL and CAPITAL using corresponding lagged values.[113]

In line with several other empirical studies, the results confirm significant labour productivity effects of product innovations in German manufacturing firms. Even after controlling for differences in material and physical capital and industry assignment, the variable which measures the output of product innovation activities significantly enters in the level and growth rate equation. It turns out that instrumenting the innovation output variable more than doubles its effect.[114] One potential explanation for this result is that the OLS estimates are downward biased due to measurement error or a negative correlation between the innovation variable and the error term. Augmenting the specification and taking potential endogeneity of the input variables into consideration leaves the results nearly unaltered.

Unfortunately, the results for process innovations are not as clear and stable as for product innovations. Without instrumenting, there is no effect of process innovations on labour productivity. Instrumenting once again leads to an increase in the coefficient which is now significant at the 10% level.[115] As one might expect, the labour productivity effect seems to be larger for process innovation than for product innovation although an F-test indicates that this difference does not reach significance at the 5% level. However, the productivity-enhancing effect vanishes if I further control for export intensity, human capital, and the group variable.

The econometric analysis further demonstrates that productivity is still – even more than 10 years after reunification – significantly lower in East German firms. As expected, firm-level productivity increases with export intensity and human capital endowment. Being in a group is also positively correlated with the productivity level.[116] As mentioned above, the coefficient of $SIZE_{02}$

---

[113] Lagged values are valid instruments as long as the error terms are not correlated over time. Blundell and Bond (2000) used a system GMM estimator. Recently, Olley and Pakes (1996) and Levinsohn and Petrin (2003) have suggested non-parametric estimation methods to control for endogeneity in total factor productivity (TFP) regressions.

[114] The predicted value for PD_OUT_{02} is highly significant in the equation for PD_OUT_{02} in the first stage (coefficient: 2.80, t-statistic: 8.69). Partial R^2 is 0.22.

[115] The predicted value for PC_OUT_{02} is highly significant in the in the equation for PC_OUT_{02} in the first stage (coefficient: 0.56, t-statistic: 2.60) but with a partial R^2 of only 0.03.

[116] I do not claim a direction of causality. Firms being part of group may be forced or may be enabled to be more efficient by their parent companies. On the other

Table 4.8: Estimation Results: Labour Productivity

Assumption	Exogeneity	Endogeneity of PD_OUT, PC_OUT		Endogeneity of PD_OUT, PC_OUT, MATERIAL, CAPITAL	
		Labour Productivity $PROD_{02}$			
Regression	(1)	(2)	(3)	(4)	(5)
const	-0.304*	0.693	-0.015	0.682	0.003
	(0.157)	(0.501)	(0.362)	(0.496)	(0.359)
$SIZE_{02}$	-0.024	-0.033	-0.028	-0.041	-0.039
	(0.022)	(0.023)	(0.021)	(0.026)	(0.026)
$MATERIAL_{02}$	0.456***	0.427***	0.427***	0.442***	0.437***
	(0.030)	(0.032)	(0.030)	(0.035)	(0.033)
$CAPITAL_{02}$	0.053***	0.036*	0.040**	0.043	0.052**
	(0.018)	(0.021)	(0.018)	(0.027)	(0.025)
PD_OUT_{02}	0.018**	0.041**	0.043***	0.040**	0.041***
	(0.007)	(0.017)	(0.014)	(0.017)	(0.014)
PC_OUT_{02}	-0.013	0.135*	0.048	0.126	0.043
	(0.013)	(0.079)	(0.056)	(0.079)	(0.056)
$EAST_{02}$	-0.231***	-0.203***	-0.212***	-0.204***	-0.213***
	(0.036)	(0.043)	(0.036)	(0.042)	(0.036)
$GROUP_{02}$	—	—	0.075**	—	0.069**
			(0.034)		(0.034)
$EXPORT_{01}$	—	—	0.204**	—	0.195**
			(0.086)		(0.086)
$HIGH_{01}$	—	—	0.248*	—	0.248*
			(0.151)		(0.148)
MILLS	0.040	0.119	0.197***	0.120	0.195***
	(0.065)	(0.079)	(0.076)	(0.078)	(0.075)
IND	yes	yes	yes	yes	yes
W_{IND}	0.003	0.002	0.0025	0.004	0.004
F_{all}	0.000	0.000	0.000	0.000	0.000
R^2_{adj}	0.694	0.597	0.674	0.607	0.677
Root MSE	0.331	0.373	0.335	0.368	0.333
Obs	522	522	522	522	522

Notes: ***, **, and * indicate significance on a 1%, 5%, and 10% level, respectively. Bootstrapped standard errors are in parentheses (50 replications are used on the whole estimation procedure). In regressions (2) and (3) the fitted values of PD_OUT and PC_OUT are used as instruments. In (4) and (5) $MATERIAL_{01}$ and $CAPITAL_{01}$ are used as additional instruments.

allows to test for the hypothesis of constant returns to scale. In all equations, this hypothesis cannot be rejected at a significance level of 5%.

4.8 Conclusion

Using the approach proposed by Crépon et al. (1998), I have analysed the relationship among innovation input, innovation output, and productivity for the period 2000-2003. The model and the information provided by the data allow a look into the "black box" of the innovation process at the firm level, not only analysing the relationship between innovation input and productivity but also shedding some light on the process in between. In comparison to previous research, I have extended the model by introducing a second knowledge production function for the outcome of process innovations (cost savings due to rationalisation innovations). This might alleviate the problem that previous studies have encountered in using an equation for product innovations as the sole output of innovation activities while the input measure (R&D or innovation expenditure) is related to both product and process innovations. Still, the best solution would involve separating product and process innovation expenditures. Furthermore, I specify a more sensible time structure of the model.

The econometric analysis indicates that selectivity and endogeneity biases seem to be important and have to be taken into account for model specification and estimation. The results have shown that firms with higher innovation efforts are able to achieve higher sales with new products. However, there is only a weak positive impact of innovation input on process innovation output. A similar result was found by Parisi et al. (2006) using a process innovation dummy variable. The econometric analysis, furthermore, highlights that, with respect to internal and external knowledge, different factors seem to be crucial for success with new products and new processes. That is, it has been shown that firms with considerable in-house capabilities for developing new products are more successful. In contrast, firms which have mainly developed their own new production technologies do not demonstrate a higher innovation success compared to firms which have developed new processes together with other firms or which have simply bought their process innovations developed by other firms. Furthermore, picking and imitating more efficient technologies from rivals seems to be a promising strategy in the case of process innovations.

In line with several other studies the results confirm that product innovations have a positive impact on labour productivity and labour productivity growth. The estimated output elasticity of knowledge capital, approximated by product innovation outcome, of about 0.04 is slightly lower than the tradi-

---

hand, if one assumes that productivity is quite persistent over time then firms might be annexed to a group because they show high productivity levels.

tional output elasticity estimated on the basis of an R&D capital stock.[117] But as has been mentioned before, these estimates were usually based on a sample of R&D-performing firms and did not correct for selectivity and endogeneity problems. However, the estimate is similar to that reported, for instance, by Crépon et al. (1998), at 0.065.

With respect to process innovations, the analysis is less clear-cut. There is weak evidence that the effect is positive and higher than that of product innovations. But admittedly, there are only few specifications in which the productivity stimulating effect of process innovations turns out to be significant.

Klette and Griliches (1996) emphasised that one problem in identifying labour productivity effects of process innovations is that one usually observes prices only at the aggregate level and not at the firm level. But, depending on competition and market power, firms pass on cost reductions to output prices, which results in a higher product output and, ceteris paribus, in higher employment. If this is the case, one may consider the estimates as a lower bound of the true effect of process innovation (Parisi et al., 2006). Nonetheless, incorporating demand side effects seems to be necessary for future research. The lack of appropriate data bar me from doing this in the present study.

Another potential drawback of the study is the assumption of a Cobb-Douglas production function. This technology assumption is widely used, in particular in the literature on productivity effects of R&D or of ICT. By definition the Cobb-Douglas specification implies a unit elasticity of substitution between the input factors and does not take the possibility into account that innovation might change the elasticity of substitution between input factors, for example, between labour and material. One point for future research is to use alternative production functions to check for the robustness of results. An alternative specification is the Translog production function which allows for more flexibility in terms of elasticities of substitution.

---

[117] Estimated output elasticity of R&D knowledge capital of about 0.06-0.2, see section 4.2.3.

Appendix C

Table 4.9: Sample by Industry

Industry	Nace	Sample					
		Total		Non-Innovative		Innovative	
		No.	%	No.	%	No.	%
Food	15-16	69	7.8	36	10.1	33	6.3
Textile	17-19	58	6.6	30	8.4	28	5.4
Wood/paper/printing	20-22	75	8.5	40	11.2	35	6.7
Chemicals	23-24	54	6.1	14	3.9	40	7.7
Plastic/rubber	25	77	8.8	33	9.2	44	8.4
Glass/ceramics	26	53	6.0	23	6.4	30	5.7
Metals	27-28	155	17.6	87	24.4	68	13.0
Machinery	29	118	13.4	33	9.2	85	16.3
Electrical engineering	30-32	65	7.4	14	3.9	51	9.8
MPO instruments[a]	33	70	8.0	19	5.3	51	9.8
Vehicles	34-35	32	3.6	6	1.7	26	5.0
Furniture/recycling	36-37	53	6.0	22	6.2	31	5.9
Obs		879	100.0	357	100.0	522	100.0

Note: [a] Medical, precision, and optical instruments.

Table 4.10: Sample by Size Class

Size Class	Sample					
	Total		Non-Innovative		Innovative	
	No.	%	No.	%	No.	%
5-9	54	6.1	33	9.2	21	4.0
10-19	121	13.8	66	18.5	55	10.5
20-49	178	20.3	96	26.9	82	15.7
50-99	129	14.7	50	14.0	79	15.1
100-199	116	13.2	43	12.0	73	14.0
200-499	153	17.4	47	13.2	106	20.3
500-999	69	7.9	14	3.9	55	10.5
1000+	59	6.7	8	2.2	51	9.8
Obs	879	100.0	357	100.0	522	100.0

Table 4.11: Definition of Variables

Variable	Type[a)]	Definition
Endogenous Variables		
$INNOSEL_{01}$	0/1	1 if the firm has positive innovation expenditure in 2001.
$INPUT_{01}$	c	Innovation input defined as innovation expenditure per employee in 2001, in logarithm.
PD_OUT_{02}	c	Product innovation output defined as sales from new products per employee in 2002, in logarithm.
PC_OUT_{02}	c	Process innovation output defined as cost reduction due to process innovations per employee in 2002, in logarithm.
$PROD_{02}$	c	Labour productivity defined as sales per employee in 2002, in logarithm.
$\Delta PROD_{03}$	c	Growth rate of labour productivity between 2002 and 2003.
Firm-Specific Exogenous Variables		
$SIZE_t$	c	Number of employees in year t with $t = 2000, 2001, 2002$, in logarithm.
$CAPITAL_{02}$	c	Physical capital defined as tangible assets in book value per employee in 2002, in logarithm.
$MATERIAL_{02}$	c	Material input defined as material costs per employee in 2002, in logarithm.
$RATING_{00}$	c	Credit rating index in 2000, originally ranging between 100 (highest creditworthiness) and 600 (worst creditworthiness), divided by 100.
AGE_{01}	c	Firm age (in years) at the beginning of the year 2001, in logarithm.
$TRAIN_{00}$	c	Training expenditure per employee in 2000, in logarithm.
$HIGH_t$	c	Human capital defined as share of employees with a university or college degree in year t with $t = 2000, 2001$, divided by 100.
$EXPORT_t$	c	Export intensity defined as exports/sales in year t with $t = 2000, 2001$.

To be continued on next page.

Table 4.11 – *continued from previous page*

Variable	Type[a)]	Definition
$EAST_t$	0/1	1 if the firm is located in East Germany in year t with $t = 2001, 2002$.
$GROUP_t$	0/1	1 if the firm belongs to a group in year t with $t = 2001, 2002$.
$FOREIGN_{01}$	0/1	1 if the firm is a subsidiary of a foreign company in 2001.
PLC_{01}	0/1	1 if the firm is a public limited company (*Aktiengesellschaft*) in 2001.
LTD_{01}	0/1	1 if the firm is a private limited liability company (*GmbH, GmbH & Co. KG*) in 2001.
$PRIVPART_{01}$	0/1	1 if the firm is a private partnership (*Einzelunternehmen, BGB-Gesellschaft, OHG, KG*) in 2001.
$PUBLIC_{98-00}$	0/1	1 if the firm received public funding for innovation projects during 1998-2000.
$PD\_INHOUSE_{00-02}$	0/1	1 if product innovations are mainly developed within the firm between 2000-2002.
$PC\_INHOUSE_{00-02}$	0/1	1 if process innovations are mainly developed within the firm between 2000-2002.
$COOP_{00-02}$	0/1	1 if the firm has innovation cooperations between 2000-2002.
PD_CUST_{00-02}	0/1	1 if the firm uses customers as source of product innovations during 2000-2002. Note that the question is on innovation sources, not only on information sources as it is usually the case in CIS. That is, customers must have triggered the product innovation.
PD_SUPP_{00-02}	0/1	Analogous definition for suppliers.
PD_COMP_{00-02}	0/1	Analogous definition for competitors.
PD_SCIEN_{00-02}	0/1	Analogous definition for sciences.
PD_REG_{00-02}	0/1	Analogous definition for regulations.
PC_CUST_{00-02}	0/1	1 if the firm uses customers as source of process innovations during 2000-2002.
PC_SUPP_{00-02}	0/1	Analogous definition for suppliers.
PC_COMP_{00-02}	0/1	Analogous definition for competitors.
PC_SCIEN_{00-02}	0/1	Analogous definition for sciences.

To be continued on next page.

Table 4.11 – *continued from previous page*

Variable	Type[a)]	Definition
PC_REG$_{00\text{-}02}$	0/1	Analogous definition for regulations.
INSPILL$_{00\text{-}02}$	c	Importance of customers, suppliers, and competitors for the success of new products during 2000-2002 relative to the industry average. The importance is measured by the sales generated through new products enabled by these sources.
IND	0/1	System of 12 industry dummies grouping manufacturing, see Table 2.1.

Exogenous Variables at Industry Level (3-digit NACE level)

HERFIN$_t$	c	Herfindahl-Hirschman Index in year t with $t = 2000, 2001$, divided by 100 to get appropriately scaled coefficients.

Exogenous Variables at Industry Level (2-digit NACE level)

LEGAL$_{98\text{-}00}$	c	Importance of the four strategic protection methods (patents, design pattern, trademarks, or copyrights) between 1998-2000. The scores for each firm ranging from 0 (not used at all) to 3 (highly important) for all three methods are summed up and divided by the maximum sum possible and averaged across each industry.
STRAT$_{98\text{-}00}$	c	Importance of the three strategic protection methods (complexity, secrecy, time-lead) between 1998-2000. Analogous construction as for LEGAL.
TECHOPP1$_{98\text{-}00}$	c	Importance of scientific information sources (universities, public or commercial research institutes) between 1998-2000. Analogous construction as for LEGAL.
TECHOPP2$_{98\text{-}00}$	c	Importance of private information sources (clients, competitors, suppliers) between 1998-2000. Analogous construction as for LEGAL.
SPILL$_{98\text{-}00}$	c	Importance of professional conferences, meetings and journals as well as exhibitions and fairs as information sources between 1998-2000. Analogous construction as for LEGAL.

Note: [a)] c denotes a continuous variable.

Table 4.12: Estimation Results: Labour Productivity Growth

Assumption	Exogeneity	Endogeneity of PD_OUT, PC_OUT	
		Labour Productivity Growth $\Delta PROD_{03}$	
Regression	(1)	(2)	(3)
const	0.032 (0.061)	0.037 (0.206)	0.111 (0.243)
$\Delta SIZE_{03}$	-0.243 ** (0.095)	-0.270 *** (0.099)	-0.272 *** (0.099)
$\Delta MATERIAL_{03}$	0.234 *** (0.061)	0.239 *** (0.060)	0.236 *** (0.060)
$\Delta CAPITAL_{03}$	-0.001 (0.012)	-0.001 (0.013)	-0.001 (0.013)
PD_OUT_{02}	0.002 (0.005)	0.035 *** (0.012)	0.033 *** (0.011)
PC_OUT_{02}	-0.013 (0.008)	-0.034 (0.040)	-0.022 (0.047)
OST_{02}	-0.013 (0.024)	-0.024 (0.030)	-0.016 (0.031)
$GROUP_{02}$	—	—	-0.005 (0.026)
$EXPORT_{01}$	—	—	-0.006 (0.062)
$HIGH_{01}$	—	—	-0.052 (0.129)
MILLS	0.061 (0.042)	0.004 (0.064)	0.001 (0.069)
IND	yes	yes	yes
W_{IND}	0.250	0.279	0.381
F_{all}	0.000	0.000	0.000
R^2_{adj}	0.256	0.143	0.149
Root MSE	0.204	0.211	0.211
Obs	375	375	375

Notes: ***, **, and * indicate significance on a 1%, 5%, and 10% level, respectively. In regressions (2) and (3) the fitted values of PD_OUT and PC_OUT are used as instruments. Bootstrapped standard errors are in parentheses (50 replications are used on the whole estimation procedure).

5

Persistence Effects of Innovation Activities[*]

5.1 Introduction

Recent empirical evidence indicates that firm performance in terms of productivity is highly skewed and that this heterogeneity is persistent over time (for an overview, see Dosi et al., 1995; Bottazzi et al., 2001; Bartelsman and Doms, 2000). Since innovation is seen as a major determinant of firm's growth, one hypothesis is that the permanent asymmetry in productivity is due to permanent differences in the innovation behaviour. However, little is known so far about the dynamics in firms' innovation behaviour, and the evidence is mostly based on patents (see Geroski et al., 1997; Malerba and Orsenigo, 1999; Cefis, 2003a).

Looking at innovation performance indicators at the aggregate or industry level, one can identify a high and quite stable share of innovators in the manufacturing as well as in the service sector in Germany over the last 10 years (see Fig. 2.1). One interesting question, however, cannot be answered by such macroeconomic numbers: Is it the same group of firms that always set themselves at the cutting edge by introducing new products and processes, or is there a steady entry into and exit from innovation activities at the firm level, with the aggregate level remaining more or less stable over time?

This chapter analyses the dynamics in firms' innovation behaviour. In particular, it focusses upon the following two research questions: First of all, is innovation persistent at the firm level? Persistence occurs when a firm which has innovated in one period innovates once again in the subsequent period. And secondly, if persistence is prevalent, what drives this phenomenon?

In principle, there are various potential sources for persistent behaviour (see Heckman, 1981a; 1981b): Firstly, it might be caused by true state dependence. This means that a causal behavioural effect exists in the sense that the decision to innovate in one period in itself enhances the probability of innovating in the subsequent period. The theoretical literature delivers several

---

[*] This chapter largely draws on Peters (2005a).

potential explanations for state-dependent behaviour. The most prominent ones relate to (i) the hypothesis of success breeds success (Mansfield, 1968), (ii) the hypothesis that innovations involve dynamic increasing returns (see, e.g., Nelson and Winter, 1982; Malerba and Orsenigo, 1993), and (iii) sunk costs in R&D investments (Sutton, 1991). Secondly, firms may possess certain characteristics which make them particularly "innovation-prone", i.e. more likely to innovate. To the extent that these characteristics themselves show persistence over time, they will induce persistence in innovation behaviour. Such firm-specific attributes can be classified into observable characteristics, such as firm size, competitive environment, or financial resources, and unobservable ones.[118] For instance, technological opportunities, managerial abilities, or risk attitudes are important for the firms' decision to innovate but are typically not observed. If these unobserved determinants are correlated over time but are not appropriately controlled for in estimation, past innovation may appear to affect future innovation merely because it picks up the effect of the persistent unobservable characteristics. In contrast to true state dependence, this phenomenon is, therefore, called spurious state dependence. And thirdly, serial correlation in exogenous shocks to the innovation decision can cause permanent behaviour over time.

The answers to both research questions are important for several reasons. First of all, they are interesting from a theoretical point of view. Endogenous growth models differ in their underlying assumptions about the innovation frequency of firms. While Romer (1990) assumes that innovation behaviour is persistent at the firm level to a very large extent, the process of creative destruction leads to a perpetual renewal of innovators in the model of Aghion and Howitt (1992). Thus, empirical knowledge about the dynamics in firms' innovation behaviour is a tool to assess different endogenous growth models (Cefis, 2003a). Furthermore, it might help to improve current theories of industrial dynamics, where some forms of dynamic increasing returns play a major role in determining degrees of concentration, the evolution of market shares, and their stability over time (Geroski, 1995). Secondly, from a managerial point of view, permanent innovation activities are seen as a crucial factor for strengthening competitiveness. And last but not least, the distinction between permanent innovation activities due to firm-inherent factors as opposed to true state dependence has important implications for technology and innovation policy. If innovation performance shows true state dependence, innovation-stimulating policy measures such as government support programmes are supposed to have a more profound effect because they do not only affect current innovation activities but are likely to induce a permanent change in favour of innovation. If, on the contrary, individual heterogeneity induces persistent behaviour, support programmes are unlikely to have long-lasting effects, and economic policy should concentrate more on measures

---

[118] Observable characteristics means known to the econometrician.

which have the potential to improve innovation-relevant firm-specific factors and circumstances.

To answer the first question, this chapter presents some stylised facts of how permanently German manufacturing and service firms innovated in the period 1994-2002. While in most of the other European countries innovation surveys take place every 4 years, the German innovation survey is annually conducted. This provides me with rather long panel data which are appropriate to study whether the innovation behaviour is persistent at the firm level. In a broader sense, this part ties in with the literature about the existence of innovation persistence effects using patents (see Geroski et al., 1997; Malerba and Orsenigo, 1999; Cefis, 2003a) and R&D indicators (Manez Castillejo, Rochina Barrachina, Sanchis Llopis, and Sanchis Llopis, 2004).

In a second step, the sources for persistent behaviour are analysed and identified by means of a dynamic random effects binary choice model. This panel data approach allows me to control for individual heterogeneity, a potential source of bias which was not taken into account in most of the previous empirical studies due to data restrictions.

This analysis contributes to the existing literature in that it is one of the first which investigates firm-level persistence using innovation data (see section 5.3) and that it is able to exploit data from a unique long panel, which are, nonetheless, internationally comparable. Furthermore, a new estimation method recently proposed by Wooldridge (2005) is applied, and the study is the first to provide empirical evidence on innovation persistence in service firms. Investigating the dynamics in the innovation behaviour of service firms is interesting not only because the service sector has experienced a rapid development over the last two decades but also from a theoretical point of view. Looking at the potential theoretical explanations for true state dependence listed above, the sunk cost hypothesis is particularly strongly related to R&D, which is less important and less common in the service sector. Thus, one hypothesis that will be investigated is that innovation activities are less permanent in this sector compared to manufacturing.

The outline of this chapter is as follows. Section 5.2 sketches some theoretical arguments in favour of and against state dependence in innovation behaviour at the firm level. Section 5.3 summarises the main empirical firm-level results so far. The panel data set underlying this study is explored in section 5.4, and section 5.5 briefly comments on some measurement issues. The following section 5.6 depicts some stylised facts about the entry into and exit from innovation activities at the firm level during the period 1994-2002. Section 5.7 presents the econometric model and its empirical implementation. It further explores the estimation methods used and sets forth the econometric results. Section 5.8 draws some conclusions on the persistence of firm-level innovation activities and discusses the main findings.

5.2 Theoretical Explanations

Economic theory provides at least three potential explanations of why innovation behaviour might demonstrate state dependence over time. The first one is the well-known hypothesis of "success breeds success". However, this view is based on different arguments in the literature. Phillips (1971), for instance, argued that successful innovations positively affect the conditions for subsequent innovations via an increasing permanent market power of prosperous innovators.[119] Mansfield (1968) and Stoneman (1983), however, emphasised that a firm's innovation success broadens its technological opportunities which make subsequent innovation success more likely. Based on this idea of dynamic intra-firm spill-overs, Flaig and Stadler (1994) developed a stochastic optimisation model in which firms maximise their expected present value of profits over an infinite time horizon by simultaneously choosing optimal sequences of both product and process innovations. Both were shown to be dynamically interrelated in this model. Another line of reasoning is the existence of financial constraints. Usually, information asymmetries about the risk and the failure probability of an innovation project exist between the innovator and external financial investors. This leads to adverse selection and moral hazard problems which usually force firms to finance innovation projects by means of internal funds (Stiglitz and Weiss, 1981). Successful innovations provide firms with increased internal funding and, hence, can be used to finance further innovations (Nelson and Winter, 1982). Common to all these various "success breeds success" theories is the notion that a firm can gain some kind of locked-in advantage over other firms due to successful innovations (Simons, 1995).

The second hypothesis is based on the idea that knowledge accumulates over time as represented by the changes in an organisation's repertories of operating and dynamic routines (Nelson and Winter, 1982). Evolutionary theory states that technological capabilities are a decisive factor in explaining innovation. Firms' innovative capabilities, in turn, are primarily determined by human capital, i.e., by the knowledge, skills, and creativity of their employees. Experience in innovation is associated with dynamic increasing returns in the form of learning-by-doing and learning-to-learn effects which enhance knowledge stocks and, therefore, the probability of future innovations. Since a firm's absorptive capacity – i.e. its ability to recognise the value of new external information as well as to assimilate and apply it to commercial ends – is likewise a function of the level of knowledge, learning in one period will, furthermore, permit a more efficient accumulation of external knowledge in subsequent periods (Cohen and Levinthal, 1990). The cumulative nature of

---

[119] In contrast to Schumpeter, who assumed that the increasing market power is a temporary phenomenon and is eroded by the entry of imitators or innovators, Phillips argued that success favours growing barriers to entry that eventually allow a few increasingly successful firms to permanently dominate an industry.

knowledge should, therefore, induce state dependence in innovation behaviour (see Nelson and Winter, 1982; Malerba and Orsenigo, 1993).[120]

The hypothesis of sunk costs in R&D investments is a third argument in favour of state dependence (see, e.g., Sutton, 1991; Manez Castillejo et al., 2004). It is stressed that R&D decisions are subject to a long time horizon, and if a firm decides to take up R&D activities, it has to incur start-up costs in building up an R&D department or hiring and training R&D staff. These fixed outlays, once made, are usually not recoverable and can, therefore, be considered as sunk costs.[121] With respect to persistence, sunk costs represent a barrier to both entry into and exit from R&D activities. Sunk costs may prevent non-R&D performers from taking up such activities because, unlike established R&D performers, potential entrants have to take these costs into account in determining their prices. Conversely, sunk costs may represent a barrier to exit for established R&D performers because they are not recovered in the case that the firm stops R&D and the firm has to incur them again if it decides to re-enter in future periods.

However, even if firms experience sunk costs or knowledge accumulation due to innovations, there are several theoretical explanations of why they may exit from innovation activities in future periods with the consequence that persistence does not emerge. The first two arguments are related to the demand-pull theory which emphasises that innovations are stimulated by demand (Schmookler, 1966). If there is, at least in the firm's perception of consumer demand, no need for further innovations due to its own previous introduction of new products or processes, the firm will at least temporarily cease to innovate. This is particularly true if a firm only offers one or a few products, and typical product life cycles are several years. Closely related is the second argument that states that unfavourable market conditions in general (i.e. expected decrease in demand) might prevent firms from carrying on with innovations, especially with respect to the timing of the market introduction of new products. This is one argument in the literature on innovation and business cycles and will be explored in more detail in section 5.6. Finally, an incumbent innovator might fear that the introduction of further new products or processes will cannibalise his rents from previous innovations and, thus, stop innovating (Schumpeter, 1942). Patent race models, for instance, predict that an incumbent invests less in R&D than challengers because it would erode current monopoly and profits (Reinganum, 1983).

---

[120] Theories which focus on how firms accumulate technological capabilities may also be considered as "success breeds success" theories since technological capabilities might substantiate sustained competitive advantages (Teece and Pisano, 1994). However, learning can also occur as a result of unsuccessful innovations.

[121] In contrast to most other kinds of sunk costs, firms can strategically decide upon the amount of R&D expenditure. Costs incurred in this manner are, therefore, referred to as endogenous sunk costs (Sutton, 1991).

5.3 What Do We Know So Far? Previous Empirical Findings

Though economic theory emphasises that innovation is an inherently dynamic process between heterogenous firms (see, e.g., Blundell et al., 1995), firm-level empirical evidence on persistence in innovation activities is scarce. The existing literature can be broadly classified into three categories according to how the authors measure innovation: patent-based, R&D-based, and innovation-based studies.

Patent-based studies have mainly focussed on the question whether innovation persistence exists, irrespective of its origin. Malerba and Orsenigo (1999) examined this question using data of manufacturing firms from six countries (France, Germany, Italy, Japan, USA, and the UK) which had requested at least one patent at the European Patent Office (EPO) between 1978 and 1991. Their results corroborated substantial entry into and exit from patent activities implying that the population of innovators changed remarkably over time. In terms of employment, entrants and exiters showed nearly the same size as incumbent innovators but, in terms of the number of patents, both were much smaller. The high entry and exit rates were associated with a large proportion of enterprises that innovated only once and than ceased to innovate further. Only a small fraction of entrants were able to persist in patent activities as time went on. However, these firms became rather large innovators (in terms of patents) over time, resulting in the fact that persistent innovators, although small in absolute numbers, accounted for an important part of all patents. The same result, that patent activities among patenting firms exhibited only a little degree of persistence, was confirmed by Geroski et al. (1997), who concentrated on patents as well but used data of UK manufacturing firms which had at least one patent granted in the US between 1969 and 1988. The majority of firms (64%) patented only once in the period, and further 34% of the firms produced patents on a sporadic base. Only 2% of the firms were found to be heavy patentees, however, they accounted for nearly half of all patents.

Cefis (1999; 2003a) used a UK sub-sample of the data set of Malerba and Orsenigo (1999) and applied a non-parametric approach based on transition probabilities matrices. Cefis and Orsenigo (2001) extended this kind of analysis to a firm-level cross-country comparison over time for the original six countries. In their studies they distinguished four states in each year: occasional (zero patents)[122], small (one patent), medium (two to five patents) and great innovators (at least six patents). They corroborated previous evidence that in general only a low degree of persistence in patenting was prevalent in all countries which, furthermore, declined as time went by. Only occasional

---

[122] Firms with zero patents in a given period are, nevertheless, referred to as occasional innovators since they had at least one patent in the whole period under consideration.

and great innovators had a high probability of remaining in their state while persistence was much lower in the intermediate classes for which a strong tendency towards the non-innovator state was ascertained. Moreover, persistence was found to differ across industries but inter-sectoral differences were, by and large, consistent across countries suggesting that persistence is at least partly technology-specific. However, cross-country differences showed up in the relationship between persistence and firm size. While a strictly positive impact was found in Italy, France, USA, and the UK, this was not observed in Japan and Germany.

In contrast to other studies, Geroski et al. (1997) also examined potential sources of persistence. To test the hypothesis of dynamic economies of scale, they focussed on patent spells, which measured the number of successive years in which a firm produced a patent. In this setting, dynamic economies of scale would imply that the probability of the spell ending at any particular time $t + \Delta t$, given it has lasted until t, decreases with the initial level of patents and with the length of time a firm has already spent in that spell. While the first relationship was confirmed by their data, the second one was rejected. All in all, their results suggested that dynamic economies might have led to more persistent patent spells but only when the threshold of initial patent activities was high enough to overcome the reversed within-spell effects. Only a few firms ever reached this threshold.

One explanation of why patent-based studies revealed only a small degree of persistence might be the well-known fact that patents measure only some aspects of innovative activity (Griliches, 1990). However, in the context of persistence analysis, patents have an additional drawback because in this kind of winner-takes-all contest, to be classified as permanent innovators, firms have to win the patent race continuously (Kamien and Schwartz, 1975). This means that patent data measure the persistence of innovative leadership rather than the persistence of innovation, as was stressed by Duguet and Monjon (2004).

Instead of patents, another strand of literature uses R&D activities. Mairesse, Hall, and Mulkay (1999) and Mulkay, Hall, and Mairesse (2001) estimated dynamic equations for physical as well as R&D investment rates. Based on samples of large French and US manufacturing firms, they found evidence that R&D investment rates are highly correlated over time, even more than physical capital investments. This reflects the inter-temporal nature of R&D and the fact that about half of the R&D expenditure consists of labour costs for R&D staff. Using a sample of small and large Spanish manufacturing firms between 1990 and 2000 and a dynamic discrete choice model, Manez Castillejo et al. (2004) asserted that past R&D experience had significantly affected the current decision to engage in R&D and interpreted this as an indication for sunk costs in building up R&D. Their results further indicated a rapid depreciation of R&D experience in that there was no significant difference between the re-entry costs of a firm that last performed R&D activities 2 or 3 years ago and a firm that had never previously conducted R&D.

Though R&D is an important input to innovation, it does not capture all aspects pertinent to innovation. Innovation activities close to the market, for instance, are not captured by the concept of R&D. Such activities of small and medium-sized manufacturing as well as service sector firms are heavily underestimated by patents as well as R&D indicators.

Hence, another strand of literature uses the broader concept implied by innovation data. So far, only a few studies have attempted to estimate the dynamics in the innovation process at the firm level, and empirical results are inconclusive. König, Laisney, Lechner, and Pohlmeier (1994) as well as Flaig and Stadler (1994; 1998) were the first to examine dynamic effects using innovation data from a panel of manufacturing firms in West Germany in the 1980s. Applying a dynamic panel probit model, empirical evidence of state dependence in process innovation activities was supported by the first study. This result was corroborated for process as well as product innovations by the second authors. Duguet and Monjon (2004) for French firms and Rogers (2004) for Australian firms also reported persistence effects. However, due to data limitations, both studies did not carry out a dynamic panel data analysis and, thus, did not control for unobserved individual heterogeneity, which leads to biased estimates if heterogeneity is present.[123]

Conversely, Geroski et al. (1997) and Raymond, Mohnen, Palm, and Schim van der Loeff (2006) could not ascertain persistence effects in the occurrence of innovations for UK and Dutch manufacturing firms. But Raymond et al. pointed out that among continuous innovators the innovation success, measured in terms of sales due to new products, had a positive impact on future success.

Among the other things highlighted, this review makes clear that previous studies solely focussed on manufacturing. One aim is, therefore, to extend this kind of analysis to a comparison between the manufacturing and service sector.

5.4 Data Set

The following analysis is based on the Mannheim Innovation Panel (MIP), whose general characteristics were set forth in more detail in section 2.1. While in most other European countries innovation surveys take place every 4 years, they are conducted annually in Germany. In manufacturing, I refer in the analysis to the surveys from 1995 to 2003; in the service sector, the first usable wave was that of 1997.[124] Thus, 9 waves in manufacturing and

---

[123] Both studies applied a cross-sectional probit approach including a dummy variable for whether the firm was an innovator in the previous period as an explanatory variable.

[124] In manufacturing, the survey started in 1993. However, due to a major refreshment and enlargement of the initial sample in 1995 and the need to construct a

7 in services are available. The data of each survey refers to the previous year, hence, I focus on the period 1994-2002 in manufacturing and 1996-2002 in the service sector. This relatively long period ensures that I can observe firms' innovation behaviour over different phases of the business cycle, and the observation period is also longer than the average product life cycle in industry.

The gross samples are constructed as panels, and about 10,000 firms in manufacturing and 12,000 service firms are questioned each year. Since participation is voluntary, response rates vary between 20 to 25%, and although the survey is designed as a panel study, one has to detect that the main part of the firms participated only once or twice.[125] Furthermore, for analysing the dynamics in firms' innovation behaviour with econometric methods, only those firms which have consecutively responded can be taken into account. Therefore, in the following I distinguish two panel data sets: Panel U is an unbalanced panel comprising all firms for which at least 4 successive observations are available, and Panel B is the balanced sub-sample. The latter is needed for estimation purposes (see section 5.7.2).

Table 5.1: Characteristics of the Unbalanced and Balanced Panel

	Manufacturing	Services
Panel U: Unbalanced Panel		
No. of observations	13,558	7,901
No. of firms	2,256	1,528
Minimum No. of consecutive observations per firm	4	4
Average No. of consecutive observations per firm	6.0	5.2
Panel B: Balanced Panel		
No. of observations	3,933	1,974
No. of firms	437	282
No. of consecutive observations per firm	9	7
Time Period	1994-2002	1996-2002

Source: Mannheim Innovation Panel; own calculations.

---

balanced panel for estimation purposes, I decided to discard the first two waves. In the service sector, the first survey took place in 1995, with a break in 1996.

[125] Table 5.16 in Appendix D2 sheds some light on the individual participation behaviour of the sampled firms. But note that the number of utilisable observations is higher than the one which would arise from the participation pattern. This can be explained by the fact that since 1998 the survey is only sent to a sub-sample of firms in even years due to cost reasons. However, to maintain the panel structure with yearly waves, the most relevant variables are retrospectively asked for the preceding year in odd years.

Table 5.1 summarises the main characteristics of both samples. Given the interest in analysing the persistence of innovation behaviour and the need to estimate a dynamic specification with a lagged endogenous variable, I have chosen to maximise the time dimension of the panel. As a result, in manufacturing as well as in the service sector this choice leads to a marked reduction in the number of observations, and the resulting panel data sets might not be representative for the total sample. To check representativeness, Tables 5.17 and 5.18 in Appendix D2 compare the distribution of firms by industry, size class, region, and innovation status in the total sample of all observations, the unbalanced panel, and the balanced sub-sample. It turns out that in manufacturing large firms with 100 or more employees are slightly over-represented in the unbalanced and balanced panel compared to the total sample while the opposite applies to the service sector. Moreover, the share of East German firms is slightly higher in both panels in manufacturing as well as in the service sector. The tables further demonstrate that the share of innovators is lower in both panels used. But, while the difference between the balanced panel and the total sample is rather small in manufacturing, it amounts to 8.5 percentage points in the service sector. That is, the service firms in the sample are less likely to engage in innovation activities. Based on these comparisons, I argue that, by and large, the panels still reflect total-sample distributional characteristics quite well in manufacturing and do not give any obvious cause for selectivity concerns. Admittedly, in the service sector, selectivity might be a more severe problem in the resulting panels since innovators are less represented.

5.5 Measurement Issues

One problem in studying state dependence in innovation behaviour with CIS data is the fact that the indicator whether a firm has introduced an innovation is related to a 3-year reference period, that is, using this indicator for annual waves would induce an artificial high persistence due to overlapping time periods and double counting.[126] Both studies of Duguet and Monjon (2004) or Raymond et al. (2006) suffer from this problem of overlapping time periods in their dependent variable. However, information on innovation expenditure is available on a yearly basis. Innovation expenditure includes outlays for intramural and extramural R&D, acquisition of external knowledge, machines and equipment, training, market introduction, design, and other preparations for product and/or process innovation activities in a given year.[127] Therefore,

---

[126] As an example, in the 2001 survey a firm is defined as an innovator if it has introduced an innovation in the period 1998-2000; in the 2002 survey this indicator is related to 1999-2001.

[127] R&D expenditure accounted for 50-55% of innovation expenditure in the period under consideration; see Gottschalk, Janz, Peters, Rammer, and Schmidt (2002).

and in contrast to the previously mentioned studies, I define an innovator as a firm which exhibits positive innovation expenditure in a given year, i.e. which decides to engage in innovation activities. This implies that I analyse the persistence in innovation input rather than in innovation outcome behaviour.

From a theoretical point of view it is not unambiguous whether state dependence in innovation behaviour should be tested in terms of an input or an output measure. The literature on sunk costs usually models the decision to invest in R&D by a rational profit-maximising firm, so that an input measure seems advisable. In contrast, the "success breeds success" hypothesis is clearly outcome-oriented. By stressing the accumulative nature of innovation and the importance of learning effects in the innovation process, the evolutionary theory is likewise rather outcome-oriented since the process of learning involves successful implementation rather than just dedicating some resources to innovation projects, see Blundell et al. (1993). Econometric evidence shows that, on average, innovation output is significantly determined by innovation input (see Crépon et al., 1998; Lööf and Heshmati, 2002; Love and Roper, 2001; Janz, Lööf, and Peters, 2004), implying that input persistence should, to a certain degree, be converted into output persistence. However, it is possible that more than one period is needed to translate innovation effort into new products or processes; furthermore, firms can not necessarily control their innovation outcome because serendipity might play an important role in the innovation process, see Kamien and Schwartz (1982) or Flaig and Stadler (1998).[128]

5.6 Stylised Facts

In what follows I want to give an answer to the first research question of "How persistently do firms innovate?". To investigate this question, transition probabilities are an appropriate method. Tables 5.2 and 5.3 show corresponding figures for the whole period and differentiated by years. First of all, it turns out that there are hardly any differences between the much larger unbalanced panel and the smaller balanced panel which has to be used for estimation purposes. Table 5.2 clearly indicates that innovation behaviour is, to a very large extent, permanent at the firm level. In the period 1994-2002, nearly 89% of innovating firms in manufacturing in one period persisted in innovation activities in the subsequent period while 11% stopped their engagement. Similarly, about 84% of non-innovators maintained this status in the following period while 16% entered into innovation activities. That also means that the probability of being innovative in period $t+1$ was about 72 percentage points higher for innovators than for non-innovators in t which can be interpreted

---

[128] I checked the robustness of my results by applying the output-oriented 3-period innovation indicator and by taking only every third survey into account, see section 5.7.5.

Table 5.2: Transition Probabilities, Whole Period[a]

| | Innovation Status in $t+1$ | | | | | |
| | Unbalanced Panel | | | Balanced Panel | | |
Innovation Status in t[b]	Non-Inno	Inno	Total	Non-Inno	Inno	Total
Manufacturing						
Non-Inno	83.6	16.4	100.0	85.3	14.7	100.0
Inno	11.2	88.8	100.0	11.2	88.8	100.0
Total	41.9	58.1	100.0	44.5	55.5	100.0
Services						
Non-Inno	82.9	17.1	100.0	83.9	16.1	100.0
Inno	29.2	70.8	100.0	30.2	69.8	100.0
Total	62.6	37.4	100.0	64.0	36.0	100.0

Notes: [a] Manufacturing: 1994-2002, service sector: 1996-2002.
[b] "Inno" means innovator as defined in section 5.5; "Non-Inno" accordingly denotes non-innovators.

as a measure of state dependence. Against the background of the sunk costs hypothesis, it is interesting that using the narrower concept of R&D expenditure, Manez Castillejo et al. (2004) found slightly higher exit rates in Spanish manufacturing for the period 1990-2000 while, not surprisingly, the entry into R&D activities is much less frequent than for innovation activities.[129]

In services, persistence effects are also clearly observable though less prevalent than in manufacturing. Non-innovative service firms had pretty much the same propensity to enter into innovation activities as manufacturing firms. However, in any given year the probability of an innovative service firm remaining in innovation activities in the subsequent year was significantly lower (70%) than for a manufacturing firm. This implies that the state dependence effect in the service sector was clearly lower with approximately 54 percentage points. Several arguments could explain this finding, one being the fact the sunk cost hypothesis is strongly related to R&D investments. However, R&D is less important and less common in most of the service sectors compared to manufacturing. This result might also occur because, on average, the time needed to develop an innovation is shorter in services and, hence, covers two calendar years less often. Alternatively, individual or industry heterogeneity, for example in the technological opportunities or in the demand for new innovations, might explain this difference.

---

[129] Manez Castillejo et al. (2004) reported transition rates for only small and large firms. Using a weighted average, one would get an exit rate of about 17% and an entry probability of 8%.

Table 5.3: Transition Probabilities by Year

Innovation Status		Years							
Year t	Year $t+1$	94-95	95-96	96-97	97-98	98-99	99-00	00-01	01-02
Manufacturing									
Non-Inno	Non-Inno	86.2	76.4	78.3	91.9	81.3	86.4	82.2	87.2
	Inno	13.8	23.6	21.7	8.1	18.7	13.6	17.8	12.8
Inno	Non-Inno	13.4	6.9	12.3	9.5	9.1	15.2	12.1	11.5
	Inno	86.6	93.1	87.7	90.5	90.9	84.8	87.9	88.5
Services									
Non-Inno	Non-Inno	–	–	68.5	87.9	81.7	84.6	82.4	90.3
	Inno	–	–	31.5	12.1	18.3	15.4	17.6	9.7
Inno	Non-Inno	–	–	24.0	35.6	20.9	34.4	29.0	30.6
	Inno	–	–	76.0	64.4	79.1	65.6	71.0	69.7

Notes: Sample: Unbalanced Panel. See also the notes of Table 5.2.

There is a related strand of literature investigating the interrelationship between business cycles and innovation activity. According to the technology-push argument, science and technology are a major driver for innovation activities and, consequently, for the business cycle; see Schumpeter (1939) or Kleinknecht (1990) for an empirical assessment. In contrast, the demand-pull hypothesis states that innovation behaviour depends on demand conditions and, thus, on the level of economic activity (Schmookler, 1966). Within this body of literature, arguments for both pro- as well as counter-cyclical relationships can be found. Pro-cyclical effects are expected to occur because cash flow as an important source of finance innovations is positively correlated with economic activity (see Himmelberg and Petersen, 1994). Furthermore, Judd (1985) argued that markets have a limited capacity for absorbing new products, thus, firms are more likely to introduce new products in prosperous market conditions. Aghion and Saint-Paul (1998) showed that firms tend to invest more in productivity growth (i.e. process innovations) during recessions, since the opportunity costs in terms of forgone profits of investing capital in technological improvements are lower during recessions. During the period 1994-2002, the German economy underwent different business cycles. 1993 was characterised by a deep recession, followed by an upswing in 1994-1995 which came to a near halt in 1996. Since 1997, economic growth steadily increased again, reaching its peak in 2000. Since 2001, the German economy has again been fighting a significant cyclical slump. Table 5.3 shows that, despite different business cycles, both the propensity to remain innovative and correspondingly the exit rates were quite stable over time in manufacturing, with one remarkable exception in the peak period 2000, where the flow out of innovating sharply increased.[130] At the same time, the entry rate into innovation activities was more volatile across the periods in manufacturing. In the service sector, the propensity to remain innovative was not only lower but also exhibited a higher variance across time.[131] However, contrasting both exit and entry rates with the annual GDP growth rate, as in Fig. 5.1, no clear pro- or counter-cyclical link to the level of economic activity can be found. One explanation could be that it is not possible to distinguish between expenditure for product innovations and for process innovations.

Fig. 5.1: Innovation Entry and Exit Rates and Business Cycles

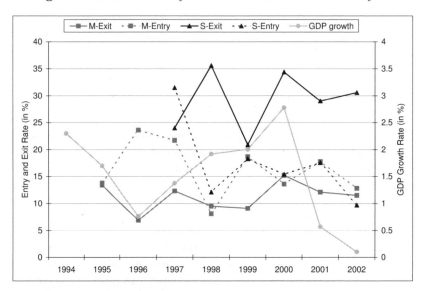

Notes: The innovation exit rate in any given year t is defined as the share of innovators in year $t - 1$ which flow out of innovation activities in year t. Similarly, the innovation entry rate in t is the share of non-innovators in year $t - 1$ which start innovation activities in year t. GDP growth denotes the annual percentage change of real GDP (in constant prices of 1995). M and S denote manufacturing and services, respectively. Sample: Unbalanced Panel.
Source: GDP growth rates: Sachverständigenrat (2004); own calculation.

---

[130] This result coincides with the decline in the share of innovators at the aggregate level, see Fig. 2.1. A main cause for this somewhat astonishing development was a severe shortage of high-qualified personnel in 2000, hampering a large number of small and medium-sized firms in their innovative efforts (see Janz, Ebling, Gottschalk, Peters, and Schmidt, 2002).

[131] The standard deviation of exit and entry rates is 2.6 and 5.1 in manufacturing and 5.8 and 7.6 in the service sector, respectively.

Table 5.4 and Fig. 5.2 provide some information on innovation persistence by size class and industry. As expected, innovation behaviour was more stable in larger firms though also relatively permanent in small firms. This result holds for manufacturing and, by and large, for service firms as well. In manufacturing 93% of the large innovative firms (with 500 and more employees) but also 67% of the small innovators (with less than 10 employees) stayed on the innovation path in the next year. The propensity to remain innovative steadily increased with firm size while, at the same time, the propensity for non-innovators to take up such activities steadily rose as well. Nevertheless, the (unconditional) state dependence effect measured as the difference between the probabilities of being innovative in period $t+1$ for innovators and for non-innovators in t was more pronounced in large manufacturing firms (approximately 72 percentage points for firms with more than 500 employees) than in small ones (59 percentage points for firms with less than 10 employees). The same qualitative picture emerges in services with a difference of 64 and 47 percentage points.

Table 5.4: Transition Probabilities by Size Class

Innovation Status		No. of Employees					
Year t	Year $t+1$	< 10	10-19	20-49	50-99	100-499	>=500
Manufacturing							
Non-Inno	Non-Inno	91.3	87.4	83.9	81.4	78.0	79.0
	Inno	8.7	12.6	16.2	18.6	22.0	21.0
Inno	Non-Inno	32.7	20.3	17.7	12.9	10.7	7.2
	Inno	67.3	79.7	82.4	87.1	89.3	92.8
Services							
Non-Inno	Non-Inno	87.1	84.6	85.3	79.6	76.0	77.1
	Inno	12.9	15.5	14.7	20.4	24.0	22.9
Inno	Non-Inno	40.5	40.4	30.7	21.4	28.8	12.8
	Inno	59.5	59.6	69.3	78.6	71.2	87.2

Notes: Sample: Unbalanced Panel. See also the notes of Table 5.2.

Fig. 5.2 further demonstrates that innovation activities at the firm level are found to be more persistent in high-technology industries though also quite permanent in some low-technology manufacturing and business-related service industries. Less surprising, the lowest exit rates from innovation activities and, hence, the most pronounced persistence can be found in R&D intensive industries, like electrical engineering (4.7%), medical instruments (5.2%), chemicals (5.6%), machinery (6.4%), or vehicles (8.2%). Exiting innovation activities is on the other hand much more likely in the wood/paper (24%), energy/water

(37.5%), or construction industry (32.8%) and in most service industries with the exception of telecommunication (13.9%) and technical services (19.2%).

Fig. 5.2: Entry into and Exit from Innovation Activities by Industry

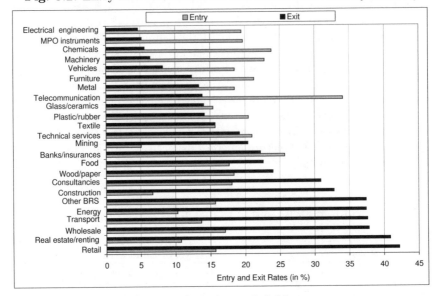

Notes: See Fig. 5.1. See Table 2.1 for industry definitions.

Finally, I shed light on the innovative history of firms. Fig. 5.3 depicts the survival rates of different innovator as well as non-innovator "cohorts"; Table 5.5 reports the number of (re-)entry into and (re-)exit from innovation. The survival rate, for instance, for the innovator cohort 1994 is the proportion of innovators in year $t = 1994$ that was still innovating in year $t + s$, for $s = 1, 2 . . . .$. In manufacturing, the 3-year survival rates were quite similar for different cohorts, amounting to 78% on average (based on the cohorts 1994 to 1999). After 5 years, on average 71% of the innovators were still innovating, and 66% of initially innovative firms (i.e. cohort 1994) were continuously engaged in innovation throughout the whole period. In services, on average only 51% of the innovators were still involved in innovation after 3 years, and the share of incessant innovators (40%) is much lower as well (even though the period for services is shorter). It turns out that, in general, the survival rates are smaller and exhibit higher variances in services.[132] Survival rates of

---

[132] For instance, the standard deviation of the 3-year survival rates of innovator cohorts amounts to 3.95 in manufacturing and 5.30 in services. Similarly, the 3-year survival rates of non-innovator cohorts are 3.65 in manufacturing and 5.6 in services.

Fig. 5.3: Survival Rates of Innovator and Non-Innovator Cohorts by Years (in %)

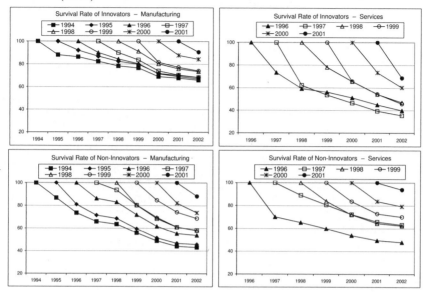

Note: Sample: Balanced Panel.

non-innovator cohorts in manufacturing turned out to be generally lower than for innovators with, for instance, 67% on average after 3 years. About 43% of the initial non-innovators kept out of innovation activities throughout the whole period. In the service sector, these last two figures were very similar with 67% and 48%.

Table 5.5 further indicates that, concerning those firms which experienced at least one change in their innovation behaviour (45% in manufacturing and 55% in services), I find a stronger tendency to return to the initial innovation status. For instance, in manufacturing 13.7% of the initial non-innovators started innovating in a later period and remained innovative while 24.2% took up such activities but then exited again. In the service sector, this tendency is even stronger with corresponding figures at 6.5% and 28.3%. Similarly, 8.9% of the initial innovators stopped their innovation engagement in a later period and remained non-innovators while 14.2% re-enter innovation activities. This implies that re-entry into innovation occurs to a non-negligible extent.

Table 5.5: Innovation History of Firms: Number of Entries into and Exits from Innovation Activities

Number of changes	Manufacturing			Services		
	Total	Non-Inno in $t = 0$	Inno in $t = 0$	Total	Non-Inno in $t = 0$	Inno in $t = 0$
0	54.9	43.1	65.9	45.0	47.8	39.8
1	11.2	13.7	8.9	13.1	6.5	25.5
2	19.0	24.2	14.2	22.7	28.3	12.2
3	8.5	10.4	6.6	10.3	7.6	15.3
4	4.8	6.6	3.1	6.4	8.2	3.1
5	1.1	1.4	0.9	1.8	0.5	4.1
6	0.5	0.5	0.5	0.7	1.1	0.0
Total	100.0	100.0	100.0	100.0	100.0	100.0

Notes: Figures are calculated as share of total firms, initial non-innovators (Non-Inno), and innovators (Inno), respectively. Sample: Balanced Panel.

5.7 Econometric Analysis

5.7.1 Econometric Model

Though interesting, transition rates only depict the degree of persistence but do not offer a clue to the causes of this phenomenon since they do not control for observed or unobserved individual characteristics. In the following I, therefore, investigate whether and to which extent the observed persistence is due to underlying differences in individual characteristics and/or due to a genuine causal effect of past on future innovations using a dynamic random effects probit model. The same model was applied for studying state dependence effects in poverty state (Biewen, 2004) or export behaviour (Kaiser and Kongsted, 2004). This panel data approach allows me to distinguish between the sources of the persistence over time observed in the data and to control for individual heterogeneity. If individual heterogeneity is present but not controlled for, the coefficients of the observed characteristics are likewise biased and inconsistent if both are correlated.

I start on the assumption that firm i will invest in innovation in period t if the expected present value of profits accruing to the innovation investment y_{it}^* is positive. The hypothesis of state dependence implies that y_{it}^* depends on the previous (realised) innovation experience $y_{i,t-1}$, i.e. $\gamma > 0$. Furthermore, it depends on some observable explanatory variables summarised in the k-dimensional row vector x_{it} and on unobservable firm-specific attributes which are assumed to be constant over time and captured by μ_i. The structural model is, thus, given by:

$$y_{it}^* = \gamma\, y_{i,t-1} + x_{it}\,\beta + \mu_i + \varepsilon_{it} \qquad i = 1,\dots,N, \qquad t = 1,\dots,T. \quad (5.1)$$

The effect of other time-varying unobservable determinants is summarised in the idiosyncratic error ε_{it}. It is assumed that $\varepsilon_{it}|y_{i0},\dots,y_{i,t-1},x_i,\mu_i$ is i.i.d. as $N(0,1)$ and that $\varepsilon_{it} \perp (y_{i0},x_i,\mu_i)$ where $x_i = (x_{i1},\dots,x_{iT})$. N is the number of firms, and the index t runs from 1 to 8 in manufacturing and 1 to 6 in services, respectively. If y_{it}^* is larger than a constant threshold (zero can be assumed without any loss of generality), I observe that firm i engages in innovation where I denotes the indicator function:

$$y_{it} = I\left[y_{it}^* > 0\right]. \quad (5.2)$$

5.7.2 Estimation Method

For estimation purposes two important theoretical and practical problems have to be solved: Firstly, the treatment of the unobserved individual heterogeneity μ_i and secondly the treatment of the initial value y_{i0}. A random effects (RE) model assumes that μ_i is random and rests on assumptions about the distribution of μ_i given the observables. A fixed effects (FE) model likewise assumes that μ_i is random but does not make any assumptions nor restriction on its distribution, making it in fact preferable. There is, however, no general solution in the literature how to estimate dynamic FE binary choice panel models because no general transformation is known how to eliminate unobserved effects; i.e., unlike in linear models, a first difference or within transformation does not eliminate μ_i in non-linear models. Honoré and Kyriazidou (2000) proposed a semiparametric estimator for the FE logit model but their estimator is extremely data demanding and cannot be used here. Carro (2006) suggested a modified maximum likelihood estimator for the dynamic probit model but the estimator is only consistent when T goes to infinity.[133] Hence, a RE model will be applied in the following analysis.

Concerning the second problem, there generally are three different ways of handling the initial condition y_{i0} in parametric dynamic non-linear models. The first one is to assume that y_{i0} is a non-random constant, which is usually not a realistic assumption because it effectively means that μ_i and y_{i0} are independent. The second solution is to allow for randomness of y_{i0}

---

[133] But, Monte Carlo studies have shown that this estimator performs quite well for 8 or more time periods. The estimator is based on the idea of getting a reparametrisation in such a way that the incidental parameters are information orthogonal to the other parameters which reduces the order of the bias of the maximum likelihood estimator without increasing its asymptotic variance (see Cox and Reid, 1987).

and to attempt to find the joint density for y_{i0} and all outcomes y_{it} conditional on strictly exogenous variables x_i. This approach starts on the joint distribution $(y_{i0}, \ldots, y_{iT}) | \mu_i, x_i$ and requires to specify the distributions of $y_{i0} | \mu_i, x_i$ and that of $\mu_i | x_i$ to integrate out the unobserved effect. However, the joint distribution can only be found in very special cases. Heckman (1981b), thus, suggested a method to approximate the conditional distribution. Another possibility is to assume that y_{i0} is likewise random and to specify a distribution of μ_i conditional on y_{i0} and x_i which leads to the joint density of $(y_{i1}, \ldots, y_{iT}) | y_{i0}, x_i$. This joint distribution allows me to apply a conditional maximum likelihood estimator – conditional on y_{i0} and x_i.[134] This was first suggested by Chamberlain (1980) for a linear autoregressive AR(1) model without covariates; Wooldridge (2005) used the same assumption to develop an estimator for dynamic nonlinear RE models, for instance dynamic RE probit, logit, or tobit models. Following this latter estimation strategy, I further assume that the individual heterogeneity depends on the initial condition and the strict exogenous variables in the following way:

$$\mu_i = \alpha_0 + \alpha_1 \, y_{i0} + \bar{x}_i \, \alpha_2 + a_i, \tag{5.3}$$

where $\bar{x}_i = T^{-1} \sum_{t=1}^{T} x_{it}$ denotes the time averages of x_{it}. Adding the means of the explanatory variables as a set of controls for unobserved heterogeneity is intuitive in the sense that one is estimating the effect of changing x_{it} but holding the time average fixed.[135] For the error term a_i I assume:

$$a_i \sim i.i.d. \; N(0, \sigma_a^2) \quad \text{and} \quad a_i \perp (y_{i0}, \bar{x}_i), \tag{5.4}$$

and, thus, $\mu_i | y_{i0}, \bar{x}_i$ follows a $N(\alpha_0 + \alpha_1 y_{i0} + \bar{x}_i \alpha_2, \sigma_a^2)$ distribution.

Having specified the distribution of the individual heterogeneity in this way, Wooldridge (2005) showed that the probability of being an innovator is given by:

$$P(y_{it} = 1 | y_{i0}, \ldots, y_{i,t-1}, x_i, \bar{x}_i, a_i) \tag{5.5}$$
$$= \Phi(\gamma \, y_{i,t-1} + x_{it} \, \beta + \alpha_0 + \alpha_1 \, y_{i0} + \bar{x}_i \, \alpha_2 + a_i).$$

Integrating out a_i in (5.5) yields a likelihood function that has the same structure as in the standard RE probit model, except that the explanatory

---

[134] The latter approach, i.e. using the joint density of $(y_{i1}, \ldots, y_{iT})$ given (y_{i0}, x_i) is not the same as treating y_{i0} as non-random though it includes the model with non-random y_{i0} as special case (see Wooldridge, 2002: 494).

[135] Instead of $\bar{x}_i$, the original estimator used $x_i = (x_{i1}, \ldots, x_{iT})$ in eq. (5.3) but time averages are allowed to reduce the number of explanatory variables (see Wooldridge, 2005).

variables are enriched by the initial condition and the time averages of the strict exogenous variables:

$$z_{it} = (1, x_{it}, y_{i,t-1}, y_{i0}, \bar{x}_i). \tag{5.6}$$

Identification of the parameters requires that the exogenous variables vary across time and individuals. If the structural model contains time-invariant regressors like industry dummies, one can include them in the regression to increase explanatory power. However, it is not possible to separate out the direct effect and the indirect effect via the heterogeneity equation unless it is assumed a priori that μ_i is partially uncorrelated with the time-constant variables. Time dummies, which are the same for all i, are excluded from $\bar{x}_i$.

The first advantage of the proposed estimator is that it is computationally attractive. The approach further allows selection and panel attrition to depend on the initial condition (innovation state). The third advantage is that partial effects are identified and can be estimated. This is not possible in semi-parametric approaches since they do not specify the distribution of individual heterogeneity on which partial effects depend. This allows me not only to determine whether true state dependence exists by referring to the significance level of the coefficient of the lagged dependent variable but also to measure the importance of this phenomenon. One problem in estimating partial effects is the fact that firm heterogeneity is unobservable. Two alternative calculation methods have been proposed to deal with this shortcoming. The first way is to estimate the partial effect as in the standard probit model and to assume that the individual heterogeneity μ_i takes its average value (PEA). That is, PEA measures the partial effect of an individual with mean heterogeneity. $E(\mu_i) = \alpha_0 + \alpha_1 E(y_{i0}) + E(\bar{x}_i) \alpha_2$ and can be consistently estimated by $\widehat{E(\mu_i)} = \widehat{\alpha}_0 + \widehat{\alpha}_1 \bar{y}_0 + \bar{x} \widehat{\alpha}_2$, where $\bar{y}_0 = \sum_{i=1}^{N} y_{i0}$ and $\bar{x} = \sum_{i=1}^{N} \bar{x}_i$. For the binary lagged dependent variable I can, therefore, calculate the marginal effect as the discrete change in the probability as the dummy variables changes from 0 to 1:

$$\widehat{PEA} = \Phi \left[\widehat{\gamma} + x_i \widehat{\beta} + \widehat{\alpha}_0 + \widehat{\alpha}_1 \bar{y}_0 + \bar{x} \widehat{\alpha}_2 \right]$$
$$- \Phi \left[x_i \widehat{\beta} + \widehat{\alpha}_0 + \widehat{\alpha}_1 \bar{y}_0 + \bar{x} \widehat{\alpha}_2 \right]. \tag{5.7}$$

This estimate suffers from the fact that the average individual heterogeneity usually only represents a small fraction of firms. Alternatively, one can calculate average partial effects (APE). The average partial effect of one explanatory variable measures the change of the expected probability of innovating at time t, either due to an infinitesimal increase in case of a continuous variable or due to a change from 0 to 1 in case of a binary variable. Importantly, the expectation is over the distribution of the individual heterogeneity

μ_i. The average partial effect (APE) for the lagged dependent variable is estimated by:

$$\widehat{APE} = \frac{1}{N}\frac{1}{T}\sum_{i=1}^{N}\sum_{t=1}^{T}\Phi\left[\widehat{\gamma}_a + x^o\,\widehat{\beta}_a + \widehat{\alpha}_{0a} + \widehat{\alpha}_{1a}\,y_{i0} + \bar{x}_i\,\widehat{\alpha}_{2a}\right]$$

$$-\frac{1}{N}\frac{1}{T}\sum_{i=1}^{N}\sum_{t=1}^{T}\Phi\left[x^o\,\widehat{\beta}_a + \widehat{\alpha}_{0a} + \widehat{\alpha}_{1a}\,y_{i0} + \bar{x}_i\,\widehat{\alpha}_{2a}\right], \qquad (5.8)$$

where the subscript a denotes the original parameter estimates multiplied by $\left(1 + \widehat{\sigma}_a^2\right)^{-0.5}$, and x^o are fixed values that have to be chosen (here sample means averaged across i and t are used for x^o). Details on how to calculate APE can be found in Appendix D1.

One limitation of the estimator is that it was derived for balanced panels which evidently reduces the number of observations included. But, using the sub-sample of balanced data still leads to consistent estimates if the dependent variables $(y_{i1}, \ldots, y_{iT})$ and s_i are independent conditional on (y_{i0}, x_i), where s_i is an indicator being 1 if the firm is observed in all periods.[136]. More critical is the fact that, as in alternative estimation methods for dynamic discrete choice panel models (e.g., Heckman 1981a; 1981b; Honoré and Kyriazidou, 2000), the consistency hinges on the strict exogeneity assumption of the regressors, and the estimator leads to inconsistent results if the distributional assumptions are not valid. Blindum (2003) and Biewen (2004) both extended the estimator to allow for endogenous dummy variables but not for a continuous variable that fails strict exogeneity which seems to be more critical in my analysis. Honoré and Lewbel (2002) and Lewbel (2005) recently proposed a semiparametric approach which does not require the strict exogeneity assumption. However, their estimator is based on the existence of one "very exogenous" regressor, and there seems to be no variable at hand that satisfies this assumption in my case.[137]

---

[136] Note that attrition is here mainly due to the voluntary character of the survey and not due to innovation.

[137] The key assumption is that of conditional independence. This means that if the values of the other covariates x_{it} are known, the conditional distribution of $\mu_i + \varepsilon_{it}$ is not altered by additional knowledge of the "very exogenous" continuous regressor v_{it}, i.e., $f(\mu_i + \varepsilon_{it}|x_{it}) = f(\mu_i + \varepsilon_{it}|x_{it}, v_{it})$. In my case the idiosyncratic errors and fixed effects capture, for instance, risk attitudes, innovation preferences, management abilities, or technological opportunities. The assumption will hold if a continuous explanatory variable exists, that is assigned to firms independently of these unobserved attributes. However, there seems to be no variable at hand that satisfies this assumption. In labour supply models, government benefits income might fulfil this requirement.

5.7.3 Empirical Model Specification

The model specification used here is similar to the specification of the selection equation of the CDM model. I, therefore, refer to the more detailed explanations in sections 4.2.1 and 4.5.1.

As was set out in section 5.5, the main dependent variable is a binary variable indicating whether the firm has positive innovation expenditure in a given period t (INNO). In subsection 5.7.5, three alternative dependent variables will additionally be used: To investigate the role of R&D activities in innovation persistence, I differentiate between R&D-performing (INNO_RD) and non-R&D-performing (INNO_NRD) innovators. Finally, I use a dummy variable indicating whether the firm has introduced a new product or process within a 3-year period (INOUT) to investigate state dependence in innovation output. See Table 5.6 for detailed variable definitions.

Theoretical and empirical studies have identified a whole array of innovation determinants; firm size and market structure are the oldest and most prominent ones (see Schumpeter, 1942). Firm size is once again measured by the log number of employees in the previous period (SIZE); the market structure is captured by the Herfindahl-Hirschmann index (HERFIN) from the previous year measured on a 3-digit level.

As explored in section 4.2.1, the innovation literature emphasises that certain firm characteristics, such as the degree of product diversification, the degree of internationalisation, the availability of financial resources, and technological capabilities, are of crucial importance for explaining innovation activities. As the data set does not contain information on product diversification for all years, I cannot take this hypothesis into account. The degree of international competition is once again measured by the export intensity (EXPORT) and the availability of financial resources is proxied by an index of creditworthiness (RATING). While a positive impact of EXPORT is expected, the hypothesis is that RATING negatively affects the propensity to innovate.

One substantial difference between the analysis in chapter 4 and the one here is that, in this case, previous innovation experience (INNO_{-1}) is taken into consideration. In addition to innovation experience, technological capabilities are mainly determined by the skills of employees. Hence, I operationalise this construct by means of three variables: the share of employees with a university degree (HIGH), a dummy variable equaling 1 if a firm has not invested in training its employees in the previous period (NOTRAIN), and the amount of training expenditure per employee (TRAINEXP).

One aim of government support programmes is to promote innovation activities. To test whether public funding induces a permanent change in favour of innovation, I further include a dummy variable equaling 1 if the enterprise has received any public financial support for innovation activities in the previous period (PUBLIC). Since all firms which receive financial support

Table 5.6: Variable Definition

Variable	Type[a)]	Definition
Alternative endogenous variables		
INNO	0/1	1 if a firm i has positive innovation expenditure in year t. Innovation expenditure includes expenditure for intramural and extramural R&D, acquisition of external knowledge, machines and equipment, training, market introduction, design, and other preparations for product and/or process innovations (main dependent variable).
INNO_RD	0/1	1 if a firm i has positive expenditure for intramural and/or extramural R&D in year t.
INNO_NRD	0/1	1 if a firm i has positive innovation expenditure in year t but no intramural and/or extramural R&D activities.
INOUT	0/1	1 if a firm i has introduced at least one product or process innovation in a 3-year period.
Explanatory variables		
Variables varying across individuals and time		
SIZE	c	Number of employees of firm i in year $t-1$, in logarithm.
LCYCLE	c	Length of product life cycle (in years) of firm's i main product in year $t-1$, in logarithm.
RATING	c	Credit rating index for firm i in year $t-1$, originally ranging between 100 (highest creditworthiness) and 600 (worst creditworthiness), divided by 100 to get appropriately scaled coefficients.
AGE	c	Age of firm i at the beginning of year t, in logarithm.
GROUP	0/1	1 if firm i belongs to a group in year t.
PUBLIC	0/1	1 if firm i received public funding for innovation projects in year $t-1$.
NOTRAIN	0/1	1 if firm i has no training expenditure in year $t-1$.
TRAINEXP	c	Training expenditure per employee (in logarithm) of firm i in year $t-1$ if NOTRAIN=0, otherwise 0.
HIGH	c	Share of employees with a university or college degree in firm i in year $t-1$, divided by 100.
EXPORT	c	Export intensity of firm i in year $t-1$ defined as exports/sales.
EXPORT2	c	Squared export intensity.

To be continued on next page.

Table 5.6 – *continued from previous page*

Variable	Type[a)]	Definition
Variables varying across industries and time		
HERFIN	c	Herfindahl-Hirschman Index in year $t-1$ on the 3-digit industry NACE level, divided by 100 to get appropriately scaled coefficients. Only available for manufacturing.
Time-constant individual-specific variables		
FOREIGN	0/1	1 if firm i is a subsidiary of a foreign company.
EAST	0/1	1 if firm i is located in East Germany.
PLC	0/1	1 if firm i is a public limited company (*AG*).
LTD	0/1	1 if firm i is a private limited liability company (*GmbH, GmbH & Co. KG*).
PRIVPART	0/1	1 if firm i is a private partnership (*Personengesellschaft, OHG, KG*).
IND	0/1	System of 15 and 9 dummies grouping industries and services, respectively, see Table 2.1.
Time-varying individual-constant variables		
TIME	0/1	System of time dummies for each year.

Note: [a)] c denotes a continuous variable.

are innovators by definition, PUBLIC is an interaction term and measures the additional effect of supported compared to non-supported innovators.

As in section 4.5.1, the estimation also controls for ownership structure by distinguishing between public limited companies (PLC), private limited liability companies (LTD), and private partnerships (PRIVPART). In addition, firm-specific variables reflecting firm age (AGE), location (EAST), whether the firm is part of an enterprise group (GROUP), and whether the group's headquarter is located abroad (FOREIGN) are included. The observed period is characterised by the catching-up process of the East German economy after reunification. At the aggregate level, the share of innovators had been found higher in East than in West Germany until the end of the 1990s (see Rammer, Aschhoff et al., 2005). Therefore, I expect a higher propensity to innovate for East German firms.[138]

As mentioned above, market or industry characteristics – alone or in combination with firm-specific features – may be important for innovation activi-

---

[138] Note that the catching-up process in East Germany was patronised by special government support programmes. Including EAST together with PUBLIC reversed the marginal effect of EAST. Though the effect is not significant at conventional levels, this gives some indication that the higher propensity to innovate in East Germany is induced by governmental support.

ties. In this context technological opportunities are expected to play a significant role. Technological opportunities are measured by the product life cycle of a firm's main product (LCYCLE) and industry dummies. The hypothesis is that firms which offer products or use production technologies that become obsolete rather soon are forced to innovate more often.

Tables 5.7 and 5.8 report the descriptive statistics of the variables used in the estimations for manufacturing and service firms, respectively. It turned out that the median firm size is much smaller in the service sector (25 employees) than in manufacturing (92 employees), which might be one explanation of the observed lower innovation persistence in services. Firm age and finan-

Table 5.7: Descriptive Statistics: Manufacturing[a]

	Unit	Mean	S.d.			Min	Max	Med
			Overall	Between	Within			
INNO	[0/1]	0.555	0.497	0.419	0.268	0	1	—
INNO_RD	[0/1]	0.465	0.499	0.442	0.231	0	1	—
INNO_NRD	[0/1]	0.090	0.287	0.163	0.236	0	1	—
SIZE[b]	No. emp.[c]	2,018.7	14,121.3	13,566.9	3,964.5	1	243,638	92
LCYCLE[b]	years	15.4	21.4	21.0	4.3	0.3	200	9.3
RATING	[Index: 1-6]	2.088	0.600	0.548	0.244	1	6	2.070 —
AGE[b]	years	21.8	23.0	22.5	4.9	0	142	13
GROUP	[0/1]	0.360	0.480	0.409	0.253	0	1	—
PUBLIC	[0/1]	0.243	0.429	0.351	0.246	0	1	—
NOTRAIN	[0/1]	0.176	0.381	0.315	0.215	0	1	—
TRAINEXP[b]	€	663.2	1,135.8	872.0	728.9	0	7,702	277.1
HIGH	[0-1]	0.110	0.136	0.117	0.069	0	1	0.067
EXPORT	[0-1]	0.196	0.246	0.232	0.083	0	1	0.071
HERFIN	[Index: 0-100]	4.7	6.1	5.6	2.4	0.1	43.2	2.4
FOREIGN	[0/1]	0.059	0.236	0.196	0.131	0	1	—
EAST	[0/1]	0.344	0.475	0.469	0.075	0	1	—
PLC	[0/1]	0.078	0.268	0.268	0.000	0	1	—
LTD	[0/1]	0.830	0.376	0.375	0.028	0	1	—
PRIVPART	[0/1]	0.085	0.279	0.278	0.028	0	1	—

Notes: [a] For the period 1995-2002. In case of lagged explanatory variables, periods used are 1994-2001. Number of observations: 3,496.
[b] Variable values shown are not log-transformed. For estimation purposes, however, a log-transformation of these variables is used to take the skewness of the distribution into account.
[c] Number of employees.

Table 5.8: Descriptive Statistics: Services[a]

	Unit	Mean	S.d.			Min	Max	Med
			Overall	Between	Within			
INNO	[0/1]	0.360	0.480	0.372	0.304	0	1	—
INNO_RD	[0/1]	0.158	0.365	0.308	0.195	0	1	—
INNO_NRD	[0/1]	0.202	0.402	0.254	0.312	0	1	—
SIZE[b]	No. emp.[c]	1,782.0	18,143.6	18,107.3	1,512.0	1	271,078	25
LCYCLE[b]	years	16.2	22.6	22.0	5.2	1	100	7
RATING	[Index: 1-6]	2.194	0.440	0.407	0.167	1	6	2.190
AGE[b]	years	22.3	21.0	20.9	2.4	1	141	14
GROUP	[0/1]	0.223	0.416	0.349	0.227	0	1	—
PUBLIC	[0/1]	0.096	0.295	0.248	0.161	0	1	—
NOTRAIN	[0/1]	0.255	0.436	0.377	0.220	0	1	—
TRAINEXP[b]	€	1,223.1	3,164.0	2,264.1	2,213.5	0	25,791	333.3
HIGH	[0-1]	0.200	0.260	0.236	0.110	0	1	0.065
EXPORT	[0-1]	0.025	0.096	0.084	0.046	0	1	0
HERFIN	[0-100]	—	—	—	—	—	—	—
FOREIGN	[0/1]	0.018	0.134	0.118	0.064	0	1	—
EAST	[0/1]	0.420	0.494	0.491	0.054	0	1	—
PLC	[0/1]	0.053	0.225	0.221	0.042	0	1	—
LTD	[0/1]	0.692	0.462	0.457	0.072	0	1	—
PRIVPART	[0/1]	0.220	0.414	0.410	0.063	0	1	—

Notes: [a] For the period 1997-2002. In case of lagged explanatory variables, the period used is 1996-2001. Number of observations: 1,692.
[b] Variable values shown are not log-transformed. For estimation purposes, however, a log-transformation of these variables is used to take the skewness of the distribution into account.
[c] Number of employees.

cial conditions on the other hand turn out be rather similar in both panels. Comparing the two industries, one further finds that manufacturing firms do invest in training more frequently than services but the average (and median) amount of training expenditure per employee is higher in service sector firms.

Furthermore, the descriptive statistics reveal that for almost all variables the variation across firms (between variation) is much higher compared to that within a firm over time (within variation) and explains the major part of the overall variance. The variables FOREIGN, EAST, PLC, LTD, and PRIVPART can vary across i and t. However, due to the fact that hardly any within variation showed up, I treated them as time-constant firm-specific variables in the estimation and include them only in eq. (5.3).

5.7.4 Econometric Results

Table 5.9 reports the estimation results of the dynamic RE probit model, including the Schumpeter determinants (size and market structure), product life cycle, and industry and time dummies as exogenous variables. It then compares the results with the static pooled model and static RE model.[139] In all following tables M_ denotes the individual time average of the corresponding variable. Note that marginal effects are reported. In the dynamic RE model they are calculated at the average value of the firm-specific error.[140] Furthermore, in the case of the static pooled model, the standard errors have been adjusted (clustered) to account for the fact that observations are not necessarily independent within firms.

The first main result is that including the lagged dependent variable is an important part of the model specification. That is, even after accounting for individual unobserved heterogeneity, the variable turns out to be highly significant in both manufacturing and services, therefore, confirming the hypotheses of true state dependence. Furthermore, the fit of the model considerably improves as can be seen in Table 5.10: The value of the likelihood function largely increases in the dynamic RE model, and the percentage of correctly predicted 1 (innovation) as well as 0 (no innovation) outcomes rises remarkably with the exception of 0 outcomes in the service sector where the already high value slightly decreases.[141] The results further show that some of the variables which are significant in the static estimation lose this property in the dynamic specification; for instance, firm size is no longer significant in services. One interpretation of this result is that firm size, which is likewise highly time-persistent, simply picks up the impact of the lagged dependent variable in the static case.

As mentioned above, one problem of the dynamic RE panel probit model is the fact that strict exogeneity of the exogenous variables is assumed. This implies that no feedback effects from the innovation variable on future values of the explanatory variables are allowed, which seems to be contestable for some of the variables usually explaining innovation behaviour, such as firm

---

[139] Note that the product life cycle concept is less common and meaningful in the service sector. The variable, therefore, exhibit a very high number of missing values which have been imputed by industry averages. Nonetheless, this variable should be treated with care in the service sector. Note that the econometric results remain nearly unaltered when this variable is excluded from the regression.

[140] However, the calculation of the marginal effect of a variable k neglects that an infinitesimal increase in x_k changes the mean value $\bar{x}_{i,k}$ as well.

[141] See Veall and Zimmermann (1996) for a discussion of the interpretation and importance of different Pseudo R^2 measures in binary choice models.

Table 5.9: Comparison: Marginal Effects in Static Pooled, Static RE, and Dynamic RE Probit Model

	Manufacturing			Services		
	Pooled Probit	Static RE Probit	Dynamic RE Probit	Pooled Probit	Static RE Probit	Dynamic RE Probit
$INNO_{-1}$	—	—	0.358*** (0.035)	—	—	0.127*** (0.044)
LCYCLE	-0.055** (0.021)	-0.089*** (0.016)	-0.052 (0.044)	0.017 (0.047)	-0.003 (0.061)	0.003 (0.109)
SIZE	0.141*** (0.014)	0.216*** (0.016)	0.129** (0.062)	0.086*** (0.014)	0.134*** (0.021)	0.019 (0.064)
HERFIN	0.018 (0.041)	0.034 (0.034)	0.050 (0.056)	—	—	—
$INNO_0$	—	—	0.535*** (0.045)	—	—	0.457*** (0.063)
M_LCYCLE	—	—	0.018 (0.050)	—	—	-0.041 (0.099)
M_SIZE	—	—	-0.035 (0.063)	—	—	0.042 (0.066)
M_HERFIN	—	—	-0.038 (0.070)	—	—	—
σ_a	—	1.861 (0.103)	0.801 (0.082)	—	1.367 (0.119)	0.928 (0.107)
ρ	—	0.776 (0.019)	0.391 (0.049)	—	0.651 (0.040)	0.463 (0.058)
LR_ρ	—	0.000	0.000	—	0.000	0.000
W_{TIME}	0.005	0.008	0.010	0.000	0.000	0.000
W_{IND}	0.000	0.000	0.000	0.000	0.000	0.000
Obs	3496	3496	3496	1692	1692	1692

Notes: ∗ ∗ ∗, ∗∗, and ∗ indicate significance on a 1%, 5%, and 10% level, respectively. Standard errors in pooled probit model are adjusted for clustering on firms. A constant (significant at the 1% level in each regression) as well as time and industry dummies are included in each regression but not reported. Marginal effects are reported. In the dynamic RE model, they are calculated at the average value of the individual-specific error. The Wald test statistics W_{IND} and W_{TIME} test for the null hypothesis that the industry and time dummies are jointly equal to zero, respectively.

Table 5.10: Comparison: Goodness-of-Fit Measures in Static Pooled, Static RE, and Dynamic RE Probit Model

	Manufacturing			Services		
	Pooled Probit	Static RE Probit	Dynamic RE Probit	Pooled Probit	Static RE Probit	Dynamic RE Probit
ln L	-1820.1	-1249.7	-1107.2	-935.2	-760.4	-722.5
ln L_{Cons}	-2402.1	-1403.1	-1403.1	-1105.5	-828.9	-828.9
R^2_{MF}	0.242	0.109	0.211	0.154	0.083	0.128
R^2_{MZ}	0.476	—	—	0.303	—	—
Obs Prob	55.5	55.5	55.5	36.0	36.0	36.0
Pred Prob	57.7	71.8	64.7	34.8	26.6	28.5
Corr Pred	71.5	69.9	85.4	72.4	72.5	77.0
Corr Pred 1	77.8	80.0	86.0	42.2	43.5	59.4
Corr Pred 0	63.7	57.4	84.7	89.4	88.8	86.8

Note: R^2_{MF} denotes McFadden's R^2, and R^2_{MZ} reports McKelvey and Zavoina's R^2 (see McKelvey and Zavoina, 1975).

size, market structure, or export behaviour. To assess the impact of including variables which potentially fail the strict exogeneity assumption on the estimated state dependence effect, I apply a stepwise procedure. That is, I start estimating an extremely parsimonious specification (1) including only LCY-CLE and industry and time dummies as exogenous variables. Specification (2) then adds the Schumpeter determinants (which underlie the comparison) and (3) incorporates some firm characteristics for which strict exogeneity seems to be satisfied.[142] Specifications (4) and (5) further include some variables that are presumably not strictly exogenous. The estimation results are summarised in Tables 5.11 and 5.12 for manufacturing and services, respectively.

It emerges from this exercise that the marginal effect of the lagged dependent variable is nearly unaltered in the different estimations. That is, even after accounting for individual unobserved heterogeneity, past innovation has a behavioural effect: Conditional on observed and unobserved firm characteristics, an innovator in $t-1$ has a probability of innovating which is approximately 36 percentage points higher than that of a non-innovator in manufacturing. For service companies, the marginal effect amounts to roughly 13 percentage points.

---

[142] I used the procedure proposed by Wooldridge (2002), i.e. I added the lead of the corresponding variable and tested on the significance of the coefficient.

Table 5.11: Robustness of Dynamic RE Probit Estimations in
Manufacturing

Regression	(1)	(2)	(3)	(4)	(5)
Structural Equation					
INNO$_{-1}$	0.364 ***	0.358 ***	0.359 ***	0.358 ***	0.333 ***
	(0.034)	(0.035)	(0.035)	(0.035)	(0.036)
LCYCLE	-0.049	-0.052	-0.057	-0.043	-0.053
	(0.044)	(0.044)	(0.045)	(0.031)	(0.044)
SIZE	—	0.129 **	0.122 **	0.111 *	0.100 *
		(0.062)	(0.062)	(0.062)	(0.061)
HERFIN	—	0.050	0.051	0.048	0.055
		(0.056)	(0.056)	(0.057)	(0.056)
RATING	—	—	-0.059	-0.066	-0.068
			(0.044)	(0.044)	(0.044)
AGE	—	—	-0.075 *	-0.071 *	-0.067 *
			(0.038)	(0.038)	(0.037)
GROUP	—	—	0.053	0.052	0.062
			(0.050)	(0.050)	(0.050)
NOTRAIN	—	—	—	-0.123	-0.116
				(0.162)	(0.160)
TRAINEXP	—	—	—	0.014	0.014
				(0.017)	(0.017)
HIGH	—	—	—	-0.100	-0.103
				(0.214)	(0.216)
EXPORT	—	—	—	0.459 ***	0.473 ***
				(0.136)	(0.130)
PUBLIC	—	—	—	—	0.174 ***
					(0.045)
TIME	yes	yes	yes	yes	yes
Individual Heterogeneity					
INNO$_0$	0.625 ***	0.535 ***	0.538 ***	0.460 ***	0.341 ***
	(0.042)	(0.045)	(0.045)	(0.045)	(0.047)
M_LCYCLE	0.023	0.018	0.021	0.030	0.017
	(0.051)	(0.050)	(0.050)	(0.050)	(0.049)
M_SIZE	—	-0.035	-0.035	-0.047	-0.056
		(0.063)	(0.064)	(0.064)	(0.063)

To be continued on next page.

Table 5.11 – *continued from previous page*

Regression	(1)	(2)	(3)	(4)	(5)
M_HERFIN	—	-0.038 (0.070)	-0.040 (0.071)	-0.038 (0.069)	-0.044 (0.067)
M_RATING	—	—	0.030 (0.062)	0.026 (0.061)	0.032 (0.059)
M_AGE	—	—	0.119 ** (0.051)	0.116 ** (0.050)	0.100 ** (0.047)
M_GROUP	—	—	0.024 (0.085)	-0.020 (0.082)	-0.026 (0.078)
FOREIGN	—	—	-0.128 (0.084)	-0.162 ** (0.083)	-0.125 (0.079)
EAST	—	—	0.016 (0.051)	0.047 (0.051)	-0.051 (0.051)
PLC	—	—	-0.209 * (0.110)	-0.201 ** (0.102)	-0.168 * (0.097)
PRIVPART	—	—	0.025 (0.069)	0.038 (0.064)	0.025 (0.060)
M_NOTRAIN	—	—	—	-0.638 *** (0.247)	-0.651 *** (0.236)
M_TRAINEXP	—	—	—	0.053 * (0.029)	0.054 ** (0.027)
M_HIGH	—	—	—	0.646 ** (0.316)	0.157 (0.312)
M_EXPORT	—	—	—	0.347 * (0.198)	0.289 (0.194)
M_PUBLIC	—	—	—	—	0.370 *** (0.091)
IND	yes	yes	yes	yes	yes
σ_a	0.876 (0.083)	0.801 (0.082)	0.792 (0.082)	0.709 (0.077)	0.623 (0.077)
ρ	0.434 (0.047)	0.391 (0.049)	0.386 (0.049)	0.334 (0.049)	0.280 (0.050)
LR_ρ	0.000	0.000	0.000	0.000	0.000
W_{TIME}	0.013	0.010	0.006	0.007	0.009
W_{IND}	0.000	0.000	0.000	0.010	0.030

To be continued on next page.

Table 5.11 – *continued from previous page*

Regression	(1)	(2)	(3)	(4)	(5)
R^2_{MF}	0.193	0.211	0.216	0.232	0.254
Obs Prob	55.5	55.5	55.5	55.5	55.5
Pred Prob	63.8	64.7	64.7	64.6	65.7
Corr Pred	83.6	85.4	85.6	86.1	87.4
Corr Pred 1	84.1	86.0	86.4	86.4	87.2
Corr Pred 0	83.0	84.7	84.7	85.7	87.7
Obs	3496	3496	3496	3496	3496

Notes: ∗∗∗, ∗∗, and ∗ indicate significance on a 1%, 5%, and 10% level, respectively. Marginal effects are reported, calculated at the average value of the individual-specific error. Columns (4) and (5) report the marginal effect of EXPORT, corrected for the fact that the original regressions also contain the quadratic term. Standard errors were calculated using the delta method. Original coefficient estimates in (4) and (5): EXPORT: 1.604 (0.784) and 1.762 (0.770), EXPORT2: -2.659 (0.906) and -2.710 (0.882). W_{IND} and W_{TIME} test for the null hypothesis that the industry and time dummies are jointly equal to zero, respectively. Estimations are based on Gauss-Hermite quadrature approximations using 8 quadrature points. The accuracy of the results have been checked using the STATA command quadchk. Most coefficients change by less than 0.01%, and none change by more than 1%, so that the model can be reliably fitted using the quadrature approach.

The results further show that the initial condition is also highly significant in both samples. This implies a substantial correlation between firms' initial innovation status and the unobserved heterogeneity.

A third important finding is that in addition to past innovation experience, knowledge provided by skilled employees has a crucial influence on generating innovations over time. In both industries the variables NOTRAIN and TRAIN, and in manufacturing also HIGH, turn out to be significant in the equation explaining individual heterogeneity across firms. That is, firms which do not invest in further training of their employees have a significantly lower propensity to innovate while for those firms which do invest an increase in average training expenditure per employee of 10% raises the probability of innovating by about 0.5 percentage points in both industries. All in all, these results confirm and highlight the role of innovative capabilities in the dynamics of firms' innovation behaviour.

Fourthly, the results provide evidence that unobserved heterogeneity is a key factor for innovation persistence. The importance of the unobserved heterogeneity in explaining the total variance can be gauged from $\rho = \sigma_a^2/(1+\sigma_a^2)$.[143] Table 5.9 has already shown that introducing the lagged dependent variable leads to a distinct reduction of the importance of the unobserved

---

[143] Note that $\varepsilon_{it}|y_{i0}, \ldots, y_{i,t-1}, x_i \sim N(0,1)$ and $\mu_i|y_{i0}, \bar{x}_i \sim N(0, \sigma_a^2)$.

heterogeneity. Unobserved heterogeneity still explains between 30 and 43% of the variance in the dependent variable in manufacturing depending on the specification of μ_i. In the service sector, this effect is in a similar range with 37 to 48%.

In addition to prior innovation experience, skills, and unobserved heterogeneity, some observed firm characteristics are also found to be crucial factors in explaining innovation. These results are, by and large, in line with the literature and with what one expected. Firms that are more financially constrained are less likely to engage in innovation. This effect is highly significant in services and slightly significant in manufacturing (p-value: 0.128 in the preferred specification (4)). Moreover, firms which receive public funding in the previous period exhibit a higher propensity to innovate in the subsequent period than innovators without financial support in both industries. In contrast, firm size is only important in manufacturing, not in the service sector. This is likewise the case for the degree of internationalisation, a result which is maybe not that surprising because exporting is less prevalent in services.[144] Firms which are more active on international markets have a higher propensity to innovate in manufacturing. However, I find an inverse U-shaped relationship for the export intensity with an estimated point of inflexion at 33% in specification (4).[145] It is also only in manufacturing that ownership matters. That is, public limited companies, in which conflicts of interests between managers and shareholders might arise, have a significantly lower conditional probability of being innovative. However, regarding the second Schumpeterian determinant, I do not find any significant impact of market concentration on innovation. But admittedly, this may be due to the fact that HERFIN is an insufficient proxy of market structure.

All in all, the model seems to fit the data quite well. The McFadden's pseudo R^2 varies between 20 and 25% in manufacturing, and based on the preferred specification (4), the model correctly predicts the innovation behaviour for 86% of the observations. This number is much higher than in the static model. Correct predictions in the service sector are likewise high with 79%. However, the model clearly performs worse in predicting the occurrence of innovation for service firms.

---

[144] I also experimented with dummy variables for the export status or export classes but in no case does export exhibit a significant impact on innovation in services.

[145] Notice that the regression for manufacturing certainly includes the export intensity as well as its quadratic term. The coefficients can be found in the notes of Table 5.11. The quadratic specification is accounted for when calculating the marginal effects in Table 5.11. That is, the marginal effect of the export intensity (x_j) is: $\widehat{PEA} = \phi[\widehat{\gamma}\, y_{i,t-1} + \widehat{\beta}_1\, x_1 + \ldots + \widehat{\beta}_j\, x_j + \widehat{\beta}_{j2}\, x_j^2 + \ldots + \widehat{\beta}_K\, x_K + \widehat{\alpha}_0 + \widehat{\alpha}_1\, \bar{y}_0 + \bar{x}\,\widehat{\alpha}_2] \cdot \left(\widehat{\beta}_j + 2\widehat{\beta}_{j2}\, x_j\right)$

Table 5.12: Robustness of Dynamic RE Probit Estimations in Services

Regression	(1)	(2)	(3)	(4)	(5)
Structural Equation					
$INNO_{-1}$	0.126 ***	0.127 ***	0.128 ***	0.128 ***	0.103 **
	(0.044)	(0.044)	(0.045)	(0.045)	(0.047)
LCYCLE	-0.009	0.003	-0.002	-0.005	-0.039
	(0.109)	(0.109)	(0.109)	(0.109)	(0.112)
SIZE	—	0.019	0.016	0.011	0.006
		(0.064)	(0.064)	(0.066)	(0.069)
RATING	—	—	-0.210 **	-0.209 **	-0.206 **
			(0.099)	(0.099)	(0.103)
AGE	—	—	0.053	0.050	0.057
			(0.060)	(0.059)	(0.062)
GROUP	—	—	0.006	0.009	0.010
			(0.063)	(0.063)	(0.066)
NOTRAIN	—	—	—	-0.060	-0.068
				(0.155)	(0.161)
TRAINEXP	—	—	—	0.003	0.007
				(0.020)	(0.021)
HIGH	—	—	—	-0.027	-0.016
				(0.127)	(0.133)
EXPORT	—	—	—	0.109	0.084
				(0.311)	(0.320)
PUBLIC	—	—	—	—	0.294 ***
					(0.102)
TIME	yes	yes	yes	yes	yes
Individual Heterogeneity					
$INNO_0$	0.532 ***	0.457 ***	0.434 ***	0.370 ***	0.335 ***
	(0.059)	(0.063)	(0.064)	(0.065)	(0.064)
M_LCYCLE	-0.047	-0.041	-0.046	-0.044	-0.021
	(0.097)	(0.099)	(0.098)	(0.099)	(0.102)
M_SIZE	—	0.042	0.021	0.022	0.021
		(0.066)	(0.068)	(0.070)	(0.073)
M_RATING	—	—	0.084	0.122	0.176
			(0.123)	(0.122)	(0.125)

To be continued on next page.

Table 5.12 – *continued from previous page*

Regression	(1)	(2)	(3)	(4)	(5)
M_AGE	—	—	-0.149 **	-0.127 *	-0.118
			(0.075)	(0.075)	(0.076)
M_GROUP	—	—	0.071	0.070	0.057
			(0.106)	(0.104)	(0.105)
FOREIGN	—	—	0.270	0.214	0.278
			(0.203)	(0.202)	(0.193)
EAST	—	—	0.040	0.022	-0.025
			(0.062)	(0.063)	(0.063)
PLC	—	—	0.216	0.211	0.281 *
			(0.166)	(0.162)	(0.158)
PRIVPART	—	—	-0.064	-0.049	-0.015
			(0.059)	(0.058)	(0.060)
M_NOTRAIN	—	—	—	-0.594 **	-0.649 **
				(0.270)	(0.273)
M_TRAINEXP	—	—	—	0.055 *	0.056 *
				(0.034)	(0.034)
M_HIGH	—	—	—	0.151	0.010
				(0.205)	(0.209)
M_EXPORT	—	—	—	0.201	0.006
				(0.428)	(0.460)
M_PUBLIC	—	—	—	—	0.528 ***
					(0.159)
IND	yes	yes	yes	yes	yes
σ_μ	0.966	0.928	0.886	0.850	0.777
	(0.109)	(0.107)	(0.105)	(0.104)	(0.102)
ρ	0.482	0.463	0.440	0.420	0.376
	(0.056)	(0.058)	(0.059)	(0.060)	(0.062)
LR_ρ	0.000	0.000	0.000	0.000	0.000
W_{TIME}	0.000	0.000	0.000	0.000	0.000
W_{IND}	0.000	0.000	0.000	0.145	0.138

To be continued on next page.

Table 5.12 – *continued from previous page*

Regression	(1)	(2)	(3)	(4)	(5)
ln L	-729.7	-722.5	-712.1	-703.9	-680.4
ln L_{Cons}	-828.9	-828.9	-828.9	-828.9	-828.9
R_{MF}^2	0.120	0.128	0.141	0.150	0.179
Obs Prob	36.0	36.0	36.0	36.0	36.0
Pred Prob	28.0	28.8	28.8	28.4	30.5
Corr Pred	76.7	77.0	78.7	79.1	80.1
Corr Pred 1	63.4	59.4	62.7	63.6	63.6
Corr Pred 0	84.3	86.8	87.7	87.9	89.4
Obs	1692	1692	1692	1692	1692

Notes: $* * *$, $**$, and $*$ indicate significance on a 1%, 5%, and 10% level, respectively. Marginal effects are reported, calculated at the average value of the individual-specific error. The Wald test statistics W_{IND} and W_{TIME} test for the null hypothesis that the industry and time dummies are jointly equal to zero, respectively. As in manufacturing, the accuracy of the results have been proved using the STATA command quadchk.

As mentioned above, partial effects at the average value of the individual effect (PEA) suffer from the fact that the average value usually represents a small fraction of firms only. To amplify what has been said so far on the importance of state dependence effects, Table 5.13 contrasts the PEA with the estimated average partial effect (APE). It is quite plain that averaging the partial effects across the distribution of the unobserved heterogeneity reduces the estimates of the state dependence effects. Section 5.6 has shown that in manufacturing the propensity to innovate in period $t + 1$ was approximately 74 percentage points higher for innovators than for non-innovators in period t in panel B (see Table 5.2). Controlling for differences in observed and unobserved characteristics, this difference reduces to 36 percentage points using PEA and 23 percentage points using APE. This implies that depending on the calculation method between nearly one third (APE) to one half (PEA) of the innovation persistence in manufacturing can be traced back to true state dependence while the rest was due to observed and unobserved characteristics. The econometric results further show that the causal effect of prior innovations on future innovations turns out to be weaker for service firms. In the service sector, the observed difference in the propensity to innovate between prior innovators and non-innovators was already lower at about 54 percentage points compared to 74 percentage points in manufacturing, and true state dependence accounts only for about 15% (APE) to 25% (PEA) of this difference.

Table 5.13: Importance of State Dependence Effects in Manufacturing and
Services

	OSD[a]	PEA[b,d]				APE[c,d]			
		$\widehat{P(1\|1)}$	$\widehat{P(1\|0)}$	$\widehat{PEA}$		$\widehat{P(1\|1)}$	$\widehat{P(1\|0)}$	$\widehat{APE}$	
				abs.	rel.			abs.	rel.
Manufacturing	74.1	79.3	43.5	35.8	48.3	68.9	45.9	23.0	31.0
Services	53.7	36.9	24.0	12.8	24.0	41.1	32.9	8.2	15.3

Notes: [a] OSD: Observed state dependence effect (in percentage points).
[b] $\widehat{P(1|1)}$ and $\widehat{P(1|0)}$ denote estimates of the probabilities $P(y_{it} = 1|y_{i,t-1} = 1, x_i, \mu_i)$ and $P(y_{it} = 1|y_{i,t-1} = 0, x_i, \mu_i)$ at the average value of μ_i.
[c] $\widehat{P(1|1)}$ and $\widehat{P(1|0)}$ are estimates of the expected probabilities of $P(y_{it} = 1|y_{i,t-1}^o = 1, x_i^o, \mu_i)$ and $P(y_{it} = 1|y_{i,t-1}^o = 0, x_i^o, \mu_i)$ where the expectation is over the distribution of μ_i.
[d] "abs." means the absolute difference $\widehat{P(1|1)} - \widehat{P(1|0)}$ in percentage points. "rel." is the absolute difference relative to the OSD.
All estimates are based on specification (4) in Tables 5.11 and 5.12.

5.7.5 Sensitivity Analysis

In this section, some further sensitivity analyses are carried out to check on the robustness of the results. Firstly, using each value $x_i = (x_{i1}, \ldots, x_{iT})$ in eq. (5.3) instead of individual time averages as originally proposed by Wooldridge (2005) leaves the results nearly unaltered. They are, therefore, not reported here but are available upon request.

Secondly, Table 5.14 differentiates between R&D-performing and non-R&D-performing innovators to examine whether persistence is mainly driven by R&D activities and whether this can explain the differences found between manufacturing and services. The results suggest that significant state dependence effects exist for both kinds of innovation activities in both samples. But as expected, state dependence effects are much higher for R&D-performing than for non-R&D-performing innovators. One astonishing result, however, is the fact that the marginal effect of past R&D experience is nearly three times higher in manufacturing with 50 percentage points than in the service sector with 16 percentage points. This relationship carries over when I calculate how much of the observed (unconditional) persistence in R&D can be explained by true state dependence. That is, in manufacturing 60.5% of the observed persistence in R&D activities is attributable to true state dependence while it is only at about 20.5% in services.[146] This points towards significant dif-

---

[146] The four one-period transition rates for R&D-performing innovators amount to 91.6% (0→0), 8.4% (0→1), 8.9% (1→0), and 91.1% (1→1) in manufacturing as

Table 5.14: Persistence of Non-R&D- and R&D-Performing Innovators

Dependent Variable	Manufacturing		Services	
	INNO_NRD	INNO_RD	INNO_NRD	INNO_RD
Structural Equation				
$INNO\_NRD_{-1}$	0.070 ***	—	0.093 ***	—
	(0.022)		(0.034)	
$INNO\_RD_{-1}$	—	0.500 ***	—	0.159 **
		(0.037)		(0.077)
LCYCLE	-0.014	-0.025	-0.093	-0.062 **
	(0.010)	(0.058)	(0.061)	(0.031)
SIZE	-0.007	0.158 **	0.011	-0.011
	(0.014)	(0.076)	(0.037)	(0.016)
HERFIN	-0.003	0.073	—	—
	(0.014)	(0.063)		
RATING	-0.006	-0.059	-0.070	-0.010
	(0.012)	(0.052)	(0.056)	(0.028)
AGE	-0.005	-0.083	0.033	-0.005
	(0.008)	(0.052)	(0.033)	(0.013)
GROUP	-0.004	0.073	0.017	-0.004
	(0.011)	(0.060)	(0.038)	(0.014)
NOTRAIN	0.020	-0.090	-0.000	-0.022
	(0.051)	(0.192)	(0.095)	(0.027)
TRAINEXP	0.004	-0.005	-0.003	0.003
	(0.004)	(0.021)	(0.012)	(0.005)
HIGH	-0.051	-0.036	-0.100	0.029
	(0.052)	(0.242)	(0.079)	(0.030)
EXPORT	-0.017	0.637 ***	-0.106	0.063
	(0.027)	(0.157)	(0.196)	(0.078)
Individual Heterogeneity				
$INNO\_NRD_0$	0.059 **	—	0.172 ***	—
	(0.026)		(0.049)	
$INNO\_RD_0$	—	0.472 ***	—	0.166 ***
		(0.061)		(0.059)
M_LCYCLE	0.012	-0.008	0.039	-0.050 *
	(0.011)	(0.066)	(0.055)	(0.028)

To be continued on next page.

Table 5.14 – *continued from previous page*

Dependent Variable	Manufacturing		Services	
	INNO_NRD	INNO_RD	INNO_NRD	INNO_RD
M_SIZE	-0.009	-0.029	-0.016	0.018
	(0.015)	(0.079)	(0.039)	(0.017)
M_HERFIN	-0.004	-0.054	—	—
	(0.017)	(0.080)		
M_RATING	0.022	-0.004	0.062	-0.010
	(0.014)	(0.073)	(0.067)	(0.033)
M_AGE	0.004	0.117 *	-0.040	-0.008
	(0.010)	(0.066)	(0.040)	(0.017)
M_GROUP	0.025	-0.088	-0.009	0.003
	(0.017)	(0.100)	(0.057)	(0.023)
FOREIGN	-0.008	-0.125	0.004	0.057
	(0.015)	(0.084	(0.088)	(0.078)
EAST	-0.016 *	0.139 **	0.033	-0.013
	(0.009)	(0.67)	(0.034)	(0.013)
PLC	0.018	-0.175 *	-0.060	0.078
	(0.027)	(0.104)	(0.045)	(0.079)
PRIVPART	0.012	-0.063	0.001	-0.018 *
	(0.016)	(0.089)	(0.032)	(0.010)
M_NOTRAIN	-0.034 **	-1.088 ***	-0.247 *	-0.061
	(0.017)	(0.345)	(0.142)	(0.056)
M_TRAINEXP	0.010 *	0.106 ***	0.016	0.003
	(0.006)	(0.037)	(0.018)	(0.007)
M_HIGH	0.115 *	0.899 **	0.089	0.030
	(0.076)	(0.374)	(0.116)	(0.043)
M_EXPORT	0.004	0.286	-0.156	0.029
	(0.042)	(0.229)	(0.250)	(0.096)
σ_a	0.590	0.828	0.689	0.713
	(0.078)	(0.105)	(0.095)	(0.178)
ρ	0.258	0.407	0.322	0.337
	(0.049)	(0.061)	(0.060)	(0.111)
LR_ρ	0.000	0.000	0.000	0.001

To be continued on next page.

Table 5.14 – *continued from previous page*

Dependent Variable	Manufacturing		Services	
	INNO_NRD	INNO_RD	INNO_NRD	INNO_RD
W_{TIME}	0.041	0.004	0.000	0.504
W_{IND}	0.504	0.017	0.308	0.126
ln L	-858.6	-820.6	-694.5	-298.5
ln L_{Cons}	-937.2	-1207.2	-761.4	-445.3
R^2_{MF}	0.084	0.320	0.088	0.330
APE: INNO_NRD	0.088	—	0.088	—
APE: INNO_RD	—	0.292	—	0.170
Obs	3,496	3,496	1,692	1,692

Notes: ***, **, and * indicate significance on a 1%, 5%, and 10% level, respectively. Marginal effects are reported, calculated at the average value of the individual-specific error. Time and industry dummies are included in each regression. The Wald test statistics W_{IND} and W_{TIME} test for the null hypothesis that the industry and time dummies are jointly equal to zero, respectively.

ferences in the characteristics of R&D activities in both industries. It might be explained by the fact that R&D projects are less important for innovation activities in services, shorter in time or that sunk costs in R&D are less important. On the other hand, in case of innovators without R&D activities, the impact of past innovation experience on the propensity to remain innovative is very much the same in manufacturing with 7 and in services with 9 percentage points. By and large, the main conclusions drawn in the previous section still hold in the separate estimations.

Moreover, as was set out in section 5.5, the results so far measured the persistence in innovation input. For manufacturing, the picture can be completed by examining the output persistence for the same set of firms. I use a dummy variable indicating whether the firm has introduced a new product or process within a 3-year period (INOUT) and take only every third survey into account to avoid overlapping periods, i.e. I used the periods 1994-1996, 1997-1999, and 2000-2002. This strategy leads to a larger reduction of the number of observations. The persistence based on this innovation output indicator is likewise high: 84.9% of innovators in one 3-year period remained an innovator in the next period while 82.8% of non-innovators maintained their status. It turns out from the econometric analysis that the lagged dependent variable is

well as 95.9% (0→0), 4.1% (0→1), 17.8% (1→0), and 82.2% (1→1) in services (the first number in parentheses is the status in period t and the second one the status in period $t+1$). The corresponding rates for non-R&D-performing innovators are 93.8% (0→0), 6.2% (0→1), 62.3% (1→0), and 37.7% (1→1) in manufacturing as well as 89.7% (0→0), 10.3% (0→1), 54.7% (1→0), and 45.3% (1→1) in services.

highly significant again, and the partial effects are very similar in magnitude, as can be seen from Table 5.15. That is, the results corroborate true state dependence in innovation output as well. Furthermore, the other main findings asserted for the innovation input are confirmed for the innovation output indicator.[147]

Table 5.15: Innovation Input and Output Persistence in Manufacturing

	Innovation Input	Innovation Output
Dependent Variable	INNO	INOUT
PEA	35.8	34.2
APE	23.0	21.5
Obs	3,496	874

Note: Estimates are based on the same specification as in column (4) in Table 5.11.

5.8 Conclusion

In this chapter I have investigated the persistence of innovation behaviour of firms based on data for German manufacturing and services during the period 1994-2002. Using the estimator recently proposed by Wooldridge (2005) for dynamic binary choice panel data models, I have analysed whether innovation behaviour shows persistence at the firm level and whether state dependence drives this phenomenon.

A first main finding is that innovation behaviour is permanent at the firm level to a very large extent. Year-to-year transition rates indicate that in manufacturing nearly nine out of ten innovating firms in one period persisted in innovating in the subsequent period and about 84% of non-innovators maintained their state in the following period. Yet, innovation is not a once and for all phenomenon. 45% of manufacturing and 55% of service firms experienced at least one change in their innovation behaviour. In general, persistence is less pronounced in the service sector and exhibits a higher variance across time. Less surprisingly, persistence turns out to be higher in larger firms and in high-technology industries but is nevertheless relatively high in small firms.

The econometric results confirm the hypothesis of true state dependence. Partial effects were calculated highlighting the importance of this phenomenon. Depending on the calculation method, about one third to one half of the difference in the propensity to innovate between previous innovators and

---

[147] Detailed results are not reported here but are available on request.

non-innovators in manufacturing can be traced back to true state dependence. In the service sector, persistence is generally less prevalent, and state dependence effects are less pronounced, yet still highly significant. The fact that innovation performance exhibits true state dependence implies that innovation-stimulating policy measures, such as government support programmes, have the potential of long-lasting effects because they do not only affect the current innovation activities but are likely to induce a permanent change in favour of innovation.

The results confirm and highlight the role of innovative capabilities on the dynamics in firms' innovation behaviour. In addition to past innovation experience, knowledge provided by skilled employees has found to be important in generating innovations over time.

The analysis further emphasise the important role of unobserved heterogeneity in explaining the persistence of innovation. Leaving out this source of persistence in the empirical analysis can lead to highly misleading results. Some observed firm characteristics like size or export behaviour (determinants which themselves show high persistence) also make some firms more innovation-prone than others.

One topic on the agenda of future research is to test for dynamic completeness, that is to extend the estimator to allow for more complex lag structures of the lagged endogenous variable. So far I have assumed that dynamics are correctly specified by a first order process.

In contrast to the results previously found using patents, this analysis has shown that innovation activities are persistent at the firm level to a large extent. One interesting question for further research is, therefore, to analyse if the persistence in firms' innovation activities carry over to an asymmetric performance across firms over time. A major issue to be addressed in this line of research will be the direction of causality, that is does the causality run from innovation to productivity or is the reverse true?

Appendix D1: Average Partial Effects

The average partial effect (APE) of one of the explanatory variables measures the change of the expected probability of innovating at time t due to an infinitesimal increase in that variable, where the expectation is over the distribution of the individual heterogeneity μ_i. The expected probability of innovating at time t, ξ_t, is given by (see Wooldridge, 2005):

$$
\begin{aligned}
\xi_t &= E_{\mu_i} \left[P(y_t = 1 | y_{i,t-1} = y_{t-1}^o, x_{it} = x_t^o, \mu_i) \right] \\
&= E_{\mu_i} \left[P(y_t = 1 | y_{t-1}^o, x_t^o, \mu_i) \right] \\
&= E_{\mu_i} \left[\Phi \left(\gamma\, y_{t-1}^o + x_t^o\, \beta + \mu_i \right) \right].
\end{aligned} \tag{5.9}
$$

Recall that x_{it} is strictly exogenous conditional on μ_i. x_t^o and y_{t-1}^o are fixed values that have to be chosen, and I use the corresponding sample means at time t averaged across i. Inserting eq. (5.3) for μ_i into eq. (5.9), one can write the expected probability of innovating in the following way, where the expectation is now over the distribution of $(y_{i0}, \bar{x}_i, a_i)$:

$$
\begin{aligned}
\xi_t &= E_{(y_{i0}, \bar{x}_i, a_i)} \left[P(y_t = 1 | y_{t-1}^o, x_t^o, y_{i0}, \bar{x}_i) \right] \tag{5.10} \\
&= E_{(y_{i0}, \bar{x}_i, a_i)} \left[\Phi \left(\gamma\, y_{t-1}^o + x_t^o\, \beta + \alpha_0 + \alpha_1\, y_{i0} + \bar{x}_i\, \alpha_2 + a_i \right) \right].
\end{aligned}
$$

Applying iterated expectations, one gets:

$$
\begin{aligned}
\xi_t = E_{(y_{i0}, \bar{x}_i)} \{ E[\Phi(\gamma\, y_{t-1}^o + x_t^o\, \beta + \alpha_0 + \alpha_1\, y_{i0} + \bar{x}_i\, \alpha_2 + a_i) \\
| (y_{i0}, \bar{x}_i)] \}
\end{aligned} \tag{5.11}
$$

Since eq. (5.11) involves the expectation of a non-linear function, the solution is generally complicated, however, under the assumption made here, Wooldridge (2005) showed that the inside expectation is equal to:

$$
\begin{aligned}
&E \left[\Phi \left(\gamma\, y_{t-1}^o + x_t^o\, \beta + \alpha_0 + \alpha_1\, y_{i0} + \bar{x}_i\, \alpha_2 + a_i \right) | (y_{i0}, \bar{x}_i) \right] \\
&= \Phi \left[\left(\gamma\, y_{t-1}^o + x_t^o\, \beta + \alpha_0 + \alpha_1\, y_{i0} + \bar{x}_i\, \alpha_2 + a_i \right) / \left(1 + \sigma_a^2 \right)^{0.5} \right] \\
&= \Phi \left[\gamma_a\, y_{t-1}^o + x_t^o\, \beta_a + \alpha_{0a} + \alpha_{1a}\, y_{i0} + \bar{x}_i\, \alpha_{2a} \right],
\end{aligned} \tag{5.12}
$$

where the subscript a denotes the original parameter multiplied by $(1+\sigma_a^2)^{-0.5}$. Thus, the expected probability of innovating at time t can be calculated as:

$$
\xi_t = E_{(y_{i0}, \bar{x}_i)} \left\{ \Phi \left[\gamma_a\, y_{t-1}^o + x_t^o\, \beta_a + \alpha_{0a} + \alpha_{1a}\, y_{i0} + \bar{x}_i\, \alpha_{2a} \right] \right\}. \tag{5.13}
$$

A consistent estimator for expression (5.13) is given by:

$$\widehat{\xi}_t = \frac{1}{N} \sum_{i=1}^{N} \Phi \left[\widehat{\gamma}_a \, y^o_{t-1} + x^o_t \, \widehat{\beta}_a + \widehat{\alpha}_{0a} + \widehat{\alpha}_{1a} \, y_{i0} + \bar{x}_i \, \widehat{\alpha}_{2a} \right], \qquad (5.14)$$

where $\widehat{\gamma}_a$, $\widehat{\beta}_a$, $\widehat{\alpha}_{0a}$, $\widehat{\alpha}_{1a}$, and $\widehat{\alpha}_{2a}$ are based on $\widehat{\gamma}, \widehat{\beta}, \widehat{\alpha}_0, \widehat{\alpha}_1, \widehat{\alpha}_2$, and $\widehat{\sigma}^2_a$, that is the conditional maximum likelihood estimators of the dynamic probit model. As can be seen from eq. (5.14), the estimator does not condition on y_{i0} or $\bar{x}_i$ but averages these out over a large cross section, which provides a consistent estimator of the mean in the population. Furthermore, the estimator is $\sqrt{N}$-asymtotically normal.

For a continuous variable j, APE_t measures the change in the expected probability of innovating at time t, ξ_t, due to an infinitesimal increase of $x_{t,j}$:

$$APE_t = \frac{\partial}{\partial x_{t,j}} E \left\{ \Phi \left[\gamma_a \, y^o_{t-1} + x^o_t \, \beta_a + \alpha_{0a} + \alpha_{1a} \, y_{i0} + \bar{x}_i \, \alpha_{2a} \right] \right\}. \ (5.15)$$

Neglecting that an infinitesimal increase in $x_{t,j}$ also changes the mean value $\bar{x}_i$, one can estimate APE_t by:

$$\widehat{APE}_t = \frac{1}{N} \sum_{i=1}^{N} \widehat{\beta}_{a,j} \, \phi \left[\widehat{\gamma}_a \, y^o_{t-1} + x^o_t \, \widehat{\beta}_a + \widehat{\alpha}_{0a} + \widehat{\alpha}_{1a} \, y_{i0} + \bar{x}_i \, \widehat{\alpha}_{2a} \right]. \ (5.16)$$

In analogy to the calculation of marginal effects in the standard probit model, APE_t of a dummy variable is estimated as the discrete change in the expected probability as the dummy variable changes from 0 to 1. For example, in the case of the lagged dependent variable:

$$APE_t = E \left[P(y_t = 1 | y^o_{t-1} = 1, x^o_t, y_{i0}, \bar{x}_i) \right]$$
$$-E \left[P(y_t = 1 | y^o_{t-1} = 0, x^o_t, y_{i0}, \bar{x}_i) \right]. \qquad (5.17)$$

A consistent estimator of expression (5.17) is given by:

$$\widehat{APE}_t = \frac{1}{N} \sum_{i=1}^{N} \Phi \left[\widehat{\gamma}_a \cdot 1 + x_t \, \widehat{\beta}_a + \widehat{\alpha}_{0a} + \widehat{\alpha}_{1a} \, y_{i0} + \bar{x}_i \, \widehat{\alpha}_{2a} \right]$$
$$- \frac{1}{N} \sum_{i=1}^{N} \Phi \left[\widehat{\gamma}_a \cdot 0 + x_t \, \widehat{\beta}_a + \widehat{\alpha}_{0a} + \widehat{\alpha}_{1a} \, y_{i0} + \bar{x}_i \, \widehat{\alpha}_{2a} \right]. \ (5.18)$$

Note that in Wooldridge (2005) the average partial effect is calculated for a specific point in time (in his example, for the year 1987). However, since the panel data set used in this study has a rather long time dimension, I would like to calculate an average APE over the whole period. In the case of the lagged dependent variable, for instance, one is interested in:

$$APE = E\left[P(y = 1|y_{i,t-1} = y^o_{-1} = 1, x_{it} = x^o, y_{i0}, \bar{x}_i)\right]$$
$$-E\left[P(y = 1|y_{i,t-1} = y^o_{-1} = 0, x_{it} = x^o, y_{i0}, \bar{x}_i)\right]. \quad (5.19)$$

In that case a consistent estimator can be yielded by averaging across i and t:[148]

$$\widehat{APE} = \frac{1}{N}\frac{1}{T}\sum_{i=1}^{N}\sum_{t=1}^{T}\Phi\left[\widehat{\gamma}_a \cdot 1 + x^o\,\widehat{\beta}_a + \widehat{\alpha}_{0a} + \widehat{\alpha}_{1a}\,y_{i0} + \bar{x}_i\,\widehat{\alpha}_{2a}\right]$$

$$-\frac{1}{N}\frac{1}{T}\sum_{i=1}^{N}\sum_{t=1}^{T}\Phi\left[\widehat{\gamma}_a \cdot 0 + x^o\,\widehat{\beta}_a + \widehat{\alpha}_{0a} + \widehat{\alpha}_{1a}\,y_{i0} + \bar{x}_i\,\widehat{\alpha}_{2a}\right].(5.20)$$

Now I insert the corresponding sample means averaged across i and t for the fixed values x^o and y^o.

[148] The author would like to thank J. Wooldridge and F. Laisney for helpful discussions on this point. Any errors remain those of the author.

Appendix D2: Tables

Table 5.16: Individual Participation Pattern

No. of Participation[a]	Total firms #	Total firms %	Total obs #	Manufacturing firms[b] #	Manufacturing obs #	Services firms[b] #	Services obs #
1	5,949	43.3	5,949	2,803	2,803	3,146	3,146
2	2,499	18.2	4,998	1,223	2,446	1,276	2,552
3	1,769	12.9	5,307	876	2,629	893	2,678
4	1,109	8.1	4,436	575	2,298	535	2,138
5	803	5.8	4,015	464	2,320	339	1,695
6	590	4.3	3,540	323	1,936	267	1,604
7	560	4.1	3,920	337	2,360	223	1,560
8	253	1.8	2,024	253	2,024	–	–
9	220	1.6	1,980	220	1,980	–	–
Total	13,752	100	36,169	7,074	20,796	6,678	15,373

Notes: [a] The number of utilisable observations is higher than that which would arise from the participation pattern. This can be explained by the fact that since 1998 the survey is only sent to a sub-sample of firms in even years due to cost reasons. However, to maintain the panel structure with yearly waves, the most relevant variables are retrospectively asked for the preceding year in odd years.
[b] Some firms have changed their main business activity which defines their industry assignment and have switched between manufacturing and services during the considered period. The number of firms is the average number of firms, calculated as the number of observations divided by the number of participation.
Source: Mannheim Innovation Panel; own calculations.

Table 5.17: Distribution of the Unbalanced and Balanced Panel in Manufacturing

Distribution by:	Panel[a)]			Difference	
	T	U	B	B-T	B-U
Total No. of Obs	27,116	13,558	3,933		
Industry[b)]					
Mining	2.0	2.1	1.7	-0.3	-0.4
Food	6.3	6.0	5.5	-0.8	-0.5
Textile	5.2	4.9	4.9	-0.3	-0.0
Wood/printing	6.7	6.5	6.4	-0.3	-0.0
Chemicals	6.6	6.8	8.7	2.1	1.9
Plastic/rubber	6.8	7.7	8.4	1.6	0.8
Glass/ceramics	4.7	5.0	5.5	0.8	0.6
Metals	13.2	13.4	11.5	-1.6	-1.8
Machinery	14.3	14.5	13.0	-1.3	-1.5
Electrical engineering	8.0	7.8	7.8	-0.2	0.0
Medical instruments	6.5	6.8	7.8	1.3	1.1
Vehicles	4.6	4.5	4.4	-0.2	-0.1
Furniture/recycling	4.2	3.6	3.8	-0.4	0.2
Energy/water	4.4	4.8	5.9	1.5	1.1
Construction	6.6	5.9	4.6	-2.0	-1.3
Size[b)]					
0-4	2.7	1.8	1.6	-1.2	-0.3
5-9	6.9	6.5	5.5	-1.3	-1.0
10-19	12.1	11.6	10.2	-1.8	-1.4
20-49	17.8	18.2	19.7	1.9	1.5
50-99	15.2	15.7	14.3	-0.8	-1.3
100-199	13.0	13.7	13.8	0.8	0.2
200-499	15.5	16.4	17.5	2.0	1.1
500-999	7.6	8.0	8.3	0.7	0.3
1000+	8.9	8.2	9.1	0.3	1.0
Region[b)]					
West	68.2	66.8	65.7	-2.6	-1.1
East	31.8	33.2	34.3	2.6	1.1
Innovators[b)]	59.3	57.8	55.1	-4.2	-2.7

Notes: [a)] T: Unbalanced panel of all firms within the period 1994-2002. U: Unbalanced panel of firms with at least four consecutive observations within 1994-2002. B: Balanced panel of firms within 1994-2002.
[b)] Calculated as share of total number of observations (in %).
Source: Mannheim Innovation Panel; own calculations.

Table 5.18: Distribution of the Unbalanced and Balanced Panel in the Service Sector

Distribution by:	Panel[a]			Difference	
	T	U	B	B-T	B-U
Total No. of Obs	20,493	7,901	1,974		
Industry[b]					
Wholesale	11.4	12.0	10.7	-0.7	-1.2
Retail	10.4	12.8	11.9	1.5	-0.8
Transport	15.4	18.8	18.8	3.4	0.0
Banks/insurances	11.1	10.0	9.2	-1.8	-0.8
Computer	8.3	6.8	7.1	-1.1	0.3
Technical services	14.4	13.5	11.5	-2.9	-2.0
Consultancies	7.8	6.7	8.2	0.4	1.5
Other BRS	13.8	12.0	12.8	-1.0	0.8
Real estate/renting	6.7	7.5	9.7	3.0	2.2
Size[b]					
0-4	7.3	7.2	9.4	2.1	2.1
5-9	13.9	15.4	14.2	0.3	1.1
10-19	17.7	19.5	19.1	1.4	0.4
20-49	19.5	22.2	20.0	0.4	-2.2
50-99	11.3	12.1	12.9	1.6	0.8
100-199	9.6	9.8	11.0	1.4	1.2
200-499	8.0	7.0	6.5	-1.5	-0.5
500-999	4.5	2.8	1.8	-2.7	-0.9
1000+	7.9	4.1	5.2	-2.7	1.1
Region[b]					
West	62.5	57.4	57.9	-4.6	0.5
East	37.5	42.6	42.1	4.6	-0.5
Innovators[b]	44.5	37.6	35.8	-8.6	-1.8

Notes: [a] T: Unbalanced panel of all firms within the period 1996-2002. U: Unbalanced panel of firms with at least four consecutive observations within 1996-2002. B: Balanced panel of firms within 1996-2002. [b] Calculated as share of total number of observations (in %).
Source: Mannheim Innovation Panel; own calculations.

6

Summary and Conclusion

The process of firms' growth – in terms of productivity or employment – is a major concern of policy makers. In this context, innovations are widely considered to play a crucial role in stimulating firms' performance. This monograph has empirically investigated the impact of innovation on firms' performance by looking at three different topics:

1. How does innovation affect the employment growth of firms?
2. Does innovation increase firms' productivity performance?
3. Do firms innovate persistently over time?

The first and second question have been intensively examined in the literature using R&D- or patent-based measures. However, more recently comprehensive innovation data sets have become available which allow a deeper look into the black box of innovation processes and their impact on productivity and employment growth. In particular, they enable a separation of the effects induced by the introduction of new or improved products from those induced by the introduction of new production technologies.

The main conclusions drawn from the empirical analyses can be summarised as follows:[149]

- The different estimates underline the benefits of product innovations on firm performance, either in terms of productivity and employment growth. Based on a new, simple multi-product model, chapter 3 has shown that the net effect of product innovations is positive and that new products have been the major driver of employment growth in manufacturing and services in the period 1998-2002. Furthermore, employment effects do not significantly differ between firms that have positioned themselves on the cutting edge by launching products that are new to the market and firms which successfully pursue product imitation strategies. Employment effects in German firms have also been found very similar to those in Spain, the

---

[149] See sections 3.7, 4.8, and 5.8 for thorough summaries.

UK, and France, thus, supporting a discernible international pattern in the firm-level association between innovation and employment. The higher average employment growth rates in the other three countries can be largely explained by higher output growth rates in existing products while in Germany employment growth can be solely (manufacturing) or for the most part (services) attributed to the introduction of new products.

Using the 3-stage approach by Crépon et al. (1998) that links innovation input, innovation output, and productivity, chapter 4 further ascertains that labour productivity and labour productivity growth are both positively correlated with the success of product innovations in German manufacturing firms. This finding corroborates recent empirical findings for France, Sweden, or the Netherlands. However, carefully controlling for selectivity and endogeneity biases, it turns out that the estimated output elasticity of knowledge capital of about 0.04, approximated by product innovation output, is slightly lower than the usual output elasticity estimated on the basis of an R&D capital stock.

- The impact of process innovations on firm performance turns out to be variable. Chapter 3 provides evidence that in manufacturing firms negative displacement effects outweigh positive compensation effects. But, not all process innovations are associated with labour reduction. Jobs are merely deteriorated through rationalisation innovations and not as a consequence of other process innovations, such as those intended to improve product quality. Although the estimated employment effects of process innovations are negative, their overall size in explaining employment changes between 1998-2002 seems to be moderate compared to other productivity enhancing strategies, like organisational changes, sales of less productive parts of the firm, acquisitions of higher productive firms, improvements in human capital, learning, or spill–over effects. In the service sector, another picture emerges. Here, process innovations are not responsible for a significant downsizing in labour. This result might be explained by the specific nature of services and their production which are typically strongly geared towards customer preferences, and thus, clearly structured production processes are often lacking. Different competitive environments of manufacturing and service sector firms might be another cause. Chapter 4 further provides weak evidence that the productivity-stimulating effect of process innovation is positive and higher than that of product innovations in German manufacturing firms.

- Based on several descriptive statistics, chapter 5 has shown that firms' innovation behaviour is persistent over time to a very large extent. This is in contrast to previous results based on patent indicators. The econometric results further reveal that innovation experience is an important driver for this phenomenon. That is, innovating in one period significantly enhances the probability of innovating in the future. The fact that innovation performance exhibits such true state dependence implies that innovation-stimulating policy programmes open up potential long-lasting effects because they do not only affect the current innovation activities but are likely to induce a permanent change in favour of innovation. Furthermore, the persistence of innovation might be one cause of the observed highly skewed and persistent productivity distribution across firms over time. If this is the case, innovation has an additional indirect effect on firms' performance. The answer to the question of whether persistency of innovation carry over to an asymmetric productivity performance across firms over time is for future research.

Abbreviations

Adj. R^2	Adjusted R^2
ALS	Asymptotic least squares
APE	Average partial effect
BRS	Business-related services
CAD	Computer-aided design
CDM	Model by Crépon, Duguet, and Mairesse
coeff.	Coefficient
CIS	Community Innovation Survey
Corr Pred	Correct prediction
df	Degrees of freedom
DWH test	Durbin-Wu-Hausman test
EU	European Union
FE	Fixed effects
FIML	Full-information maximum likelihood
FRA	France
GDP	Gross domestic product
GER	Germany
GMM	General method of moments
HGB	Handelsgesetzbuch
i.i.d.	independently and identically distributed
IV	Instrumental variable
ICT	Information and communication technologies
ILO	International Labour Organisation (Internationale Arbeitsorganisation)
LM	Lagrange multiplier
LR	Likelihood ratio
ln L	Log-likelihood function
marg. eff.	Marginal effect
max	Maximum
med	Median
min	Minimum

MIP	Mannheim Innovation Panel
MPO	Medical, precision, and optical instruments
MSE	Mean squared error
NACE	Nomenclature générale des activités économiques dans les Communautés Européennes (Standard Classification of Industries in Europe)
Obs	Number of observations
OECD	Organisation for Economic Co-operation and Development (Organisation für wirtschaftliche Zusammenarbeit und Entwicklung)
OLS	Ordinary least squares
OSD	Observed state dependence effect
PEA	Partial effect at average value
R&D	Research and experimental development
RE	Random effects
RMSE	Root mean squared error
s.d.	Standard deviation
SPA	Spain
TFP	Total factor productivity
UK	United Kingdom
US	United States of America
ZEW	Centre for European Economic Research (Zentrum für Europäische Wirtschaftsforschung)
2SLS	Two-stage least squares
3SLS	Three-stage least squares

List of Figures

List of Tables

References

Abramovsky, L., J. Jaumandreu, E. Kremp, and B. Peters (2004), *National Differences in Innovation Behaviour: Facts and Explanations. Results Using Basic Statistics from CIS 3 for France, Germany, Spain and United Kingdom*, mimeo, Madrid.

Acemoglu, D., P. Aghion, and F. Zilibotti (2006), Distance to Frontier, Selection and Economic Growth, *Journal of the European Economic Association* 4(1), 37–74.

Aghion, P., N. Bloom, R. Blundell, R. Griffith, and P. Howitt (2005), Competition and Innovation: An Inverted-U Relationship, *Quarterly Journal of Economics* 120(2), 701–728.

Aghion, P. and P. Howitt (1992), A Model of Growth Through Creative Destruction, *Econometrica* 60(2), 323–351.

Aghion, P. and G. Saint-Paul (1998), Virtues of Bad Times: Interaction Between Productivity Growth and Economic Fluctuations, *Macroeconomic Dynamics* 2(3), 322–344.

Ahn, S. (2002), *Competition, Innovation and Productivity Growth: A Review of Theory and Evidence*, OECD Economics Department Working Papers 317, Paris.

Almus, M., S. Prantl, and D. Engel (2000), The ZEW Foundation Panels and the Mannheim Enterprise Panel (MUP) of the Centre for European Economic Research (ZEW), *Schmollers Jahrbuch* 120(2), 301–308.

Arnold, J. M. (2005), *Productivity Estimations at the Plant Level: A Practical Guide*, mimeo, Milan.

Arnold, J. M. and K. Hussinger (2005), Export Behavior and Firm Productivity in German Manufacturing: A Firm-Level Analysis, *Review of World Economics* 141(2), 219–243.

Aschhoff, B., C. Rammer, B. Peters, and T. Schmidt (2005), *Aufnahme/Ausweitung von Innovationsaktivitäten 2004/2005. Kurzbericht zur Innovationserhebung 2004*, Mannheim.

Baily, M. N., C. Hulten, and D. Campbell (1992), Productivity Dynamics in Manufacturing Plants, *Brookings Papers on Economic Activity: Microeconomics* 1992, 187–249.

Bartelsman, E. and P. Dhrymes (1998), Productivity Dynamics: U.S. Manufacturing Plants 1972–1986, *Journal of Productivity Analysis* 9(1), 5–34.

Bartelsman, E. and M. Doms (2000), Understanding Productivity: Lessons from Longitudinal Microdata, *Journal of Economic Literature* 38(3), 569–594.

Baum, C., M. Schaffer, and S. Stillman (2003), Instrumental Variables and GMM: Estimation and Testing, *Stata Journal* 3(1), 1–31.

Becker, W. and J. Peters (2000), *Technological Opportunities, Absorptive Capacities and Innovation*, Volkswirtschaftliche Diskussionsreihe 195, Augsburg.

Beise-Zee, M. and C. Rammer (2006), Local User-Producer Interaction in Innovation and Export Performance of Firms, *Small Business Economics* 27(2–3), 207–222.

Bernard, A. B. and B. Jensen (1999), Exceptional Exporter Performance: Cause, Effect or Both?, *Journal of International Economics* 47(1), 1–25.

Bernard, A. B. and J. Wagner (1997), Exports and Success in German Manufacturing, *Review of Word Economics* 133(1), 134–157.

Bertschek, I. and U. Kaiser (2004), Productivity Effects of Organizational Change: Microeconometric Evidence, *Management Science* 50(3), 394–404.

Biewen, M. (2004), *Measuring State Dependence in Individual Poverty Status: Are There Feedback Effects to Employment Decisions and Household Composition?*, IZA Discussion Paper 1138, Bonn.

Bishop, P. and N. Wiseman (1999), External Ownership and Innovation in the United Kingdom, *Applied Economics* 31(4), 443–450.

Blechinger, D., A. Kleinknecht, G. Licht, and F. Pfeiffer (1998), *The Impact of Innovation on Employment in Europe – An Analysis Using CIS Data*, ZEW Dokumentation 98-02, Mannheim.

Blechinger, D. and F. Pfeiffer (1999), Qualifikation, Beschäftigung und technischer Fortschritt. Empirische Evidenz mit den Daten des Mannheimer Innovationspanels, *Jahrbücher für Nationalökonomie und Statistik* 218(1+2), 128–146.

Blindum, S. W. (2003), *Relaxing the Strict Exogeneity Assumption in a Dynamic Random Probit Model*, CAM Working Papers 2003-04, Copenhagen.

Bloom, N., R. Sadun, and J. van Reenen (2007), *Americans Do I.T. Better: US Multinationals and the Productivity Miracle*, NBER Working Papers 13085, Cambridge, MA.

Blundell, R. and S. Bond (2000), GMM Estimations with Persistent Panel Data: An Application to Production Functions, *Econometric Reviews* 19(3), 321–340.

Blundell, R., R. Griffith, and J. van Reenen (1993), *Knowledge Stocks, Persistent Innovation and Market Dominance: Evidence from a Panel of British Manufacturing Firms*, IFS Working Paper W93/19, London.

Blundell, R., R. Griffith, and J. van Reenen (1995), Dynamic Count Data Models of Technological Innovation, *The Economic Journal* 105(429), 333–344.

Blundell, R., R. Griffith, and J. van Reenen (1999), Market Share, Market Value and Innovation in a Panel of British Manufacturing Firms, *Review of Economic Studies* 66(3), 529–554.

Bond, S., D. Harhoff, and J. van Reenen (2003), *Investment, R&D and Financial Constraints in Britain and Germany*, CEP Discussion Paper 0595, London.

Bottazzi, G., G. Dosi, M. Lippi, F. Pammolli, and M. Riccaboni (2001), Innovation and Corporate Growth in the Evolution of the Drug Industry, *International Journal of Industrial Organization* 19(7), 1161–1187.

Bound, J., C. Cummins, Z. Griliches, B. H. Hall, and A. B. Jaffe (1984), Who Does R&D and Who Patents, in: Griliches, Z. (Ed.), *R&D, Patents and Productivity*, Chicago, 21–54.

Bound, J., D. Jaeger, and R. Baker (1995), Problems with Instrumental Variables Estimation when the Correlation Between the Instruments and the Endogenous Explanatory Variable is Weak, *Journal of the American Statistical Association* 90(430), 443–450.

Brockhoff, K. (1998), *Forschung und Entwicklung: Planung und Kontrolle*, 5. edn., Munich.

Brouwer, E. and A. Kleinknecht (1997), Measuring the Unmeasurable: A Country's Non-R&D Expenditure on Product and Service Innovation, *Research Policy* 25(8), 1235–1242.

Brouwer, E., A. Kleinknecht, and J. Reijnen (1993), Employment Growth and Innovation at the Firm Level. An Empirical Study, *Journal of Evolutionary Economics* 3(2), 153–159.

Brynjolfsson, E. and L. Hitt (1996), Paradox Lost? Firm-Level Evidence on the Returns to Information Systems Spending, *Management Science* 42(4), 541–558.

Brynjolfsson, E. and L. Hitt (2000), Beyond Computation: Information Technology, Organizational Transformation and Business Performance, *Journal of Economic Perspectives* 14(4), 23–48.

Carro, J. M. (2006), Estimating Dynamic Panel Data Discrete Choice Models with Fixed Effects, *Journal of Econometrics,* forthcoming.

Cassiman, B. and R. Veugelers (2002), R&D Cooperation and Spillovers: Some Empirical Evidence from Belgium, *American Economic Review* 92(4), 1169–1184.

Cefis, E. (1999), *Persistence in Innovative Activities. An Empirical Analysis*, Ph.D. thesis, European University Institute, Florence.

Cefis, E. (2003a), Is There Persistence in Innovative Activities?, *International Journal of Industrial Organization* 21(4), 489–515.

Cefis, E. (2003b), Persistence in Profitability and in Innovative Activities, *Rivista Internazionale Di Scienze Sociali* 111(1), 19–37.

Cefis, E. and L. Orsenigo (2001), The Persistence of Innovative Activities. A Cross-Countries and Cross-Sectors Comparative Analysis, *Research Policy* 30(7), 1139–1158.

Chamberlain, G. (1980), Analysis of Covariance with Qualitative Data, *Review of Economic Studies* 47(1), 225–238.

Chennells, L. and J. van Reenen (1999), *Has Technology Hurt Less Skilled Workers? An Econometric Survey of the Effects of Technical Change on the Structure of Pay and Jobs*, IFS Working Paper W99/27, London.

Chennells, L. and J. van Reenen (2002), Technical Change and the Structure of Employment and Wages: A Survey on the Microeconometric Evidence, in: Greenan, N., Y. L'Horty, and J. Mairesse (Eds.), *Productivity, Inequality and the Digital Economy: A Transatlantic Perspective*, Cambridge, MA, 175–224.

Clark, K. B. (1987), Managing Technology in International Competition: The Case of Product Development in Response to Foreign Entry, in: Spence, M. and H. Hazard (Eds.), *International Competitiveness*, Cambridge, MA, 9–30.

Cohen, W. M. (1995), Empirical Studies of Innovative Activity, in: Stoneman, P. (Ed.), *Handbook of the Economics of Innovation and Technological Change*, Oxford, 182–264.

Cohen, W. M. and S. Klepper (1992a), The Anatomy of Industry R&D Intensity Distributions, *American Economic Review* 82(4), 773–799.

Cohen, W. M. and S. Klepper (1992b), The Tradeoff Between Firm Size and Diversity in the Pursuit of Technological Progress, *Small Business Economics* 4(1), 1–14.

Cohen, W. M. and S. Klepper (1996), A Reprise of Size and R&D, *The Economic Journal* 106(437), 925–951.

Cohen, W. M. and R. Levin (1989), Empirical Studies of Innovation and Market Structure, in: Schmalensee, R. and R. D. Willig (Eds.), *Handbook of Industrial Organization*, Vol. 2, Amsterdam, 1059–1107.

Cohen, W. M., R. Levin, and D. Mowery (1987), Firm Size and R&D Intensity: A Re-Examination, *Journal of Industrial Economics* 35(4), 543–463.

Cohen, W. M. and D. A. Levinthal (1989), Innovation and Learning: The Two Faces of R&D, *The Economic Journal* 99(397), 569–596.

Cohen, W. M. and D. A. Levinthal (1990), Absorptive Capacity: A New Perspective on Learning and Innovation, *Administrative Science Quarterly* 35(1), 128–158.

Cox, D. R. and N. Reid (1987), Parameter Orthogonality and Approximate Conditional Inference, *Journal of the Royal Statistical Society* 49(1), 1–39.

Crépon, B., E. Duguet, and J. Mairesse (1998), Research Innovation and Productivity: An Econometric Analysis at the Firm Level, *Economics of Innovation and New Technology* 7(2), 115–158.

Criscuolo, C. and J. Haskel (2003), *Innovations and Productivity Growth in the UK: Evidence from CIS2 and CIS3*, CeRiBA Discussion Paper EBPF03-3(10), London.

Criscuolo, C., J. Haskel, and M. Slaughter (2005), *Global Engagement and the Innovation Activities of Firms*, NBER Working Paper 11479, Cambridge, MA.

Czarnitzki, D. and K. Kraft (2004a), Firm Leadership and Innovative Performance: Evidence from Seven EU Countries, *Small Business Economics* 22(5), 325–332.

Czarnitzki, D. and K. Kraft (2004b), Management Control and Innovative Activity, *Review of Industrial Organization* 24(1), 1–24.

Davidson, R. and J. MacKinnon (1993), *Estimation and Inference in Econometrics*, New York.

De Loecker, J. (2004), *Do Exports Generate Higher Productivity? Evidence from Slovenia*, Licos Discussion Paper 151/2004, Leuven.

Dosi, G. (1988), Sources, Procedures, and Microeconomic Effects of Innovation, *Journal of Economic Literature* 26(3), 1120–1171.

Dosi, G. (1997), Opportunities, Incentives and the Collective Patterns of Technological Change, *The Economic Journal* 107(444), 1530–1547.

Dosi, G., O. Marsili, L. Orsenigo, and R. Salvatore (1995), Learning, Market Selection and the Evolution of Industrial Structures, *Small Business Economics* 7(6), 411–436.

Duguet, E. and S. Monjon (2004), *Is Innovation Persistent at the Firm Level? An Econometric Examination Comparing the Propensity Score and Regression Methods*, Cahiers de la Maison des Sciences Economiques v04075, Paris.

Easterbrook, F. (1984), Two Agency-Cost Explanations of Dividends, *American Economic Review* 74(4), 650–659.

Ebling, G., S. Gottschalk, N. Janz, and H. Niggemann (2000), *Prospects of the German Economy – Innovation Activities in Manufacturing and Mining. Survey 1999*, Mannheim.

Ebling, G. and N. Janz (1999), *Export and Innovation Activities in the German Service Sector: Empirical Evidence at the Firm Level*, ZEW Discussion Paper 99-53, Mannheim.

Engel, D. and M. Keilbach (2007), Firm Level Implications of Early Stage Venture Capital Investment – An Empirical Investigation, *Journal of Empirical Finance* 14(2), 150–167.

Entorf, H. and W. Pohlmeier (1990), Employment, Innovation and Export Activity: Evidence from Firm-Level Data, in: Florens, J.-P., M. Ivaldi, J.-J. Laffont, and F. Laisney (Eds.), *Microeconometrics: Surveys and Applications*, Oxford, 394–415.

Eswaran, M. (1994), Cross-Licensing of Competing Patents as a Facilitating Device, *Canadian Journal of Economics* 27(3), 689–708.

Eurostat (1992), *Nace Rev. 1*, Paris.

Eurostat (2004), *Innovation in Europe. Results for the EU, Iceland and Norway*, Luxemburg.

Evenson, R. E. and L. E. Westphal (1995), Technological Change and Technology Strategy, in: Chenery, H. and T. Srinivasan (Eds.), *Handbook of Development Economics*, Vol. 3A, Amsterdam, 2209–2299.

Falk, M. (1999), *Technological Innovations and the Expected Demand for Skilled Labour at the Firm Level*, ZEW Discussion Paper 99-59, Mannheim.

Falk, M. and K. Seim (2000), Workers' Skill Level and Information Technology: A Censored Regression Model, *International Journal of Manpower* 22(1,2), 98–120.

Falk, M. and K. Seim (2001), The Impact of Information Technology on High-Skilled Labour in Services: Evidence from Firm-Level Panel Data, *Economics of Innovation and New Technology* 10(4), 289–323.

Felder, J., G. Licht, E. Nerlinger, and H. Stahl (1996), Factors Determining R&D and Innovation Expenditure in German Manufacturing Industries, in: Kleinknecht, A. (Ed.), *Determinants of Innovation: The Message from New Indicators*, London, 125–154.

Fitzenberger, B. (1999), International Trade and the Skill Structure of Wages and Employment in Germany, *Jahrbücher für Nationalökonomie und Statistik* 219(1/2), 67–89.

Flaig, G. and M. Stadler (1994), Success Breeds Success. The Dynamics of the Innovation Process, *Empirical Economics* 19(1), 55–68.

Flaig, G. and M. Stadler (1998), On the Dynamics of Product and Process Innovations. A Bivariate Random Effects Probit Model, *Jahrbücher für Nationalökonomie und Statistik* 217(4), 401–417.

Franz, W. (2006), *Arbeitsmarktökonomik*, 6. edn., Berlin.

Freeman, C. and L. Soete (1997), *The Economics of Industrial Innovation*, 3. edn., London.

Garcia, A., J. Jaumandreu, and C. Rodriguez (2002), *Innovation and Jobs: Evidence from Manufacturing Firms*, mimeo, Madrid.

Gemünden, H. G., P. Heydebreck, and R. Herden (1992), Technological Interweavement: A Mean of Achieving Innovation Success, *R&D Management* 22(4), 359–376.

Geroski, P. A. (1995), What Do We Know About Entry?, *International Journal of Industrial Organization* 13(4), 421–440.

Geroski, P. A. and A. Jacquemin (1988), The Persistence of Profits: A European Comparison, *The Economic Journal* 98(391), 375–389.

Geroski, P. A., J. van Reenen, and C. F. Walters (1997), How Persistently Do Firms Innovate?, *Research Policy* 26(1), 33–48.

Gibrat, R. (1934), *Les Inégalités Économiques; Applications: Aux Inégalités des Richesses, à la Concentration des Enterprises, aux Populations des Villes, aux Statistiques des Familles, etc., d'une Loi Nouvelle, la Loi des l'Effet Proportionnel*, Paris.

Gottschalk, S., N. Janz, B. Peters, C. Rammer, and T. Schmidt (2002), *Innovationsverhalten der deutschen Wirtschaft: Hintergrundbericht zur Innovationserhebung 2001*, ZEW Dokumentation 02-03, Mannheim.

Greenan, N. and D. Guellec (2000), Technological Innovation and Employment Reallocation, *Labour* 14(4), 547–590.

Griffith, R., E. Huergo, J. Mairesse, and B. Peters (2006), Innovation and Productivity Across Four European Countries, *Oxford Review of Economic Policy* 22(4), 483–498.

Griliches, Z. (1986), Productivity, R&D and Basic Research at the Firm Level in the 1970s', *American Economic Review* 76(1), 141–154.

Griliches, Z. (1990), Patent Statistics as Economic Indicators: A Survey, *Journal of Economic Literature* 28(4), 1661–1707.

Griliches, Z. (1994), Productivity, R&D and the Data Constraint, *The American Economic Review* 84(1), 1–23.

Griliches, Z. (1995), R&D and Productivity: Econometric Results and Measurement Issues, in: Stoneman, P. (Ed.), *Handbook of the Economics of Innovation and Technological Change*, Oxford, 52–89.

Griliches, Z. (1998), *R&D and Productivity: The Econometric Evidence*, Chicago.

Griliches, Z. and F. Lichtenberg (1984), R&D and Productivity Growth at the Industry Level: Is There Still a Relationship?, in: Griliches, Z. (Ed.), *R&D, Patents and Productivity*, Chicago, 465–496.

Griliches, Z. and J. Mairesse (1983), Comparing Productivity Growth: An Exploration of French and U.S. Industrial and Firm Data, *European Economic Review* 21(1–2), 89–119.

Griliches, Z. and J. Mairesse (1984), Productivity and R&D at the Firm Level, in: Griliches, Z. (Ed.), *R&D, Patents and Productivity*, Chicago, 339–374.

Grupp, H. (1997), *Messung und Erklärung des technischen Wandels. Grundzüge einer empirischen Innovationsökonomik*, Berlin.

Hagedoorn, J. (2002), Inter-Firm R&D Partnership: An Overview of Major Trends and Patterns Since 1960, *Research Policy* 31(4), 477–492.

Hahn, J. and J. A. Hausman (2002), A New Specification Test for the Validity of Instrumental Variables, *Econometrica* 70(1), 163–189.

Hahn, J. and J. A. Hausman (2003), *IV Estimation with Valid and Invalid Instruments*, MIT Department of Economics Working Paper 03-26, Cambridge, MA.

Hall, B. H., F. Lotti, and J. Mairesse (2006), *Employment, Innovation, and Productivity: Evidence from Italian Microdata*, UNU-MERIT Working Papers 2006-043, Maastricht.

Hall, B. H. and J. Mairesse (1995), Exploring the Relationship Between R&D and Productivity in French Manufacturing Firms, *Journal of Econometrics* 65(1), 263–293.

Hall, B. H. and R. H. Ziedonis (2001), The Patent Paradox Revisited: An Empirical Study of Patenting in the U.S. Semiconductor Industry, 1979-1995, *RAND Journal of Economics* 32(1), 101–128.

Hall, R. (1990), Invariance Properties of Solow's Productivity Residual, in: Diamond, P. (Ed.), *Growth/Productivity/Unemployment – Essays to Celebrate Bob Solow's Birthday*, Cambridge, MA, 71–112.

Harhoff, D. and G. Licht (1994), Das Mannheimer Innovationspanel, in: Hochmuth, U. and J. Wagner (Eds.), *Firmenpanelstudien in Deutschland: Konzeptionelle Überlegungen und empirische Analysen*, Tübingen, 255–284.

Harris, R. (1991), Technological and Regional Policy: A Case Study of Northern Ireland, *Applied Economics* 23(4A), 685–696.

Harrison, R., J. Jaumandreu, J. Mairesse, and B. Peters (2005), *Does Innovation Stimulate Employment? A Firm-Level Analysis Using Comparable Micro Data on Four European Countries*, MPRA Discussion Paper 1245, Munich.

Hauschildt, J. (2004), *Innovationsmanagement*, 4. edn., Munich.

Hausman, J. A. (2001), Mismeasured Variables in Econometric Analysis: Problems from the Right and Problems from the Left, *Journal of Economic Perspectives* 15(4), 57–68.

Heckman, J. J. (1976), The Common Structure of Statistical Models of Truncation, Sample Selection and Limited Dependent Variables and a Simple Estimator for Such Models, *Annals of Economic and Social Measurement* 5(4), 475–492.

Heckman, J. J. (1979), Sample Selection Bias as a Specification Error, *Econometrica* 47(1), 153–162.

Heckman, J. J. (1981a), Heterogeneity and State Dependence, in: Rosen, S. (Ed.), *Studies in Labour Markets*, Chicago, 91–139.

Heckman, J. J. (1981b), Statistical Models for Discrete Panel Data, in: Manski, C. and D. McFadden (Eds.), *Structural Analysis of Discrete Data with Econometric Applications*, Cambridge, MA, 114–178.

Hempell, T. (2003), Innovation im Dienstleistungssektor, in: Janz, N. and G. Licht (Eds.), *Innovationsforschung heute – Die Mannheimer Innovationspanels*, ZEW Wirtschaftsanalysen, Vol. 63, Baden-Baden, 149–184.

Hempell, T. (2004), What's Spurious, What's Real? Measuring the Productivity Impacts of ICT at the Firm Level, *Empirical Economics* 30(2), 427–464.

Henderson, R. (1993), Underinvestment and Incompetence as Responses to Radical Innovation: Evidence from the Photolithographic Alignment Equipment Industry, *Rand Journal of Economics* 24(2), 248–270.

Himmelberg, C. P. and B. C. Petersen (1994), R&D and Internal Finance: A Panel Study of Small Firms in High-Tech Industries, *Review of Economics and Statistics* 76(1), 38–51.

Honoré, B. and E. Kyriazidou (2000), Panel Data Discrete Choice Models with Lagged Dependent Variables, *Econometrica* 68(4), 839–874.

Honoré, B. and A. Lewbel (2002), Semiparametric Binary Choice Panel Data Models Without Strictly Exogenous Regressors, *Econometrica* 70(5), 2053–2063.

Howell, J. R. (1984), The Location of Research and Development: Some Observations and Evidence from Britain, *Regional Studies* 18(1), 13–29.

Janz, N. (2003), Innovationserfolge und die Aneignung von Innovationserträgen, in: Janz, N. and G. Licht (Eds.), *Innovationsforschung heute – Die Mannheimer Innovationspanels*, ZEW Wirtschaftsanalysen, Vol. 63, Baden-Baden, 73–112.

Janz, N., G. Ebling, S. Gottschalk, and H. Niggemann (2001), The Mannheim Innovation Panels (MIP and MIP-S) of the Centre for European Economic Research (ZEW), *Schmollers Jahrbuch* 121(1), 123–129.

Janz, N., G. Ebling, S. Gottschalk, and B. Peters (2002), Die Mannheimer Innovationspanels, *Allgemeines Statistisches Archiv* 86(2), 189–201.

Janz, N., G. Ebling, S. Gottschalk, B. Peters, and T. Schmidt (2002), *Innovation Activities in the German Economy – Report on Indicators from the Innovation Survey 2001*, Mannheim.

Janz, N., H. Lööf, and B. Peters (2004), Firm Level Innovation and Productivity – Is There a Common Story Across Countries?, *Problems and Perspectives in Management* 2, 184–204.

Jaumandreu, J. (2003), *Does Innovation Spur Employment? A Firm-Level Analysis Using Spanish CIS Data*, mimeo, Madrid.

Jefferson, G. H., B. Huamao, G. Xiaojing, and Y. Xiaoyun (2006), R&D Performance in Chinese Industry, *Economics of Innovation and New Technology* 15(4/5), 345–366.

Jensen, M. C. and W. H. Meckling (1976), Theory of the Firm: Managerial Behavior, Agency Costs and Ownership Structure, *Journal of Financial Economics* 3(4), 305–360.

Jovanovic, B. (1982), Selection and the Evolution of Industry, *Econometrica* 50(3), 649–670.

Judd, K. L. (1985), On the Performance of Patents, *Econometrica* 53(3), 567–585.

Kaiser, U. (2000), New Technologies and the Demand for Heterogeneous Labor: Firm-Level Evidence for German Business-Related Services, *Economics of Innovation and New Technology* 9(5), 465–484.

Kaiser, U. (2001), The Impact of Foreign Competition and New Technologies on the Demand for Heterogeneous Labor: Empirical Evidence from the German Business-Related Services Sector, *Review of Industrial Organization* 19(1), 109–120.

Kaiser, U. and H. C. Kongsted (2004), *True Versus Spurious State Dependence in Firm Performance: The Case of West German Exports*, CEBR Working Paper 2004-07, Copenhagen.

Kamien, M. I. and N. L. Schwartz (1975), Market Structure and Innovation: A Survey, *Journal of Economic Literature* 13(1), 1–37.

Kamien, M. I. and N. L. Schwartz (1982), *Market Structure and Innovation*, Cambridge, MA.

Katsoulacos, Y. S. (1984), Product Innovation and Employment, *European Economic Review* 26(1/2), 83–108.

Kleinknecht, A. (1987), Measuring R&D in Small Firms: How Much Are We Missing?, *Journal of Industrial Economics* 36(2), 253–256.

Kleinknecht, A. (1990), Are There Schumpeterian Waves of Innovations?, *Cambridge Journal of Economics* 14(1), 81–92.

Kleinknecht, A. and T. P. Poot (1992), Do Regions Matter for R&D?, *Regional Studies* 26(3), 221–232.

Klette, T. J. and S. E. Forre (1998), Innovation and Job Creation in a Small Open Economy – Evidence from Norwegian Manufacturing Plants 1982-1992, *Economics of Innovation and New Technology* 5(2), 247–272.

Klette, T. J. and Z. Griliches (1996), The Inconsistency of Common Scale Estimators when Output Prices Are Unobserved and Endogenous, *Journal of Applied Econometrics* 11(4), 343–361.

Klette, T. J. and S. Kortum (2004), Innovating Firms and Aggregate Innovation, *Journal of Political Economy* 112(5), 986–1018.

Kline, S. J. (1985), Innovation Is Not a Linear Process, *Research Management* 28(4), 36–45.

Klomp, L. and G. van Leeuwen (2001), Linking Innovation and Firm Performance: A New Approach, *International Journal of the Economics of Business* 8(3), 343–364.

Knight, K. E. (1967), A Descriptive Model of Intra-Firm Innovation-Process, *The Journal of Business* 40(4), 478–496.

König, H. and J. Felder (1994), Innovationsverhalten der deutschen Wirtschaft, in: Zoche, P. and D.-M. Harmsen (Eds.), *Innovation in der Informationstechnik für die nächste Dekade. Bedarfsfelder und Chancen für den Technologiestandort Deutschland*, Karlsruhe, 35–64.

König, H., F. Laisney, M. Lechner, and W. Pohlmeier (1994), On the Dynamics of Process Innovative Activity: An Empirical Investigation Using Panel Data, in: Oppenländer, K.-H. and G. Poser (Eds.), *The Explanatory Power of Business Cycle Surveys*, Avebury, 243–262.

König, H., G. Licht, and H. Buscher (1995), Employment, Investment and Innovation at the Firm Level, in: OECD (Ed.), *The OECD Jobs Study – Investment, Productivity and Employment*, Paris, 67–81.

Kortum, S. and J. Lerner (2000), Assessing the Contribution of Venture Capital to Innovation, *Rand Journal of Economics* 31(4), 674–692.

Krugman, P. (1979), A Model of Innovation, Technology Transfer and the World Distribution of Income, *Journal of Political Economy* 87(2), 253–266.

Kukuk, M. and M. Stadler (2001), Financing Constraints and the Timing of Innovations in the German Services Sector, *Empirica* 28(3), 277–292.

Lerner, J., J. Tirole, and M. Strojwas (2007), The Design of Patent Pools: The Determinants of Licensing Rules, *RAND Journal of Economics,* forthcoming.

Levin, R. C., W. M. Cohen, and D. C. Mowery (1985), R&D Appropriability, Opportunity and Market Structure: New Evidence on Some Schumpeterian Hypotheses, *American Economic Review* 75(2), 20–24.

Levinsohn, J. and A. Petrin (2003), Estimating Production Functions Using Inputs to Control for Unobservables, *Review of Economics Studies* 70(2), 317–342.

Lewbel, A. (2005), *Simple Endogenous Binary Choice and Selection Panel Model Estimators*, Boston College Working Papers in Economics 613, Boston.

Lichtenberg, F. (1995), The Output Contributions of Computer Equipment and Personnel: A Firm-Level Analysis, *Economics of New Technology and Innovation* 3(3/4), 201–217.

Lichtenberg, F. and D. Siegel (1990), The Effects of Leveraged Buyouts on Productivity and Related Aspects of Firms Behaviour, *Journal of Financial Economics* 27(1), 165–194.

Link, A. (1981), Basic Research and Productivity Increase in Manufacturing: Additional Evidence, *American Economic Review* 71(5), 1111–1112.

Llorca Vivero, R. (2002), The Impact of Process Innovations on Firm's Productivity Growth: The Case of Spain, *Applied Economics* 34(8), 1007–1016.

Lööf, H. and A. Heshmati (2002), Knowledge Capital and Performance Heterogeneity: A Firm Level Innovation Study, *International Journal of Production Economics* 76(1), 61–85.

Lööf, H., A. Heshmati, R. Asplund, and S. Naas (2003), Innovation and Performance in Manufacturing Industries: A Comparison of the Nordic Countries, *Journal of Management Research* 2, 5–36.

Love, J. H., B. Ashcroft, and S. Dunlop (1996), Corporate Structure, Ownership and the Likelihood of Innovation, *Applied Economics* 28(6), 737–746.

Love, J. H. and S. Roper (2001), Location and Network Effects on Innovation Success: Evidence for UK, German and Irish Manufacturing Plants, *Research Policy* 30(4), 643–661.

Lucas, R. E. (1988), On the Mechanics of Economic Development, *Journal of Monetary Economics* 22(1), 3–42.

Maddala, G. (1983), *Limited-Dependent and Qualitative Variables in Econometrics*, Cambridge, MA.

Maidique, M. (1980), Entrepreneurs, Champions and Technological Innovation, *Sloan Management Review (Winter)* 21(2), 59–76.

Mairesse, J., B. H. Hall, and B. Mulkay (1999), Firm-Investment in France and the United States: An Exploration of What We Have Learned in Twenty Years, *Annales d'Economie et de Statistiques* 55–56, 27–67.

Mairesse, J. and P. Mohnen (2005), The Importance of R&D for Innovation: A Reassessment Using French Survey Data, *The Journal of Technology Transfer* 30(1-2), 183–197.

Mairesse, J. and M. Sassenou (1991), R&D and Productivity: A Survey of Econometric Studies at the Firm Level, *STI Review* 8, 9–43.

Malerba, F. and L. Orsenigo (1993), Technological Regimes and Firm Behaviour, *Industrial Corporate Change* 2(1), 45–71.

Malerba, F. and L. Orsenigo (1999), Technological Entry, Exit and Survival: An Empirical Analysis of Patent Data, *Research Policy* 28(6), 643–660.

Manez Castillejo, J. A., M. E. Rochina Barrachina, A. Sanchis Llopis, and J. Sanchis Llopis (2004), *A Dynamic Approach to the Decision to Invest in R&D: The Role of Sunk Costs*, mimeo, Valencia.

Mansfield, E. (1968), *Industrial Research and Technological Innovation: An Econometric Analysis*, New York.

McKelvey, R. and W. Zavoina (1975), A Statistical Model for the Analysis of Ordinal Level, *Journal of Mathematical Sociology* 4(1), 103–120.

Mueller, D. C. (1967), The Firm's Decision Process: An Econometric Investigation, *Quarterly Journal of Economics* 81(1), 58–87.

Mueller, D. C. (1977), The Persistence of Profits Above the Norm, *Economica* 44(176), 369–380.

Mulkay, B., B. H. Hall, and J. Mairesse (2001), Firm Level Investment and R&D in France and the United States: A Comparison, in: Deutsche Bundesbank (Ed.), *Investing Today for the World of Tomorrow: Studies on the Investment Process in Europe*, New York, 229–273.

Nelson, R. R. (1959), The Simple Economics of Basic Scientific Research, *Journal of Political Economy* 67(3), 297–306.

Nelson, R. R. (1981), Research on Productivity Growth and Productivity Differences: Dead Ends and New Departures, *Journal of Economic Literature* 8(4), 1137–1177.

Nelson, R. R. (1988), Modelling the Connections in the Cross-Section Between Technical Progress and R&D Intensity, *RAND Journal of Economics* 19(3), 478–485.

Nelson, R. R. (1991), Why Do Firms Differ, and How Does It Matter?, *Strategic Management Journal* 12(Winter Special Issue), 61–74.

Nelson, R. R. and S. Winter (1982), *An Evolutionary Theory of Economic Change*, Cambridge, MA.

Nickell, S. (1999), Product Markets and Labour Markets, *Labour Economics* 6(1), 1–20.

OECD (2002), *Frascati Manual: 2002, Proposed Standard Practice for Surveys on Research and Experimental Development*, 6. edn., Paris.

OECD (2005a), *OECD Economic Outlook*, Vol. 77, Paris.

OECD (2005b), *OECD Factbook 2005*, Paris.

OECD (2005c), *OECD Science, Technology and Industry Scoreboard*, Paris.

OECD and Eurostat (1997), *Oslo Manual: Proposed Guidelines for Collecting and Interpreting Technological Innovation Data*, 2. edn., Paris.

OECD and Eurostat (2005), *Oslo Manual: Proposed Guidelines for Collecting and Interpreting Technological Innovation Data*, 3. edn., Paris.

Olley, S. and A. Pakes (1996), The Dynamics of Productivity in the Telecommunications Equipment Industry, *Econometrica* 64(6), 1263–1298.

Pagan, A. R. and D. Hall (1983), Diagnostic Tests as Residual Analysis, *Econometric Reviews* 2(2), 159–218.

Pakes, A. and Z. Griliches (1984), Patents and R&D at the Firm Level: A First Look, in: Griliches, Z. (Ed.), *R&D, Patents, and Productivity*, Chicago, 55–71.

Parisi, M. L., F. Schiantarelli, and A. Sembenelli (2006), Productivity, Innovation and R&D: Micro Evidence for Italy, *European Economic Review* 50(8), 2037–2061.

Patel, R. and K. Pavitt (1995), Patterns of Technological Activity: Their Measurement and Interpretation, in: Stoneman, P. (Ed.), *Handbook of the Economics of Innovation and Technological Change*, Oxford, 14–51.

Peters, B. (2003), Innovation und Beschäftigung, in: Janz, N. and G. Licht (Eds.), *Innovationsforschung heute – Die Mannheimer Innovationspanels*, ZEW Wirtschaftsanalysen, Vol. 63, Baden-Baden, 113–148.

Peters, B. (2004), *Employment Effects of Different Innovation Activities: Microeconometric Evidence*, ZEW Discussion Paper 04-73, Mannheim.

Peters, B. (2005a), *Persistence of Innovation: Stylised Facts and Panel Data Evidence*, ZEW Discussion Paper 05-81, Mannheim.

Peters, B. (2005b), *The Relationship Between Product and Process Innovation and Firm Performance. Microeconometric Evidence*, mimeo, Mannheim.

Petit, R. (1995), Employment and Technological Change, in: Stoneman, P. (Ed.), *Handbook of the Economics of Innovation and Technological Change*, Oxford, 366–408.

Pfeiffer, F. and M. Falk (1999), *Der Faktor Humankapital in der Volkswirtschaft, Berufliche Spezialisierung und Technologische Leistungsfähigkeit*, ZEW Wirtschaftsanalysen, Vol. 35, Baden-Baden.

Phillips, A. (1971), *Technology and Market Structure: A Study of the Aircraft Industry*, Lexington.

Rammer, C. (2004), *Unternehmensdynamik in Deutschland 1995-2003: Die Rolle forschungs- und wissensintensiver Branchen und eine Einordnung im internationalen Vergleich*, ZEW Studien zum deutschen Innovationssystem 11, Mannheim.

Rammer, C., B. Aschhoff, T. Doherr, B. Peters, and T. Schmidt (2005), *Innovation in Germany – Results of the German Innovation Survey 2004*, Mannheim.

Rammer, C. and G. Metzger (2003), *Unternehmensdynamik in forschungs- und wissensintensiven Wirtschaftszweigen in Deutschland und der deutsche Wagniskapitalmarkt*, ZEW Studien zum deutschen Innovationssystem 14, Mannheim.

Rammer, C., B. Peters, T. Schmidt, B. Aschhoff, T. Doherr, and H. Niggemann (2005), *Innovationen in Deutschland. Ergebnisse der Erhebung 2003 des Mannheimer Innovationspanels*, ZEW Wirtschaftsanalysen, Vol. 78, Baden-Baden.

Raymond, W., P. Mohnen, F. Palm, and S. Schim van der Loeff (2006), *Persistence of Innovation in Dutch Manufacturing: Is It Spurious?*, UNU-Merit Working Paper 2006-011, Maastricht.

Regev, H. (1998), Innovation, Skilled Labour, Technology and Performance in Israeli Industrial Firms, *Economics of Innovation and New Technology* 5(2-4), 301–323.

Reinganum, J. F. (1983), Uncertain Innovation and the Persistence of Monopoly, *American Economic Review* 73(4), 741–748.

Roberts, E. B. (1987), Introduction: Managing Technological Innovation – A Search for Generalizations, in: Roberts, E. B. (Ed.), *Generating Technological Innovation*, New York, 3–21.

Rogers, E. (1995), *Diffusion of Innovations*, 4. edn., New York.

Rogers, M. (2004), Networks, Firm Size and Innovation, *Small Business Economics* 22(2), 141–153.

Romer, P. (1986), Increasing Returns and Long-Run Growth, *Journal of Political Economy* 94(5), 1002–1037.

Romer, P. (1990), Endogenous Technological Change, *Journal of Political Economy* 98(5), 71–102.

Rottmann, H. and M. Ruschinski (1998), The Labour Demand and the Innovation Behaviour of Firms, *Jahrbücher für Nationalökonomie und Statistik* 217(6), 741–752.

Ruud, P. (1986), Consistent Estimation of Limited Dependent Variable Models Despite Misspecification of Distribution, *Journal of Econometrics* 32(1), 157–187.

Sachverständigenrat (2004), *Jahresgutachten 2004/05: Erfolge im Ausland – Herausforderungen im Inland*, Wiesbaden.

Sachverständigenrat (2005), *Jahresgutachten 2005/2006: Die Chance nutzen – Reformen mutig voranbringen*, Wiesbaden.

Sapir, A., P. Aghion, G. Bertola, M. Hellwig, J. Pisani-Ferry, D. Rosati, J. Vinals, and H. Wallace (2003), *An Agenda for a Growing Europe. Making the EU Economic System Deliver*, Report of an Independent High Level Group established at the initiative of the President of the European Commission, Brussels.

Scherer, F. M. (1965), Firm Size, Market Structure, Opportunity and the Output of Patented Inventions, *American Economic Review* 55(5), 1097–1125.

Scherer, F. M. (1967), Market Structure and the Employment of Scientists and Engineers, *American Economic Review* 57(3), 524–531.

Schmookler, J. (1966), *Invention and Economic Growth*, Cambridge, MA.

Schumpeter, J. A. (1934), *The Theory of Economic Development*, Cambridge, MA.

Schumpeter, J. A. (1939), *Business Cycles*, 2 edn., New York.

Schumpeter, J. A. (1942), *Capitalism, Socialism and Democracy*, New York.

Schumpeter, J. A. (1947), The Creative Response in Economic History, *Journal of Economic History* 7(2), 149–159.

Scott, J. T. (1984), Firm Versus Industry Variability in R&D Intensity, in: Griliches, Z. (Ed.), *R&D, Patents and Productivity*, Chicago, 233–245.

Shapiro, C. (2001), Navigating the Patent Thicket: Cross Licences, Patent Pools, and Standard Setting, in: Jaffe, A. B., J. Lerner, and S. Stern (Eds.), *Innovation Policy and the Economy*, Vol. 1, Cambridge, MA, 119–150.

Shea, J. (1997), Instrument Relevance in Multivariate Linear Models: A Simple Measure, *Review of Economics and Statistics* 79(2), 348–352.

Simons, K. (1995), *Shakeouts: Firm Survival and Technological Change in New Manufacturing Industries*, Ph.D. thesis, Carnegie Mellon University, Pittsburgh.

Smolny, W. (1998), Innovations, Prices and Employment – A Theoretical Model and an Empirical Application for West German Manufacturing Firms, *Journal of Industrial Economics* XLVI(3), 359–381.

Smolny, W. (2002), Employment Adjustment at the Firm Level. A Theoretical Model and Empirical Investigation for West German Manufacturing Firms, *Labour* 16(4), 65–88.

Smolny, W. and T. Schneeweis (1999), Innovation, Wachstum und Beschäftigung – Eine empirische Untersuchung auf der Basis des ifo Unternehmenspanels, *Jahrbücher für Nationalökonomie und Statistik* 218(3+4), 453–472.

Spence, M. (1984), Cost Reduction, Competition and Industry Performance, *Econometrica* 52(1), 101–121.

Spiezia, V. and M. Vivarelli (2002), Innovation and Employment: A Critical Survey, in: Greenan, N., Y. L'Horty, and J. Mairesse (Eds.), *Productivity, Inequality and the Digital Economy*, Cambridge, MA, 101–131.

Staiger, D. and J. Stock (1997), Instrumental Variables Regression with Weak Instruments, *Econometrica* 65(3), 557–586.

Statistisches Bundesamt (a), *Bevölkerung und Erwerbstätigkeit*, Fachserie 1, Reihe 4.2.1, different years, Wiesbaden.

Statistisches Bundesamt (b), *Betriebe, Beschäftigte und Umsatz des Verarbeitenden Gewerbes sowie des Bergbaus und der Gewinnung von Steinen und Erden. Ergebnisse der Betriebe, Beschäftigte, Umsätze nach Wirtschaftszweigen und Beschäftigtengrößenklassen*, Fachserie 4, Reihe 4.1.2, different years, Wiesbaden.

Statistisches Bundesamt (c), *Beschäftigte, Umsatz und Investitionen der Unternehmen und Betriebe des Verarbeitenden Gewerbes sowie des Bergbaus und der Gewinnung von Steinen und Erden*, Fachserie 4, Reihe 4.2.1, different years, Wiesbaden.

Statistisches Bundesamt (d), *Beschäftigte, Umsatz, Investitionen und Kostenstruktur der Unternehmen in der Energie- und Wasserversorgung*, Fachserie 4, Reihe 6.1, different years, Wiesbaden.

Statistisches Bundesamt (e), *Beschäftigung, Umsatz und Investitionen der Unternehmen im Baugewerbe*, Fachserie 4, Reihe 5.2, different years, Wiesbaden.

Statistisches Bundesamt (f), *Beschäftigung, Umsatz, Aufwendungen, Lagerbestände, Investitionen und Warensortiment im Handel*, Fachserie 6, Reihe 4, different years, Wiesbaden.

Statistisches Bundesamt (g), *Eisenbahnverkehr*, Fachserie 6, Reihe 2, different years, Wiesbaden.

Statistisches Bundesamt (h), *Statistik der Personenbeförderung im Straßenverkehr*, Fachserie 6, Reihe 3, different years, Wiesbaden.

Statistisches Bundesamt (i), *Binnenschifffahrt*, Fachserie 6, Reihe 4, different years, Wiesbaden.

Statistisches Bundesamt (j), *Statistik des Luftverkehrs*, Fachserie 6, Reihe 8, different years, Wiesbaden.

Stifterverband für die Deutsche Wissenschaft (2004), *FuE-Datenreport 2003/04: Forschung und Entwicklung in der Wirtschaft*, Essen.

Stiglitz, J. E. and A. Weiss (1981), Credit Rationing in Markets with Imperfect Information, *American Economic Review* 71(3), 393–410.

Stoneman, P. (1983), *The Economic Analysis of Technological Change*, New York.

Stoneman, P. (1995), Introduction, in: Stoneman, P. (Ed.), *Handbook of the Economics of Innovation and Technological Change*, Oxford, 1–13.

Suits, D. B. (1984), Dummy Variables: Mechanics Versus Interpretation, *Review of Economics and Statistics* 66(1), 177–180.

Sutton, J. (1991), *Sunk Costs and Market Structure*, Cambridge, MA.

Teece, D. J. (1986), Profiting from Technological Innovation: Implications for Integration, Collaboration, Licensing, and Public Policy, *Research Policy* 15(6), 286–305.

Teece, D. J. and G. Pisano (1994), The Dynamic Capabilities of Firms: An Introduction, *Industrial and Corporate Change* 3(3), 537–555.

Tirole, J. (2000), *The Theory of Industrial Organization*, 11. edn., Cambridge, MA.

van Leeuwen, G. (2002), *Linking Innovation to Productivity Growth Using Two Waves of CIS*, STI Working Paper 2002/8, Paris.

van Leeuwen, G. and L. Klomp (2006), On the Contribution of Innovation to Multi-Factor Productivity Growth, *Economics of Innovation and New Technology* 15(4/5), 367–390.

van Reenen, J. (1997), Employment and Technological Innovation: Evidence from U.K. Manufacturing Firms, *Journal of Labor Economics* 15(2), 255–284.

Veall, M. and K. F. Zimmermann (1996), Pseudo-R2 Measures for Some Common Limited Dependent Variable Models, *Journal of Economic Surveys* 10(3), 241–259.

Verbeek, M. (2000), *A Guide to Modern Econometrics*, West Sussex.

Vernon, R. (1966), Investment and International Trade in the Product Cycle, *Quarterly Journal of Economics* 80(2), 190–207.

von Hippel, E. (1988), *The Sources of Innovation*, New York.

Witte, E. (1973), *Organisation für Innovationsentscheidungen*, Göttingen.

Wooldridge, J. M. (2002), *Econometric Analysis of Cross Section and Panel Data*, Cambridge, MA.

Wooldridge, J. M. (2005), Simple Solutions to the Initial Conditions Problem in Dynamic Nonlinear Panel Data Models with Unobserved Heterogeneity, *Journal of Applied Econometrics* 20(1), 39–54.

Zimmermann, K. F. (1991), The Employment Consequences of Technological Advance, Demand and Labour Costs in 16 German Industries, *Empirical Economics* 16(2), 253–266.